Unknowing and the Everyday

SUFISM AND KNOWLEDGE IN IRAN

Seema Golestaneh

DUKE UNIVERSITY PRESS   *Durham and London*   2023

Designed by Matthew Tauch
Project Editor: Ihsan Taylor
Typeset in Arno Pro by Westchester Publishing Services

Library of Congress Cataloging-in-Publication Data
Names: Golestaneh, Seema, [date] author.
Title: Unknowing and the everyday : Sufism and knowledge in Iran / Seema Golestaneh.
Description: Durham : Duke University Press, 2023. | Includes bibliographical references
and index.
Identifiers: LCCN 2022030463 (print)
LCCN 2022030464 (ebook)
ISBN 9781478019534 (paperback)
ISBN 9781478016892 (hardback)
ISBN 9781478024170 (ebook)
Subjects: LCSH: Sufism—Iran. | Sufis—Religious life—Iran. | Mysticism—Islam—Iran. | Iran—
Religious life and customs. | Iran—Social life and customs—21st century. | BISAC: SOCIAL
SCIENCE / Anthropology / Cultural & Social | HISTORY / Middle East / Iran
Classification: LCC BP188.8.I7 G65 2023 (print) | LCC BP188.8.I7 (ebook) |
DDC 297.4—dc23/eng/20220817
LC record available at https://lccn.loc.gov/2022030463
LC ebook record available at https://lccn.loc.gov/2022030464

Cover art: Azita Panahpour, *Shattered Poems No. 27*, 2017. Acrylic on canvas,
44 in. × 56 in. × 1 in. Courtesy of the artist.

DUKE UNIVERSITY PRESS GRATEFULLY ACKNOWLEDGES THE HULL MEMORIAL
PUBLICATION FUND OF CORNELL UNIVERSITY, WHICH PROVIDED FUNDS TOWARD
THE PUBLICATION OF THIS BOOK.

This book is dedicated to

Lila, Nasser, and Parisa

(Maman, Baba, Abji)

CONTENTS

ACKNOWLEDGMENTS

I owe my greatest debt to all those who shared their wisdom, thoughts, ideas, and dreams with me. In this text, they go entirely unnamed, and it is from this place of strange obfuscation that this project takes shape. These individuals were endlessly generous in so many ways, carving time out of their busy days, always demonstrating infinite patience and kindness with me. Some I met only a few times, and others I have had the great pleasure and honor of weaving into my life. I can only offer these words in the text as a too poor thank-you to all those who go unrecognized here.

A great deal of gratitude is owed to my own "masters of the path" who have provided both guidance and inspiration. I must first thank my PhD advisor, Marilyn Ivy, whose support, intellectual rigor, and inspiring approach to the discipline of anthropology have been as invaluable as they have been instrumental. For her guidance and insight, and for believing in me before I believed in myself, I will always be grateful. An enormous debt is owed as well to Brinkley Messick, who guided me through the daunting terrain of Islamic studies, and from whom I could have asked for no richer an education. His deep enthusiasm for the field and reassuring nature were truly invaluable. Setrag Manoukian has read more iterations of this project than anyone else, and I could not be more grateful to have as an interlocutor and mentor someone whose intellectual acumen and insight into the anthropology of Iran and Islam is matched only by his kindness and generosity of spirit. His work inspired from the earliest stages of my research, and continues to do so today. Michael Taussig, who introduced me to anthropology as a first-year undergraduate at Barnard College, continues to provoke and surprise in the most unexpected of ways. This project was also greatly enhanced by conversations with Rosalind Morris on the ethnographic imagination and anthropological ethics, Severin Fowles on the possibilities of thinking through materiality and aesthetics, Brian Larkin on sound and mediation, and with the late Peter Awn on the question of language and Islamic mysticism.

As a postdoc at Connecticut College, I was able to pause and think more slowly about the project as a whole, a reframing that was enhanced by conversations with Catherine Benoit, Sheetal Chhabria, Eileen Kane, David Kim, Christopher Steiner, and Sufia Uddin. Augustine O'Keefe was a wonderful friend who made suburban living infinitely better. I learned greatly from my colleagues at my first tenure-track job at the Central Eurasian Studies Department at Indiana University, whose inspiring work allowed me to put my project in conversations with historians and literature scholars of the early modern and modern Persianate world. For this, I thank Margaret Graves, Paul Losensky, Asma Afsaruddin, Huss Banai, Gardner Bovingdon, Jamsheed Choksy, Devin DeWeese, Marianne Kamp, Ron Sela, and Nazif Shahrani. I will always be grateful for Purnima Bose's mentorship and friendship while at Indiana and beyond. She was under no obligation to take me under her wing, but I am so appreciative that she did. And who knew I would meet one of my very favorite interlocutors and intellectual partners in crime, Nur Amali Ibrahim, in the wilds of the Midwest. Similarly, I thank Clémence Pinaud, my favorite wild woman, for her irreverence, kindness, and unfailing support.

At Cornell, I have had the extremely good fortune to encounter individuals as generous as they are intellectually gifted, especially my colleagues in the Department of Near Eastern Studies, from whom I have learned a great deal. Extra thanks are due to Jonathan Boyarin, Lori Khatchadourian, Ziad Fahmy, and Deborah Starr for their mentorship and friendship. I have also benefited greatly from conversations with colleagues in the Department of Anthropology, who have been so welcoming, as well as Anne Blackburn, Iftikhar Dadi, Andrew Hicks, Chiara Formichi, Durba Ghosh, Mostafa Minawi, Tejasvi Nagarja, Juno Salazar Parrenas, Eric Tagliocozzo, Noah Tamarkin, and Robert Travers. A special thank-you to Begum Adalet, David Bateman, Anndrea Matthews, Prachi Patankar, Natasha Raheja, and Parisa Vaziri for being such wonderful company and making life in the northern lands so much fun.

This project has benefited immensely from those who have read chapter drafts, including Anne Blackburn, Jonathan Boyarin, Marina Antic, Margaret Graves, Guadeloupe Gonzalez, Michelle Hwang, Nur Amali Ibrahim, William McAllister, Setrag Manoukian, Izabela Potapowicz, David Powers, Ayana O. Smith, Anand Taneja, and Darryl Wilkinson. Thanks to all for the labor of reading often very inchoate thoughts and gnarly sentences. I am particularly grateful to Emilio Spadola for his insightful comments on an early draft of the entire manuscript. Of course, before (and while) there is the writing process there is speaking, and as such this project has been shaped by conversations with Sonia Ahsan-Tirmzi, Elizabeth Angell, Randi Asher, Hasan Azad, Jon Carter, Deniz Duruiz, Partha Chatterjee, Julia Fierman, Sayo Ferro, Aimee Genell, Behrooz Ghamari-Tabrizi, Guangtian Ha, Niloofar Haeri, Pedram Khosronejad, Seung Jung Kim, Christine Marrewa Karwoski, Jason Mohaghegh, Amir Moosavi, Olivia Nichols, Stefania Pandolfo, Gaurav Pant, Swatika Rajaram, Zainab Saleh, Annika Schmeding, Christina Sornito Carter, Matthew West, and Tyler Williams. I am particularly fortunate to have wrestled through ideas with Neda Bolourchi, Fatima Mojaddedi, and Manuel Schwab. I learned so much from the brilliant Sarah Vaughn, especially how to think anthropologically, and always had such fun while doing it. I am thankful for the hours and hours spent talking with and learning from Farbod Honarpisheh, my fellow *shahrestani*, about Iran, aesthetics, politics, and everything under the sun. And to my dissertation writing group, Robert Brink, Joel Bordeaux, Shannon Garland, Benjamin Johnson, Sarah Lazur, and José Antonio Ramírez Orozco, who somehow made writing on a sunny Sunday in August seem like a good idea. Arunabh Ghosh's kindness and forbearance supported this project during a critical phase, and for this I am grateful.

This research required me to learn how to listen to music and sounds in ways unfamiliar to me, and I first encountered new ways of listening during my time at WKCR-FM NY and my conversations with its brilliant, eccentric, and wholly lovable volunteer staff. The station could not have existed without the tireless efforts of Benjamin Young and the late Phil Schapp, and their lifelong commitment to the strangest of all musical sounds.

In graduate school, two individuals were beyond instrumental in shaping my writing process. William McAllister's support and reassurance, as well as his ability to finagle a working space for his late-stage PhD students still hanging around the joint, could not have been more invaluable. As intellectually curious as he is kind, I wish there were more people in the academy like Bill. Dr. Shirley Matthews and her "Getting Things Done" working group at Columbia taught me to re-think my writing process and I have never looked back. There was a reason we all referred to her as "Saint Dr. M."

This project was made possible through the generous support of several institutions and programs: the Institute for Religion, Culture, and Public

Life, the Columbia University Graduate School of Arts and Science Dissertation Travel Grant, the Middle East Institute Dissertation Writing Fellowship, the Interdisciplinary Center for Innovative Theory and Empirics (INCITE)'s Mellon Dissertation Fellowship, the Mellon C3 Minority Postdoctoral Fellowship, and Indiana University's College of Arts and Humanities Institute Research Fellowship. I appreciate the backing of each institution and fellowship in making possible this endeavor from the earliest initial stages of fieldwork through publication. A version of chapter 5 appeared in the *Journal of the American Academy of Religion,* and I thank the editors for the opportunity and reviewers for their thoughtful comments. I am grateful to Elizabeth Ault, my editor at Duke University Press, for all her support, encouragement, insights, and good humor in guiding this project to fruition. Benjamin Kossak, and the entire production team were so helpful, and it was a pleasure to work with them. I am especially appreciative of the endless patience and guidance of Ihsan Taylor; I truly could not have asked for a better project editor.

To my hosts in Iran, who include family biological and adopted, I will be forever indebted. Their companionship and help in navigating the trials and tribulations of life in Iran made my time there immeasurably better. Thank you to Vida Khanum Shahnasser, Ahmad Agha Tabaizadeh, Khanoom Sadat Golestaneh, Hajj Agha Mahmood Golestan, Agha Hossein Vatani, and Khanum Hediye Mohadammadian. To my friends in Iran, *saale bad dar Kerman.* To my many, many family members, who went out of their way to include me in an endless array of gatherings of various persuasions, insisted on making the long drive to the airport to pick me up despite my protestations, and made sure they brought to my attention every single iteration of "Sufi" they could, I owe a tremendous amount. In particular, I wish to thank Akhtar Golestaneh, Mansour Golestaneh, Houshang Shahnasser, Yekta Amiri, Diba Fesharaki, Setare Golestaneh, Soheil Golestaneh, Elnaz Kamazani, Nasser Kamazani, Rameen Kamazani, Marjan Masoudi, Farzaneh Norouzi, Hamid Shahnasser, Mina Shahnasser-Kamazani, Sanaz Shahnasser, Soheil Shahnasser, Venous Shahnasser, Shahnaz Shahramfar, Ali Tabaizadeh, Mohammad Tabaizadeh, Shayan Tabaizadeh, and Shirin Tabaizadeh. Double thanks are owed to my aunt Khanoom Vida Shahnasser for parsing through innumerable mystical texts with me at various libraries and bookstores, and for the great kindness she has always bestowed upon me. And to my late grandmother Parichehreh, whose love was so strong that I still feel it acutely some twenty-eight years after she is gone, and who forever shaped the way I view Iran and faraway worlds different from my own.

This book would not have been possible without the support of my closest friends. Thank you to Zoe Kelly-Nacht, who has done everything from read chapter drafts to laugh at the absurdity of it all, and always with such warmth. I thank Anand Taneja for always being such a supportive friend, for our conversations that cover everything from *al-ghayb* to silly jokes, and for his inspiring work. My writing group, who have become so much more, Michelle Hwang, Ama Awowti, and Tamar Blickstein have listened to the painful minutiae of the progression of this project, from earliest chapter drafts to book copyedits, with infinite patience and always a kind and encouraging word. What a gift I have in them. I am so grateful for my decades-long friendships with Leanne Tory-Murphy and Laura Waldman, who always inspire with their thoughts and ideas, equal parts wise and irreverent, and always deeply ethical. Sophia-Stamatopoulou Robbins and Kaet Heupel's enthusiasm for anthropological thinking and insightful and compassionate ways in which they view the world make them an incomparable joy to be around.

Most importantly, I thank my family. The nonhuman are family too, so thank you to Maggie and Lily B for being my best friends and protectors, and for always putting everything in perspective. To my brother-in-law Elliot, whose good cheer always provides a welcome respite from the difficulties of writing. To my sister Parisa, for whom selflessness seems to come as second nature, for her tireless support and unwavering belief in my abilities, I express my deepest gratitude. If only everyone had a sister like I do, what a better world it would be. Little Siavash has brought our family a joy like no other. Together we will write some books that have more pictures in them. I am indebted to my baba Nasser, the last of the poets, who instilled in me a steadfast belief in the transformative power of the written word, and whose great sacrifices have made it that much easier for me to take on a line of work that did not seem an option to him. And how does one thank a mother? My maman Lila, who has stood with me like no other, aiding me in this endeavor in every conceivable fashion and yet still in more ways than she knows. The love that she has bestowed upon me has formed the lens through which I see the world.

And to Darryl, whom I could thank for doing everything for this project from the most tiresome of copyedits to speaking through the thorniest of conceptual arguments, for tirelessly expressing his unwavering belief in me and this book, for sharing in all the highs and lows, but whom ultimately, I will thank for being himself. The Sufis have taught me the beauty of the unknown, and I could ask for no better companion to venture into these open waters with together.

For all the shortcomings of this text I bear sole responsibility, as they are mine and mine alone.

Sometimes, in Isfahan, a river appears. When it is there, it runs straight through the heart of the city, from west to east. The river Zayandeh runs 400 kilometers long and in the city of Isfahan proper it is between 150 and 300 meters wide, and hundreds of years ago the Shahs built six footbridges so that people and horses could cross it with ease. Since then, the wide banks have been transformed into parks full of flowers and greenery.

Today, however, sometimes these footbridges are not necessary because the river has been rerouted to Qom Province, to provide water for farmers there feeling the effects of desertification. And so, for months at a time, Zayandeh's bed is completely dry and hence passable by foot, cracks in the earth noticeable as you make the strange and unsettling walk across it, as if you are walking across a moonscape in the middle of a lush park. Sometimes football games pop up in the wide expanse of the river where a current once ran.

When the water returns, the people come out in droves to its banks, as if to see for themselves that the rumors are true: the river had come back to Isfahan. Families small and large, groups of young people, gaggles of girls and boys, old men in blazers and wool hats, ladies in elegantly draped black chadors; all are present. When the waters first started being rerouted, the opening and closing of the river was more dramatic; people were brought to tears at the return of the waters, as if overcome with relief that indeed it was real, it was real, the river was a river once more, a current flowed through Isfahan again, and all was water, light, and sound. Now the inhabitants have become accustomed to the unpredictable rhythms of their fickle river, and while its reappearance is still met with gratitude, it is not as quite as heartrending as during those initial years.

And yet, what a river it is. When the river Zayandeh is full and flowing in springtime, and the flowers are in full bloom, to walk the

banks of the river of Isfahan is to experience a beauty of historical pro-
portions. There is an easy serenity to these riverbanks; the gardens are
not ostentatious or overly manicured, but as relaxed and easy as a sigh.
The flowers' heady perfumes transport you somewhere so that you are at
once deeply present, immersed as you are in the sensory perception of the
present time and place, and very much elsewhere, all at the same time.

And those imagined things which are common and proverbial among people of any group, village, or town should not be disregarded openly as long as they are the subjects of attention. For, as a result of the attention paid to them by these souls, they give rise to some effects.

HAJJ SHEIKH MUHAMMAD HASAN SALIH 'ALI SHAH,
SPIRITUAL LEADER OF THE NIMATULLAHI SULTANALISHAH
SUFI ORDER, *PAND-E SALEH*, 1939

Introduction

Isfahan
August 2012

It was Friday, the day of rest, but Elaheh had still gone to work. A young woman in her late twenties, she had a degree in architectural design but, unable to find work in her field of choice, had two jobs instead: one working in a half-time IT position, the other tutoring high school students in math. She also did some Web design on the side when the opportunity presented itself, and it was a meeting with a potential client for this specialty that she had attended today. Needless to say, she was tired.

I had wanted to talk to Elaheh about her experiences with Sufism and, despite her fatigue, she did not cancel our meeting. She was not born into a "family of Sufis" (*khanevade darvishi*), but had started attending meetings some years ago after hearing about them from a friend, and said she had called herself a Sufi for several years now. We spoke about her love of the "endlessness of meanings" (*tamoom nadare*) in the Qur'an and Persian poetry (*adabiyat*), the constant remembrance of the mysteries of God at all times, and how meetings left her with "an open heart" (*del baz*). Given her busy and unpredictable schedule, however, she did not make the meetings as regularly as she would have liked. The meetings themselves, held either Thursday night or Friday, had also grown increasingly infrequent and irregularly scheduled—sometimes alternating weeks, other times occurring several weeks in a row then nothing—which also made going more difficult.

"Whenever I go, I always enjoy myself. Especially when the readings are of [the poet] Sa'adi, and I like how those things they say have great application [amal] for me. . . . But it's hard to coordinate sometimes: I don't know when I will have the time, and also if there is a meeting at all that week. So, you see, it's both my being able to go, and they being able to have a meeting! But I always try to go when I can, it's good for my spirit [ruhiyeh]!" Compounding the issue was that Elaheh had applied for a master's degree program in Malaysia and was waiting to hear if she had been accepted, and, in the event of her admittance, if there was also scholarship money. She was doubtful about her chances for acceptance, however, and she had heard a rumor that Malaysian universities were taking fewer Iranian students these days, because of "something to do with Russia." Despite the uncertainties she faced, she remained upbeat: "I will always love mysticism, and God willing I can continue, perhaps even on my own, but I'm just not sure about my plan for next year. For now I'll keep going, though, and then we will see what happens later."

We started our way back to the street to catch the bus when two young boys selling fortunes (fal) on scraps of papers approached us: "Four fortunes for a toman, ma'am; come on then, buy something from me!" I turned over a bill to the boys and Elaheh and I both took a fortune. As is always the case, the "fortune" was actually a verse from a poem. I read mine aloud first. It was from Mawlana, also known as Rumi:

> Andam keh mara beh gherd-e to doran ast
> Saqi o sharab o qadah-o dor an ast
> Vandam keh tora tajjali-e ehsan ast
> Jan dar heyrat cho Musi-e Umran ast.

> The moment in which I turn round and round, circulating
> It is the age of wine, the wine-bearer, and the cup
> And in that moment of kindness which you have made manifest
> In amazement I am like Moses, son of Umran.

Elaheh rolled her eyes and laughed: "This one is always drunk!" she said, meaning Rumi. She turned to hers next. It was yet another by Rumi:

> Ey aql boro keh aqel inja nist
> Ghar moy shavo moy-e to ra ghunja nist

Ruz amad o ruz har cheraghi keh furokht
Dar sholeh-e aftab joz rusva nist.

O reason, begone! There is no wiseman here
There is no room for you here, even for the finest of your hairs
The day has come, and whatever lamp gives light
Is shamed by the face of the sun's bright glare.

"Not exactly his best," I remarked, unimpressed. After a moment had passed, Elaheh expressed her disagreement: "No, you see, it's actually kind of interesting. Light and the intellectual are always supposed to go together, right?" Here she used the Persian word for intellectual: *roshanfekr*, literally "the light thinker" or "the lit thinker." She began to speak more quickly and more impassionedly: "But Rumi is saying that the reasoned thinking of the intellectual will always be less than that of the sun, the light and knowledge of God. This is what we must think about: there is always that which is beyond what we are thinking!" And at this declaration of one's own limitations, Elaheh seemed overjoyed.

What does it mean, to think "there is always that which is beyond what we are thinking"? To not only recognize that the cognitive capabilities of the intellectual pales in comparison to the knowledge of God, but then to position oneself at that very threshold, that precipice where the capabilities of human thought are said to end? In other words, what does it mean to recognize the endpoint of human thinking not as a terminus but as a beginning? Within certain iterations of the Islamic mystical tradition, to better understand and approach this mode of thought one must utilize a specific type of knowledge. This type of knowledge is called *ma'rifat*, an epistemology often called gnosis in English but which I translate here as "unknowing."

Over the course of nearly a decade of fieldwork in Iran, including an extended period of time from 2009 through 2011, I worked with various Sufi groups whose members were deeply invested in this form of unknowing, among other ideas. I say "this form" because the understandings and interpretations of *ma'rifat* are myriad and vast, but for the sake of this project I use the word to indicate the particular hermeneutic stance of my interlocutors.

Intriguingly, what I found was that discussions of *ma'rifat* were not only relegated to the page but that interpretations of *ma'rifat* spilled out onto the street, accompanying its practitioners into situations foreseen and unforeseen, into the smallest corners of life and its widest expanses, just as countless theological concepts before it have also been carried in the pockets of their practitioners. Mysticism has too often been dismissed as only belonging to the world of the abstract and far removed from the socio-material realm; my interlocutors instead discussed its potential for *amal*, application.

And so, the question arises: How does one utilize a type of knowledge that contests the finality of thought in the context of the everyday?

Understanding Unknowing

What is unknowing (*ma'rifat*)? It is a concept that is first and foremost based on the affirmation of the unknowability of God, that it is ultimately impossible for humans to fully understand the divine. And yet rather than consider this fact an obstacle to contemplating the nature of the divine and other related matters, these Sufis firmly position themselves at this juncture in developing their epistemologies. They operate from a position of accepting and emphasizing that there will always be that which we do not know. Thus, we might posit non-knowledge not as a form of anti-knowledge or metaknowledge but rather as *an awareness of that which we do not know, an engaged awareness that we know nothing*.

While I think it is fair to assert that the vast majority of Muslims would agree that God is inherently unknowable, these Sufi groups take this conceit as the foundation of their broader epistemology. For the contemporary sheikh Seyed Mustafa Azmayesh, the interminable nature of the journey of Sufism is perhaps its most defining feature: "The road to God is endless because God is infinite. Constantly we have to go on and accept to go on. When you stop you are no longer a Sufi."[1] My friend Elaheh's interpretation of the Rumi poem expressed a similar faith in the endlessness of meaning, where a reminder of the limits of the human intellect, being made cognizant of this often forgotten fact, was a source not of melancholy but of joy.

Within non-knowledge there remains some elemental form of understanding, a self-conscious awareness, but it is an awareness that something remains unresolved, something remains unanswered. Hajj Nur'Ali Tabandeh, the highest spiritual authority figure (*qotb*) of the Nimatullahi Soltanalishahi Sufi Order, who passed away in December 2019, offers the following definition of *ma'rifat* emphasizing the lack of finality that it invokes: "Literally, *erfan* is knowing. Yet knowing has different stages . . . gnosis is not an absolute matter. It is something that, as the philosophers say, is graduated [*tashkiki*] such as light and faith, which have degrees. . . . More than anything else . . . this process continues endlessly."[2] Here then we see one of the first aspects of unknowing: that it contests the finality of thought, suggesting an intimation of knowing as a process without endpoint, and that there will always exist that which we do not know. Far from advocating the removal of knowledge, this form of thinking, where thought is compelled to its limit, rather emancipates thinking as an automatic, systematic means to an end, and allows it to operate as a constantly searching, ceaselessly critical investigative device. What surfaces then is a new mode of thinking, one that, through its need to question, is able to conceive of a wholly different conception of reality. Above all else, unknowing must be understood as a fundamentally *generative* enterprise, one wherein the finality of conventional knowledge is supplanted by an unresolvable dilemma until ultimately all thought operates as a formless, generative endeavor, speculating upon that which it does not know, moving forward into the "nothing," until all life is lived at the level of an improvisatory gesture.

Unknowing is exactly that: it causes one to *unknow* something; it takes a seemingly concrete and finite entity and unravels it, blurs its ends and beginnings, renders the once familiar into the unfamiliar, and, in some cases, puts its very existence into question. As the eleventh-century writer Ahmad Ghazzali explained in his famous treatise *Sawaneh*: "This station is beyond the limit of knowledge (*aql*) and the allusive expression of knowledge cannot reach it, any more than its outward expression (*ebarat*). However, the allusion of mystical epistemologies (*ma'rifat*) will indicate it, for unlike knowledge, the boundaries of which are all well-constructed, the boundaries of mystical epistemology lead to ruin. Here is the dashing of waves of the ocean of love, breaking on themselves and returning to themselves."[3] This ruination of boundaries, of that which is contained, is seen throughout this book.

At the heart of the project are four ethnographic case studies. In each instance, I trace the affective and sensory dimensions of *ma'rifat* as it influences the mystics' understanding of text and authority, the self, memory, and place. I speak with two sheikhs whose belief in the endlessness of meanings found in works of poetry, the ultimate unknowability of text, leads them to confirm the limits of their own authority, as interpreters and subsequently as spiritual leaders. Listening practices within the musical *zekr* ritual demonstrate a reconfiguration of the self as an unbound entity, a move toward a destabilization of subjectivity, a "loss of self" in a postcolonial context where a "return to the self" has long been championed by Iranian thinkers like Ali Shariati and Jalal Al-e Ahmad. A small collective of mystics actively attempt to overturn a memory of a difficult event, summoning a "willful amnesia" that both dovetails with and diverges from other forms of remembrance (*zekr*) in postwar Iran. Finally, a residential neighborhood is rendered unfamiliar as a group of young people reimagine the space through movement, reviving a literal interpretation of the idea of *sargardan*, intentional wandering.

I hence approach unknowing in two ways: as object of study but also as critical lens, utilizing the Sufis' own mystical epistemology to guide me in understanding and interpreting my ethnographic case studies. In this way, the project of this book is to demonstrate the ways in which mystical thought is rendered manifest in Iran today, and how unknowing unravels the borders of the material. In doing so, the Sufis reaffirm not only the supremacy of God's omniscience but also their belief in the illusory nature of reality. I should reiterate that *ma'rifat* is a hugely complex category with thousands of definitions of what it might entail. In this text, however, unless otherwise noted, when I refer to *ma'rifat* I refer to the specific interpretation of *ma'rifat* of my interlocutors, and I have translated it here as "unknowing" to better reflect their particular hermeneutic stance.[4]

Guiding me in my analysis are the following questions: What are the possibilities and limitations—intellectually, ethically, politically—contained in the application of *ma'rifat*? In what ways is this interpretation and utilization influenced by the larger sociopolitical context of postrevolutionary Iran and how, in turn, does it influence this same arena? More broadly, what is the role of Sufism in late modernity, and how might such a question be answered anthropologically?

In some sense, this book is more an ethnography of an idea or, perhaps more accurately, an ethnography of an interpretation of a theological concept, than an exhaustive study of what might be called "Iranian Sufism" in and of itself.[5] Such a framing is not intended to downplay the role of my interlocutors—as if I am emphasizing abstract knowledge at the cost of those who generate it—but rather to allow my primary subject matter to be their interpretations and applications of said knowledge. An ethnography of an interpretation traces how theories of *ma'rifat* are understood and interpreted, applied and utilized, influence and subsequently are influenced by the larger sociopolitical context in which they operate, arise out of particular historical contingencies—in other words, carries out all the things an ethnography must do.

In doing so, I find myself in conversation with other recent anthropologies of Islam focused upon the ineffable and the unseen, where communities or individuals are concerned with planes of existence that are difficult if not impossible to access (at least for the anthropologist). Amira Mittermaier's artful and far-reaching study of dreams and dreaming in Egypt has proved an incomparable guide as she investigates a realm—the world of dreams—that is at once "radically inassimilable" to her interlocutors while demonstrating how this space of alterity acts as a site of engagement for them, leading to profound reconfigurations of what might be classified as real and unreal, self and nonself, and more. Other examples of anthropologies of the invisible include Anand Taneja's elegiac exploration of the interactions between *jinns*—spirits made of smokeless fires—and the Hindu and Muslim visitors of the medieval Firoz-Shah Kotla shrine in contemporary Delhi who consult them, demonstrating how supernatural entities keep alive histories otherwise effaced by the Indian government. Alireza Doostdar offers no less than an historically informed anthropology of *al-ghayb*, that dominion of the concealed and unseen, as a window into contemporary debates concerning rationality and scientific thought in Iran. And finally, Stefania Pandolfo's magisterial *Knot of the Soul* bears witness to the tribulations of the souls of individuals living "in the proximity of madness,"[6] wherein she explores that which, oftentimes explicitly by definition, eludes human understanding. How are we to approach such topics, as anthropologists and ethnographers but also as writers? How can such experiences be rendered legible to ourselves and to others? When the subject matter is the formulation and interactions of multiple realities (and perhaps nonrealities), the researcher must look for evidence, beyond that which is immediately available. As Pandolfo writes in the overture to part 3 of *Knot of the Soul*, "The Jurisprudence of the Soul": "I was clear that I could not write based on his [the Imam's] practice, or even his teachings and explications alone. In the watermark of his words, there was an archive that I had the responsibility of addressing, on its own terms, and in terms of the questions and concepts that had guided my own search."[7] Here, Pandolfo points out that in the Imam's words there is an entire corpus of knowledge that must be addressed, viewed on its own terms but also through the lens of her own reading. A watermark can be seen, but it remains ever vague.

The dream-world, the spirit-world, the world of the unconscious: these are all realms the majority of individuals can never fully inhabit but are able to encounter or at least engage with through a variety of methods and an equally diverse set of consequences. Moreover, what I find compelling in these texts is that each phenomenon—dreams, *jinns*, souls, knowledge— acts as an object of ethnographic inquiry in its own right, rather than solely as an avenue or entryway to understanding some other determining force: electoral politics, economics, infrastructure. This is not to say that these more ephemeral phenomena are apolitical in any sense, or are divorced from or unaffected by the contexts in which they operate, far from it; I simply suggest that the political or some other larger determining force does not exhaust them as subjects of ethnographic inquiry or, to put it differently, the political does not *wholly* shape or determine their significance. Indeed, my objective here is to trace the ways that these Sufis in Iran engage with difficult-to-access mystical epistemologies, ones that often may be retrieved only through much effort and dedication. In other words, I examine the ways in which that which is intangible—namely, abstract thought in the form of philosophical ideas—is rendered material in such a way as to leave its mark upon the social realm, and it is this act of rendering in which I am most interested. My intention is not to explicate the ways in which these case studies provide merely an example or an uncritical and unthinking implementation of a predetermined conceit, but to examine how these epistemological matrices are first interpreted and then applied to the specific context at hand. What this requires is an activation of the religious imaginary, one to generate an envisioning of a world that is in conversation with, yet not entirely restricted to, the larger sociopolitical context in which those who imagine belong.

The Sufi Ties That Bind

I began my work with Sufis in 2007, with a longer period of research in late 2009 through 2011. The Green Movement, the series of large-scale protests prompted by the 2009 presidential election, were largely in the rearview mirror at this point, and though they continued to act as a point of conversation, as all current events do, they otherwise did not affect my research. It was not my first extended trip to Iran, either, as I had spent summers at my grandmother's house in Isfahan, experiencing the country as many children of the diaspora do, through the joy of large family gatherings, ice cream cones and picnics in the park, being a little scared and secretly delighted when the power went out, and enjoying the company of hordes of cousins, bringing with us many pairs of jeans as gifts, the trendy ones still in short supply in the waning days of the Iran-Iraq War and the years after. In other words, the holiday version of Iran. It was only when I was in my early twenties that I started to venture outside my large circle of relations. No one in my extended family is part of any Sufi order, but it was through networks of friends and family that I met some of my initial interlocutors; in other cases, I approached Sufi groups myself, without any intermediary. All my interlocutors were incredibly gracious with their time, but it is a testament to these latter groups' generosity of spirit that they were so open and welcoming to a complete stranger.

At this point, I must introduce my interlocutors with more specificity. This study is not focused upon a single Sufi order,[8] nor does it purport to be an exhaustive overview of what might be called "organized Sufism" within Iran. My interlocutors include members of groups of varying sizes and organizational structures, all of whom have their own different spiritual leaders. Because I worked with mystics in the cities of Isfahan, Kerman, and Tehran, a regional specificity is lacking as well. In all but one of my case studies, I make no mention of which city my interlocutors are located in or when exactly the interviews took place. This is an intentional blurring, done to provide more cover for my interlocutors.

There are, however, certain characteristics shared by all my interlocutors. They are all ethnically Persian, and hence part of the majority ethnic group of Iran.[9] Unlike other Sufi groups in Iran, such as the Sunni Kurdish Qaderis, my interlocutors are indistinguishable from the rest of the ethnic Persian population in terms of their phenotypical appearance, their names, and the language they speak. They also all identify, resolutely and without fail, as followers of Twelver Shiʿism, the state religion of Iran. They are Shiʿi Sufis, meaning they follow all the tenets of Twelver Shiʿism,[10] but either have a particular hermeneutic stance toward said tenets and/or believe in certain conceptual matrices that may be seen as outside "mainstream" Shiʿi thought (although of course the Sufis themselves always argue that any and all of their beliefs are perfectly within the guidelines of Twelver Shiʿism). I will think through these differences in more detail in chapter 1.

More compelling than this set of ethnic, linguistic, and "sect" characteristics shared between my interlocutors, however, are those of the conceptual variety. As such, all my interlocutors share the following traits: (1) all identify the fourteenth-century sheikh Shah Nimatullah Vali as a key intellectual grandfather; (2) they read and discuss a similar corpus of texts, and, most significantly; (3) they express similar interpretations of key mystical concepts despite belonging to different orders. The ties that bind these groups are thus more literary and conceptual than organizational or immediately empirical. In privileging the conceptual over the structural, I aim to foreground the groups' intellectual output, as well as the source material that helps formulate their ideas and interpretations, in my study. In other words, texts and interpretative stance are the criteria by which I have organized these mystical orders into a somewhat cohesive collection of case studies. Unknowing thus emerges as a trans-order phenomenon; it does not belong to a single group or specific sheikh; it is not relegated to mystics of any particular class background or training. Of course, this is not to say that many self-identified Sufis, in Iran and elsewhere, would surely disagree with this interpretation of ma'rifat; it is not a universal interpretation. Indeed, a more comprehensive study would provide examples of other Sufis' alternative understandings of the concepts explored in this study, and that is something that is surely lacking. Still, that this interpretive stance operates across these disparate groups indicates that a hermeneutic trend is currently operating today. The case studies of this book are thus a fragmentary portrait of contemporary Sufi practice in Iran, a series of isolated snapshots that give clues to a larger, unseen whole.

As previously mentioned, all my interlocutors consider themselves followers of Shah Nimatullah Vali (d. 1431), and either use the moniker "Nimatullahi" or trace their spiritual lineage (*selsele*) back to him. To be clear, this does not mean they are part of the same order nor does it mean they share an identical spiritual lineage. But the shared claiming of Shah Nimatullah Vali is significant for two reasons: (1) it indicates the potential for some shared epistemologies; and (2) it ties them more directly to the organized mysticism of a Sufi order (*tariqeh*),[11] meaning a collective of students and teachers following a more codified school of mystical thinking that has typically been in place for some generations prior, as opposed to other forms of "mystical practice." Iterations of the Nimatullahi Order have existed within Iran or South Asia since the fifteenth century, and by identifying as such my interlocutors lay claim to and view themselves as part of a broader tradition of organized Sufism.[12] This is in contrast to many individuals in contemporary Iran who feel a predilection for mysticism but who may or may not identify as Sufi (*darvish*), a phenomenon I explain in greater detail in chapter 1. Indeed, "mysticism" in Iran is a shape-shifter, existing in a number of disparate but interconnected categories: religio-philosophical mysticism taught in the seminaries (*erfan* and *tasavvuf*), literary and musical mysticism (*erfan*), New Age health and psychology, as well as the organized group practices (*sufigari*) that are the focus of this study. This self-identifying as Nimatullahi, however, distinguishes my interlocutors from other individuals in Iran who are invested in mysticism (usually *tasavvuf* or *erfan*), including those following mystically inflected self-help programs and writings, a trend thoughtfully investigated by Alireza Doostdar through both anthropological and historical lenses,[13] as well as those authors who write about what Niloofar Haeri has termed "simple *erfan*" or "simple mysticism" (*erfan-e sadeh*).[14] Haeri has outlined this phenomenon of lay authors, meaning they are neither clerics nor professors, who write prayer books in Persian on the subject of mysticism in plain prose, making them accessible to a much broader readership than the more dense, philosophically oriented prose that often characterize writings on mysticism. In self-identifying as *darvish* or *faqir* specifically and in laying claim to having ties to Shah Nimatullah Vali—either nominally or genealogically—these Sufis are putting themselves firmly in a different category than the two other groups. There is a specific genealogy being invoked here, and all the accompanying identifying factors as well: literary, philosophical, and hierarchical.

The second trait shared by all the Sufis in my case studies is their similar interpretations of key mystical concepts, despite the fact that they follow different sheikhs. Of particular importance is their adherence to the idea that Sufi knowledge (*ma'rifat*), or unknowing as I am calling it, remains an open-ended phenomenon, where the mystery of God is seen not as limitation but as opportunity. Such an idea, although certainly not exclusive to these Iranian Sufis, is not universally accepted within all forms of Islamic mysticism, with luminaries such as Abu-Hamid al-Ghazzali and Mulla Sadra proving key objectors.

The third point of convergence between my interlocutors is the use of similar textual materials. As is the case with many Islamic groups, the majority of the Sufis' time together is spent reading, discussing, and/or analyzing different texts, and so an overlap in reading material is not an insignificant fact. The interpretation of this constellation of textual material forms the bedrock of their practices, and as one navigates with heavenly bodies so too do these written works provide the guidance the Sufis may use to move through life.

The use of shared textual materials also demonstrates a shared affinity for particular intellectual debates and discourses. This is not to say that their "reading lists" were entirely identical; there were certainly divergences—in terms of genre, in terms of favored writers—but there was enough overlap of texts that I was able to make note of it.

There is also a cross-pollination of literatures between the groups, meaning many of the mystics read and discussed texts by twentieth- and twenty-first-century Sufi sheikhs other than their own. For example, I found the works of Javad Nurbakhsh, the psychologist who founded his own order in the 1970s and left Iran during the early days of the revolution, were still in relatively heavy circulation and in every group there were at least a few who were familiar with his work.[15] Such a finding speaks against narrow definitions of "saint worship" and the supposedly single-minded devotion students give to their leader, where the disciples accept the word of their spiritual authority figure as the beginning and end of debate.

Other literatures read by sheikhs or members of the groups with whom I worked include the writings of members of the Safi Ali Shahi Order and the Soltan Ali Shahi Order. All read the poetry of Shah Nimatullah Vali, the aforementioned intellectual grandfather. While his writings are not widely read amongst the broader population, the fifteenth-century sheikh's poetry is not obscure by any means—volumes of his collected works can be found in mainstream Iranian bookstores like City of Books (Shahr-e Ketab). The works of the sixth Shi'i imam, Imam Jafar al-Sadeq, and key Shi'i clerics such as Ayatollah Khomeini, Allameh Sayyed Mohammad Tabatabai, and Seyed Mohammad Husayn Husayni Tihrani were also of interest to some—if not all—members of each of the groups with which I worked. Of course, the works of many medieval Persian poets are heavily read and discussed by the Sufis as well. The analysis of poetry, medieval or otherwise, is extraordinarily common in Iran, regardless of one's religiosity or educational background, from those who may identify as atheist to the most devout practitioners of "mainstream" Twelver Shi'ism (whatever that may be). Haeri, Shams, Olszewska, Manoukian, and Fischer have all traced the ways in which poetry and specific forms of knowledge derived from poetry (sometimes called poetics or poesis) occupy places in the Iranian imagery both expected and unexpected,[16] appearing in everything from television game shows and art house cinema to prayer circles and refugee cultural organizations, university and seminary settings, and debates at bus stops. The infiltration of poetry and poetics into contemporary Iranian life cannot be underestimated, and this book contributes to this ever-growing and thoughtful genre with a focus on the role of poetry for a particular group of readers, here Sufis.

The Sufis refer to themselves by a variety of names: gnostics (*arif/urafa*), paupers (*faqir/fuqara*), wayfarers or wanderers (*salik/salik-ha*), darvish (also pauper or, alternatively, one who travels "door to door"), Sufis, and, to a much lesser extent, students (*murid*). The different collectives with which I worked often referred to themselves most frequently with one specific moniker, such that some preferred *faqir* while others used *darvish*. Generally, however, the name *faqir*, or pauper, indicating that one exists in a state of "spiritual poverty," was used the most frequently. Outside of Sufi circles, Iranians almost exclusively used the term *darvish* or Sufi.

Finally, and most significantly for this study, I counter assertions of Sufi "exceptionalism," which argues that mystics are not in conversation with other Islamic debates and discourses, a claim which could not be further from the truth. In this book, I explore how Iranian Shiʻi mystical epistemologies have similarities and differences with the conceptual matrices of their non-Sufi, Twelver Shiʻi counterparts. Indeed, it is vital to remember that within Qom, the home of mainstream and state-run Shiʻite seminaries (*howzeh*),[17] students have been able to study mysticism (*tasavvuf*) with teachers—both inside and outside the classroom—since the city's reemergence as a site of Shiʻi scholarship in the early 1920s.[18] More recently, there have been a number of more prominent clerics within the seminaries of Mashhad that espouse a more esoterically oriented view, which I discuss briefly in chapter 1. While it would require another book entirely to more exhaustively trace convergences and divergences between philosophies of Sufi orders and the staggering output of ideas from the seminaries, I do hope my modest contribution to such an endeavor here highlights the fact that mystical thought does not operate in a vacuum.

Transfigurations of the Self

The enemy of Sufism (*faqr*) is the devil of the self, which appears in various forms. Do not be taken in by the deceptions of the self, for it is possible that it may take on the appearance of being pleasing to God.

HAZRAT MAHBUB ALISHAH (D. 1997)

Remember God so much that you are forgotten. Let the caller and the called disappear; be lost in the call.

RUMI

The self as an enemy to be avoided, the self as a thing to be dissolved, the self as a false mirror of understanding: these are typical injunctions for those who subscribe to the mystical path. As previously mentioned, the primary objective of Sufism is union with God (*tawhid*) through the acquisition of non-knowledge. As such, something which is both a cause and a consequence of this increased proximity to God is the transformation of the self. This altering of subjectivity, which can range from a quieting of self-involved patterns of thought (self-pity, envy, etc.) to an extinguishing of subjectivity (*fana*) entirely, is something for the faithful to work toward and achieve. This of course necessitates the questions of exactly *how* one goes about dissolving their own subjectivity (*fana*), their own sense of self, and how exactly one manages to usher in a form of consciousness where the self has been dislodged as the origin point and source of all things.

The answer is twofold, and involves an understanding of multiple forms of subjectivity. The first mode of subjectivity is similar to that which is found in studies of what has been called ethical self-fashioning, a phenomenon masterfully explored in works by Charles Hirschkind, Saba Mahmood, Lara Deeb, and others. This aspect of one's self is dedicated to proper ethical comportment (*akhlaq*, the *shari'at*) and involves reading and analyzing textual materials. It is a type of selfhood recognizable by many as the liberal autonomous subject, contained and centered, with the self as the sun in the Copernican model of consciousness. Moreover, the trope of "cultivation" is also appropriate here, as many Sufis work tirelessly to try to educate themselves about mystical epistemologies, attending classes or sessions and reading through materials, working to increase their knowledge and achieve the realization of their full scholarly potential. There is an active engagement here, a dedication of time and energy to create an ethical and knowledgeable self whose boundaries are discernible and whole.

And then there is another form of subjectivity, one a bit more porous and opaque, that is dedicated to its own dissolution. This element of the self is seen as contingent upon but also resolutely distinct from the type just described. While proper ethical comportment and obtaining scholarly knowledge—the domain of the worldly self—are understood to be important, they are considered to be only the (necessary) first step in achieving *tawhid*. To continue forward on the path toward *tawhid* requires the capturing of a form of subjectivity that cannot be developed solely through careful study and good deeds—a fact relayed to me time and time again by many of my interlocutors—but by making oneself vulnerable, by allowing oneself to be exposed to a certain existential and ontological register; it is as if one has undergone a long and potentially difficult journey and then arrived at a destination where such journeying, such efforts are no longer effective. Peppered throughout the mystical literatures is the language of surrender and submission; rather than develop the self, one must abandon it, and what of course makes this all the more difficult is that even this cannot be an act of pure volition. But it is only with this form of radical subjectivity/nonsubjectivity that one is able to experience and obtain unknowing (*ma'rifat*).

According to the Sufis, there is a clear hierarchy between these different forms of self and the corresponding forms of knowledge and knowledge production with which they are engaged. As Sheikh Alizadeh, one of my key interlocutors, told me, "If you just want to learn how to be an ethical person, a person of substance (*adam-e dorost va hesabi*), to pray correctly, maybe learn more about the Qur'an, there are a hundred thousand religious teachers who can do that. If you want to learn of the loss of self (*bikhudi*) and nonexistence (*naboodi*), then you turn to the mystics (*fuqaha*)!" For Sheikh Alizadeh, activities like studying the Qur'an and aspirations of living an ethical life are presented as almost unremarkable undertakings, "*just* learn[ing] how to be an ethical person," (emphasis mine), in contrast to learning about nonexistence, which seems to be the domain, or at least the specialty, of those who have embarked on the mystical path (*tariqeh*). Many other individuals with whom I spoke, including Sheikh Noroozi, described *fana*, the annihilation of the self, as the "next stage" or the "next step" in the process toward *tawhid, following* the cultivation of an ethical self. Among the Soltanalishahi Order, the *qotb* Hazrat Hajj Nur'Ali Tabandeh Majzub'alishah described in an introductory text: "In Islam, Sufism or gnosis (*erfan*) is the inward dimension of the religion, like the seed of a nut whose shell is the outward rules (*shari'at*) and whose seed is the path (*tariqeh*),"[19] at once privileging the *tariqeh* as the "seed" and depicting the *shari'at* as the protective outer shell guarding the treasure inside. In these cases, all embrace the importance of ethics and the self-contained and self-directed subjectivity that it requires, but all also emphasize the equal and often greater significance of the unbounded and unknown self that the *tariqeh*, the mystical path, entails.

A number of recent works that have explored the phenomenon of nonautonomous selves in other Islamic settings have been extremely instructive for my own project. In her study of the social life of dreams in contemporary Egypt, Amira Mittermaier considers subjectivity in light of the fact that dreams are said to "come" to her interlocutors rather originate within them, therein tracing the ways that the self is understood to be formulated by external forces as well as internal forces. This is a community of individuals who value being "acted upon"—primarily by those spirits and saints who visit them in their dreams—where the self emerges as a *site for interaction* between the Real and Unreal worlds rather than a wholly self-contained entity. Borrowing from Godfrey Lienhardt's classic study, Mittermaier describes the phenomenon of "being acted upon" as an "ethics of passion": "The ethics of passions that emerges from my interlocutors' dream stories not only undoes the notion of a unified subject but also draws attention to the role of an Elsewhere in constituting the subject, and with it to elements of unpredictability and contingency."[20] In other words, the vicissitudes of the self are contingent upon not only internal processing but external processing as well.

The destabilization of subjectivity is also a major theme in Stefania Pandolfo's ethnography of madness, in which her interlocutors are suffering from "maladies of the soul" alternately caused by *jinn* possession, the trauma of war, and emotional abuse.[21] Those who experience this form of dislocation of the self, however, are in stark contrast to the Sufis with whom I worked in that the former experience great pain and suffering, and are actively looking to reestablish an equilibrium within themselves, whereas the latter are striving to *activate* this potentially unsettling experience. Pandolfo's interlocutors understand the cause of their maladies as arising from something external to themselves; whether they be from malevolent spirits or from the devastation of violence, these undoings are caused by that which is exterior to body and consciousness. In this sense, it seems as though the soul (*nafs*) is being undermined, which is quite different from the actions undertaken by the mystics with whom I worked, where the dissolution of the self is something that is, at least in part, self-driven.

Outside of the Islamic context (but within the Iranian context), Setrag Manoukian offers the idea of "the impersonal," considering what it might mean to conduct ethnography where selves are not bounded entities, where the self does not exist at all, but where the self once was there exist moments (and perhaps records) of exchange. Manoukian develops this critical lens in response to his interlocutors in Shiraz, Iran, who understand poetry as a way of existence, and Manoukian takes this assertion seriously, viewing it as an epistemic challenge, rather than simply as metaphor or empty language. He writes:

In Iran, poetic traditions are relevant in constructing an existential ground for recognition. Beyond political and religious differences, Iranians habitually recur to poetry when existential matters are at play ... it is the impersonal force of poetry that structures a mode of existence in which form and life become inseparable. Shiraz poet Mansur Awji ... explained to me that while a poet needs an equal measure of effort and inspiration to compose verses, one cannot control the combination of circumstances in which poetry comes, if it comes at all. These poetic occurrences are neither active movements from the inside towards the outside, a sovereign self-expression, nor passive recipients of messages from the outside to the self.[22]

Here, the composition of the poetry is not wholly the result of either interior or external forces, but it arises instead from something in between. Similarly, as the mystics of this study work to dislodge their subjectivity, the "who" that is doing the "work" becomes ever more unclear, a form of engagement with the world neither entirely fully active or fully passive.

In this book I frequently refer to "transformation," and by this I mean a transfiguration of the self that occurs simultaneously at the divine and existential registers. The transformation of the self at the levels of the Real (*haqiqat*) is seen as a fundamentally distinct as well as more significant cultivation of the self than that which occurs at the level of ethics. Indeed, if one is to take seriously the idea that the acquisition of *ma'rifat* and achievement of *tawhid* require no less than the dissolution of subjectivity, then we must entertain forms of thinking and thought that operate without subjectivity, a form of thought that seems impossible by standards of Western consciousness. By considering unknowing, this book expands on those forms of Islamic selfhood/non-selfhood that do not fit so easily into self-cultivation, and at the same time challenge, perhaps in a more radical fashion, the notion of the liberal autonomous subject.

The Real and the Unreal

Sheikh Noroozi led a modestly sized group of followers and they would meet to discuss, among many other things, theories of the nature of reality (*haqiqat*). Effervescent and irascible, he would illustrate the ways that intimate experiences with and of God can occur in more quotidian moments.

"If you listen closely, sometimes even in the din of the streets (*sar-a seda-ye khiyaban*), you can hear the sound of '*Hu*.'[23] But then in that same moment it will disappear. You will ask yourself: Did you really hear it? Maybe you did and maybe you did not. Was it really there? Were *you* really there? Was it just the wind, playing tricks? Was it the sound of your own heartbeat, echoing through your ears? While you are waiting to cross the street, can you hear the *Hu*? Even if you are not 100 percent sure, even if all you have understood really is a strange question, for a moment, you will not be in this world."

Later I discussed Sheikh Noroozi's lecture with Shohreh, a homemaker and mother in her forties who regularly attended his gatherings. "I like the reminder of thinking about union with God (*tawhid*), that it can happen in this world too, just from a strange noise on a street corner. I mean, of course not fully, but we can have moments, we can get a little closer. It's so beneficial to remember the world of Truth (*haqiqat*; the divine realm), just thinking this other world is there and is possible. Here, in the Unreal (*alam-e khiyali*), it changes the time you spend on the little street corner, makes it a new experience."

At the core of Nimatullahi Sufism there lies a central idea: that existence is composed of two separate but interrelated realms: the Real (*haqiqat*) and the Unreal (*khiyali, vehmi*).[24] In contrast to many post-Enlightenment discourses, the Real is the world of the divine, of the unseen and the imperceptible, while everything else in the universe—humanity, plants, animals, mountains, deserts—are inhabitants of the Unreal. It is also essential to understand that the Real and the Unreal exist simultaneously. A common idea within Sufi literatures is that the Real is available to us but is merely veiled, and therein concealed, from the Unreal. It is the goal of Sufism to remove this veil and become ever closer to the Real, the world of God, therein achieving *tawhid*, union with God.

As Sheikh Noroozi explains it, the reception of a passing sound, one which you are not entirely sure you have heard at all, is enough to transport you to another world. This other world is the world of the Real (*haqiqat*), the world of the divine. You must listen for this sound, or "listen closely" as Sheikh Noroozi advises, and even then you will not be sure you have heard it at all. It will cause you to question yourself and your surroundings, inspiring a small vertigo, so that your heartbeat, the wind, and the disparate sounds of the street might take the shape of one another.

Reports of feeling unmoored and unsettled when one is becoming closer to the Real are extremely common throughout Sufi literatures; leaving behind the illusory plane of the profane world, this Unreal, is not without side effects, it would seem. And yet despite any discomfort that might accompany this questioning of the self that occurs in approaching the Real, it is seen by Shohreh as something to be desired. Indeed, Shohreh does not focus on the lack of clarity that Sheikh Noroozi describes, but notes instead her appreciation of the reminder that opportunities for union with God (*tawhid*) might occur even in the most quotidian moments, in this case instigated by an unidentified noise on the street. This moment is then able to transform the experience of the street corner, suggesting that even the mere remembrance of the Real can impact the experience of the Unreal.

This interplay between the Real and the Unreal, especially as it relates to materiality, is an important theme in three out of four of my case studies. To recap, the world in which humanity resides is fundamentally Unreal, meaning illusory and fictive, and to affirm such a belief in the *unreality* of the world is a simultaneous confirmation of the *reality* of God and the inherent supremacy of the divine realm. Moreover, an acceptance of the illusory nature of reality allows for a certain kind of imaginative capability, one that sometimes involves the questioning of the ontological and/or existential status of people, places, things, and even the self. Of course, these imaginings do not occur in a vacuum, but are influenced by the specific contexts in which the imaginer operates, whether that influence is personal, sociopolitical, or something else. It is important to remember that this is an active process, as one must always remember to listen closely.

Textual Ethnography and the Hermeneutic Imagination

Much of my time in "the field" was spent with an open book in my lap, sitting around with other tome-laden individuals, shifting our gazes up and down from the pages in front of us to one another. Sometimes there was a leader to these discussions, and sometimes there was none. Sometimes the mood of these reading groups was relaxed and contemplative, full of slow movements and the gentle turning of pages, and other times they could be charged and electric, slightly raised voices puncturing the air, potential energy radiating from those waiting their turn to speak. In most of these meetings the topic at hand was poetry. All the groups were thoughtful, and a privilege to attend.

While I was very interested in the discussions that occurred in these reading groups, I also wished to understand how the ideas and themes debated also influenced my interlocutors' lives outside of the reading groups, just as many ethnographies of religion have previously done. In this book, I strive to understand the disparate forms of social phenomena—both knowledge and practices—that arise from texts and textual practices specifically, where the written word is seen as both the result of and source of cultural formations. In other words, to consider what it means to approach textual materials—here religio-philosophical texts—as a form of anthropological evidence.

In addition to those classic texts, which understood literacy as a form of technology and power,[25] many have analyzed reading as a critical act which itself is "culturally and historically determined," as Jonathan Boyarin has articulated, tracing the intersections between knowledge production and the literary and hermeneutic imagination.[26] Influential works like those of Fischer and Abedi and Brinkley Messick demonstrated how intellectual debates, often centered around questions and interpretations of specific textual materials, might be rendered legible by historically informed anthropological research, combining ethnography with analyses of religious texts.[27]

Since then, many others have followed suit, especially in considering how reading determines subject formation.[28] In recent years, the reading and nonreading of documents, especially of the bureaucratic variety, has also drawn substantial attention,[29] and of course there is much "non-knowing" that occurs in bureaucracy, and those who privilege reading practice over content.[30]

This book draws most heavily from those studies that trace the intersections between cultural production and the literary and hermeneutic imagination. Of particular importance is the role of poetry, especially medieval Persian poetry, which my interlocutors read alongside the Qur'an, the Hadith, and other texts of religious authority. Setrag Manoukian explores how Iranians are able to view themselves as subjects and subjects-in-history through engagement with and composition of poetry. Far from constituting a genre that is divorced from the sociocultural realm, Manoukian demonstrates how "poetry is the form in which Iranians experience themselves as subjects endowed with the power to act and live in the world."[31] While I found my interlocutors to take a similar stance toward poetry, my work is less concerned with the historical and genealogical contingencies of the relationship between self and poetry within Iran as Manoukian's work demonstrates, and more focused upon poetry as an affirmation and purveyor of a particular type of knowledge for these Iranian Sufis. I will explain.

There are certain characteristics that define the poetry my interlocutors read: ambiguity of meaning, multiplicity of meaning, words that may or may not adhere to their literal definitions, a sensitivity to rhythm, rhyme, and speed. This does not even include the further nuances that these poems can take on when they are performed orally, each reader adding their unique interpretation in the way they utter aloud the poem. Of course, it is not only poetry that utilizes these tropes—one only has to read the prose works of more esoterically minded theologians to encounter similarly abstruse epistemologies—but these literary traits are most consistently found in poetic genres. It is the genre of writing that is perhaps the most uncompromising in its multiplicities of meanings and, as a result, most conducive to Sufi epistemologies of unknowing.

Moreover, within this multiplicity of meanings there is a more specific hermeneutic stance that many Islamic mystics adopt. Poetry, like esoteric interpretations of the Qur'an, is seen as containing esoteric meanings and exoteric meanings; in other words, poems contain meanings both hidden and transparent.[32]

What is vital to understand is that this interpretative lens, of hidden meanings and transparent meanings, is directly tied to the idea of the world as being composed of two separate but intertwined realms: the Real and the Unreal. In other words, poetry is reflective and emblematic of the nature of reality as a whole. The Real, the world of the divine, is analogous to the hidden meaning of the poem, so much so that the Real is often referred to as the hidden (*al-ghayb*). Just as one must strive to gain access to the Real—the realm of the divine—so too must the reader work toward accessing the hidden meaning of the text. Similarly, the transparent meanings of the text are as readily available as the Unreal—the profane—world around us; still providing valuable insights, but not quite as transformative as those insights found in hidden meanings.

In this way, each poem is a microcosm of the world. Simultaneously self-contained and infinite, possessing an endless array of meanings, some surface level and easily accessible, others requiring more dexterity of thought. The Sufis' interpretation of poetry is directly influenced by the way they interpret the world, such that their hermeneutics and ontological critical lenses are one and the same. As such, what I wish to demonstrate in *Unknowing and the Everyday* is that this particular critical lens of the Real and the Unreal arises from the page but also extends beyond it, as the goal of textual ethnography is to trace the intersections between cultural production and the hermeneutic imagination. This is seen most clearly in chapter 2 when I speak with two sheikhs who discuss the relationship between hermeneutics and religious authority, both agreeing that the multiplicity of meanings, the endlessness of meanings, of poetry complicates notions of religious authority.

It is one thing to have an admiration and predilection for poetry as many Iranians do, believing it to hold valuable life lessons and complex ideas, as Niloofar Haeri and Michael Fischer have thoughtfully investigated.[33] It is another thing to believe that poetry is a reflection of reality as a whole, and as such can be used to transform the self at the divino-existential registers. As one of my interlocutors told me about his relationship with the poet Hafez, "You cannot simply read Hafez [to understand him], you must *live* with him." Ultimately, I agree with Manoukian's assertion, stated above, that the Iranians view poetry as a means by which to experience themselves as subjects in the world. I am only applying a more specific hermeneutic stance here.

As previously mentioned, I also draw from Sufi publications and literatures as a critical lens; in other words, using passages and quotes from their own literature in understanding my case studies. As such, the primary sources I am utilizing include the sermons, decrees, epistles, essays, and poetry written by the Sufi sheikhs of the order in the twentieth and twenty-first centuries, with a particular focus given to (1) texts that were written by sheikhs during the past twenty years and (2) texts that are widely read by all lay Sufis. Many of these works are self-published by a Sufi publishing house, Entesharat-e Haqiqat.

My focus is narrowed further still to the works of *qotbs* (literally "pole" or "axis" but indicating highest religious authority) of the contemporary era, with special attention given to the writings of those still active or very recently passed. In this sense, I am working backward through the chain of succession. By focusing on the work of the sheikhs and *qotbs* created in recent memory, my goal is not only to begin to outline the current debates and discourses within Iranian Sufism, but also to track those ideas which have been encountered with more frequency by lay Sufis (*darvish*) in Iran. For this reason, I draw more heavily from sermons and also introductory texts, which, as I was informed by elders of the order, receive the most circulation among their members. Of particular importance is the short treatise *Saleh's Advice* (*Pand-e Saleh*). Written in 1939 by the *qotb* Saleh Alishah (1891–1966), *Saleh's Advice* broadly outlines the group's epistemologies and, to a lesser extent, best practices. The majority of the texts used here are thus available in Sufi bookstores and libraries, meaning those adjacent to a meeting place (*khaneqah*), public libraries, and, to a lesser extent, private bookstores, and a not insignificant number of them have been made available online. In addition, I draw from works of poetry of the medieval canon that are highly familiar and widely read by my interlocutors: namely, Rumi, Attar, Sa'adi, Hafez, Hallaj, Baba Taher, and several prominent Sufi philosophers,[34] such as Junayd Baghdadi, Sayyed Haydar Amoli, Ahmad Ghazzali, Bastami, and Shah Nimatullah Vali.[35]

Aesthetics and Affect

In order to trace these aforementioned intangible theories, I hope to provide a more material object of study by investigating the realm of sensorial affect, with a specific focus on the uses of intentional listening (*sama*). Moreover, in addition to providing a concrete analytical endpoint, audition is considered an absolutely central practice for many of my interlocutors, existing not as a passive mode of reception but as a highly intentional act that possesses near-infinite transformative capacities. Put more simply, listening is considered a strategy to achieve the experience of *ma'rifat* in that it provides a conduit, a cipher by which to unravel that moment of interaction between the individual and the material world. Furthermore, it may be argued that the type of knowledge inherent in aesthetic experience—that strange information gathered from touching, tasting, seeing, hearing, smelling—is very much analogous to the experience of unknowing: it needs to be experienced before it can be understood. I further situate my analysis within what might be called Islamic aesthetic theory, where I draw from both canonical and contemporary writings of the Sufis focused on the philosophies of music and listening. In this way, rather than carry out an analysis of the auditory itself, I trace instances and experiences of unknowing as they are generated through sensorial affect. For it is through the affect, or the impact or response, imparted onto someone or something that we are able to see the transformative capacities inherent in sensoriality.

I draw from a number of literatures concerned with the intersection of aesthetics and anthropology. Indeed, as audition is an undoubtedly essential part of Islamic practice, it has been analyzed through the lens of various subjects: from the initial revelation of the Qur'an to the call to prayer,[36] to the complex sermon tradition[37]—and I do hope to expand upon the specifics of mystical *sama* with other interpretations of the uses of audition in Islam. Here, I draw from work about Islamic soundscapes such as those by Charles Hirschkind, Brian Larkin, Naveeda Khan, and Emilio Spadola.[38]

Outside of the Islamic studies category, my work is situated within the world of auditory anthropology, or "anthropologies of sound,"[39] which not only focus upon music, sound, and listening as objects of inquiry, but also analyze the ways in which the auditory influences and is influenced by the broader sociopolitical realm. In other words, they follow James Clifford's question: "Suppose that, instead of seeing those places, these anthropologists had heard them: how would they have theorized their encounters with the other?"[40] From this conjecture it is made apparent that such an endeavor would not simply result in a cataloging of the particular sounds of an environment, but rather would affect the way in which this environment was approached critically, as we remember Attali's declaration to "theorize through sound."[41] By theorizing through intentional listening, and by extension through the prism of a particularized aesthetic experience, one is therein able to merge both perception and the production of critical thought together into one instantiation of consciousness, until it is difficult to identify one from the other. Similarly, this project closely follows the work of Michael Taussig,[42] which considers not only the aesthetic experience as the object and method of inquiry, but also looks to the transformative capabilities of affect in regards to the anthropological inquiry more broadly.

Chapter Overview

Each chapter of this book, with the exception of the first, analyzes an individual case study. These chapters all begin with an ethnographic anecdote that describes the event or practice in question. This is then followed by an analysis that traces the ways that particular mystical concepts present within the case studies are applied to navigate the socio-material realm. In utilizing this rhetorical technique, I adopt a more miniaturist stance, taking individual stories and unraveling them, ethnographically, rather than exploring broader themes present within my research. This is perhaps a less explicit mode of analysis, one that asks too much of the reader to try to knit these disparate strands of ethnography together themselves, but in doing so I feel I am avoiding laying claim to essentialisms about the Iranian Sufi community, or at least doing so slightly less than might be otherwise. Moreover, given the abstracted nature of certain aspects of mysticism, I find beginning each chapter with an ethnographic anecdote provides more solid ground upon which to venture into the chapter's investigation. Or, perhaps more accurately, it is a reminder that the goal is to mine the concepts and epistemologies at play within the ethnographic narratives and not the other way around, and so the analysis unfolds as such. As Deleuze has written: "Empiricism is by no means a reaction against concepts. . . . On the contrary, it undertakes the most insane creation of concepts ever."[43] It is in this spirit that I foreground my chapters in the socio-material realm, Unreal though it may be to the Sufis themselves.

CHAPTER ONE: SUFISM IN IRAN, IRAN IN SUFISM

My first chapter explores the complexities behind the category of "mysticism" within Iranian intellectual and political history, the legacies of this convoluted history, and the prevalence of mystical thought outside of Sufi circles. In sharp distinction to designations of Sufism as "heterodox" and their non-Sufi "mainstream" counterparts as "orthodox," Iranian intellectual histories demonstrate no such clear bifurcation. I begin by analyzing the ambiguity surrounding the terms Sufism (*sufigari*), literary mysticism (*erfan*), and scholarly mysticism (*tasavvuf*), and the subsequent difficulty involved in categorizing a person or group as Sufi or not within the Iranian popular imagination. I then provide an overview of the history of the Nimatullahi Sufi Order since the late nineteenth century, with a focus on the complicated history between certain branches of the Nimatullahi Sufi Order and the reigning political and theological authorities in Iran, highlighting how these relationships have varied drastically over time. From here, I highlight strains of Shi'i clerical commitment to mystical thought through the twentieth century, touching upon two of the most famous members of the mystically inclined clergy (*ulama*): Ayatollah Ruhollah Khomeini and Allameh Sayyed Mohammad Tabatabai. I also draw on scholarship that explores the relationship between the seminaries (*howzeh*) and Sufi Orders in the mid-twentieth century, mysticism in the popular imagination as seen through self-help movements and popular fiction, and recent publications by mystically inclined clerics in Mashhad. While *Unknowing and the Everyday* does highlight several instances where Iranian mystical thought diverges from "mainstream" Twelver thought, by establishing this broader theological and sociohistorical landscape of Iran, I hope to highlight how the mysticism of my interlocutors is simultaneously convergent with and divergent from other forms of "Islamic thought" (considered broadly) within contemporary Iran.

My second chapter analyzes the transformative power of textual interpretation (*tafsir*) for two Sufi reading groups. In particular, I trace the ways the Sufis' unique understanding of spiritual authority is directly tied to their methods of *tafsir*. The members of these Sufi poetry reading groups believe that the *tafsir* of a text leads not to the correct answer in regard to its meaning, but to yet more difficult questions contained therein. The text is in a sense endless, its words able to convey countless ideas that lead to ever deeper philosophical musings the further one goes in one's analysis. Thus, employing a hermeneutic method not dissimilar to many modern and postmodern literary theorists of the twentieth century, the Sufis adhere to an interpretative framework for understanding Persian poetry that mimics their understanding of knowledge as an exercise without limit or finality. Furthermore, this understanding of *tafsir* holds vast consequences not only for the possibilities contained within the text, but also the ways in which the Sufis view the one who leads the reading group and guides them in analysis: their sheikh. Indeed, in contrast to the mainstream Ja'fari Shi'i clerics (*mojtahed-ha*), whose authority is directly derived from their training and the fact that they are able to interpret sacred texts more accurately than lay people, therein providing the best answers to their students, the Sufi sheikhs engage with a different form of authority. It is their ability to guide their students (*taleban*) to find the appropriate *questions*, rather than provide them with the most accurate *answers* for a text that distinguishes them. Of course, anyone who has witnessed pedagogical sessions with ulama know that many of them are also hesitant to provide straightforward answers, similarly reveling in contradictions and complications, and yet I would argue that this form of pedagogy is never tied in any way to a questioning of their authority as a whole. Hence, this chapter examines these Sufi groups' methods of literary analysis, and the ways in which they apply to their broader ideas of gnosis and spiritual authority.

CHAPTER THREE: UNKNOWING OF SELF, UNKNOWING OF BODY

My third chapter investigates the relationship between the Sufi remembrance ritual (*zekr*), sensorial engagement, and sociopolitical identity. More specifically, I analyze how the Sufi idea of annihilation of the self (*fana*), achieved through the bodily *zekr* ritual, has been reinterpreted by my interlocutors in one of two ways: The first group articulates their understandings of *fana* in largely theological terms, discussing concepts like the quieting of the lower soul (*nafs-e ammara*) and the turn to nonexistence. The second group, in contrast, describes their experience of *fana* as the loss of a much more socialized self, interpreting the loss of self as the loss of what might be called identity politics or the self in society. In the final part of this section, I compare these Sufis' desire to destabilize subjectivity with calls by prerevolutionary Iranian intellectuals Jalal Al-e Ahmad and Ali Shariati to "return to the self." How might these thinkers, both of whom advocate for a complex restoration of the self within a postcolonial context, where they understand the "loss" of self not as something to be desired but the outcome of, in part, colonial hegemony, reflect upon these mystics longing for an extinguishment of the self? I conclude the chapter by turning my attention to those Sufi aesthetic theories that expound upon the relationship between intentional listening and the transformation of the self specifically, understanding the ways that bodily and sensorial engagement might invoke a momentary alternative to the sociopolitical subject.

CHAPTER FOUR: UNKNOWING OF MEMORY

My fourth chapter traces an instance of the destruction of a Sufi meeting place (*khaneqah*) by the local authorities in the city of Isfahan in February 2009 and the Sufis' response not to mourn the site, but to actively and deliberately forget it in order to disavow the material in favor of the spiritual. A shrine that was used as a site for Thursday and Friday prayer meetings, it was housed in the Takhteh-Foulad Cemetery that had recently been dubbed an Islamic Heritage Site by UNESCO (the United Nations Educational, Scientific, and Cultural Organization). Following this designation, the local authorities began to transform the cemetery into a tourist site and destroyed the shrine on the grounds of "beautification" of the neighborhood. Within this chapter, my focus is hence twofold: (1) an analysis of the Sufis' reaction to the actions of the authorities, both before and after the demolition; and (2) how such commemoration differs from that of memorialization processes of the Iranian state. Regarding the former, I analyze the order's curious decision to "remember to forget" the site. More specifically, the sheikhs advised their followers not to mourn the loss of the site but to actively try to forget it, arguing that the material structure was not important. From here, I examine how this command to "remember to forget" is tied to both Sufi ideals of the relationship between remembrance and forgetting and Ja'fari Shi'i ideals of remembrance. I use this discussion as a jumping-off point to explore the ways in which this technique of commemoration exhibits both similarities and differences to the Islamic Republic's own exercises in the construction of public memory.

CHAPTER FIVE: UNKNOWING OF PLACE

My fifth and final chapter focuses on the relationship between concepts of wandering, intentional listening, and techniques of spatial formation as seen through the establishment and rotation of meeting places. As authorities continue to frown upon public gatherings, Sufis have sought alternative methods of convening that allow them to create and maintain an autonomous space while still complying with government regulations. One informal Sufi youth group, meaning one operating without the involvement of a sheikh or other spiritual leader, does so by meeting in private homes and rotating locations each week to avoid attention from the authorities. More notably, rather than let the participants know the exact address of the meeting place, each week they announce a nearby intersection at which to meet and then proceed to broadcast music to allow the members to locate the site by listening and hence "following" the sounds. While texting and telephone calls are ultimately used to find the exact address, in this chapter I examine (1) the ways that ideas of existential wandering are implemented to help resolve a matter of state interference, (2) the formation of a Sufi soundscape, and (3) the broader impact for the creation of such a collective space within postrevolutionary Iran.

POSTSCRIPT: IMPROVISATIONS

I conclude my book by thinking about the utilization of unknowing through the lens of improvisation. In musical improvisation, one draws upon one's prior training to instantaneously react to the immediate present. Similarly, the Sufis turn to their own mystical philosophies and ideas of gnosis to navigate the sociopolitical realm, responding to external actors by drawing upon their own training in real time. By drawing parallels between aesthetic and social improvisation, the postscript reaffirms the ways in which the contemporary Iranian mystical experience is in conversation with the sociopolitical realm, as well as the intricate relationship between religious, aesthetic, and sociopolitical narratives in Iran.

1 Sufism in Iran, Iran in Sufism

> We find certain scholars . . . denying the validity of mysticism and thus
> depriving themselves of a form of knowledge. It is regrettable. . . . It
> is regrettable that some of the *ulama* should entertain those suspicions
> and deprive themselves of the benefits to be gained from the study of
> mysticism. . . . Those who wear cloaks and turbans and denounce the
> mystics as unbelievers do not understand what they are saying;
> if they did, they would not denounce them.
>
> AYATOLLAH KHOMEINI, *ISLAM AND REVOLUTION* (1981)

It was always difficult to discern which moments of my time in Iran
comprised "fieldwork" and which didn't; more often than not they
snuck up on me.

I had missed my friend's Nahid's birthday party, and I wanted to
stop by to see her and give her a small present. She worked as a teller
in a bank and usually got home around 4 p.m., so I met her at her
house a little while later. After some time, Nahid's sister Farahnaz, a
middle school teacher, stopped by, wanting to borrow a dress to wear
to a wedding. I had met her only before in passing, and she joined us
now for tea. She inquired about my research and, after I gave her an
overview, she nodded and thought for a moment, then remarked:
"That's very interesting. You know, I'm kind of like a Sufi." To this her
sister gave her a look, somewhere between skepticism and bemuse-
ment. "Really? Since when are you a Sufi?"

"Well, see, isn't my bachelor's degree in Persian literature? And I used to go to those poetry meetings at Mrs. Nabavinejad's house, with that guy with the beard who played *daf* [frame drum]? Now that guy was really a Sufi!"

Nahid remained unconvinced: "That just means you like *adabiyat* (Persian literature)!

"No, but those meetings with that man, those were different! With his *daf* drum, he sang those poems, we would go into a state [*hal*], and he was always very calm. And remember for a while, right after college, I would only wear a white *rusari* [a headscarf]?"

At this her sister laughed heartily. "Oh, well then, a white *rusari!* This means a *real* Sufi! See, Seema, your research is done! Right here before you is the great mystic [*darvish*]! Truly Madame Professor [*khanoom ostad*] can tell you all you need to know!"

Farahnaz laughed too, embarrassed now, and said, turning to me, "So rude, this one! Come on, I just said I was *like* a Sufi!"

An interest in poetry, the wearing of white, the slow collapse into a heightened emotional state (*hal*) . . . all cues that conveyed the spirit of a more enigmatic form of Islamic worship for Farahnaz (if not enough to convince Nahid). What defines a mystic, or mysticism in general, in Iran is not so easily delineated and, beyond the confines of this sisterly debate, has in fact been a point of contention within Iran for centuries. Indeed, sometimes these murky definitions result in debates like the one expressed here by Farahnaz and Nahid, where the line between mysticism and New Age ideals gets blurred, a topic thoughtfully explored by Alireza Doostdar,[1] and other times the stakes of what is and what is not mysticism can be much higher.

There is first the term *sufigari*, which most closely approximates what might be called "organized Sufism." In addition to *sufigari*, however, is the much more nebulously defined category of "mysticism" in all its myriad instantiations—primarily understood to involve the categories of *erfan* and *tasavvuf* alongside that of *sufigari*. Each of these terms provides a site of contested meaning, with disparate political and theological entities laying claim to possessing the definitive version. The contestations over these terms goes back until at least the early modern Safavid era (AD 1500–1720), and these assertions over the definition of mysticism have led to lasting effects in the ways that the categories of Sufism, *erfan*, and *tasavvuf* are viewed in Iran today. While *erfan* and to a lesser extent *tasavvuf* are accepted as essential and revered elements of Iranian culture (*farhang*), *sufigari* will elicit a much more mixed response, with some denouncing it and others defending it.

At this point, however, I would like to be clear that when I discuss denouncements of *sufigari* it is something quite different than a dismissal of mysticism as a whole. Too often Sufism and especially mysticism are labeled the "heterodox" counterpart to the "orthodoxy" of the Shiʻi clergy (ulama), but really any such statements are nothing less than a gross mischaracterization. There is a long history of mystical ideas being discussed within the seminaries in the twentieth century, which continues today. Similarly, certain sheikhs and *qotbs* within Nimatullahi Iranian Sufi Orders had ties to the seminaries, expressing interest in those conceptual matrices such as law and ethics which are not not typically understood to be the jurisdiction of Sufis (at least by those unfamiliar with the cross-pollination of ideas between mystics and nonmystics).

Moreover, that which may be categorized as "mysticism" in Iran has been discussed and advocated for by those in the highest seats of power and the most vulnerable members of society, both before and after the advent of the Islamic Republic, from the supreme leader (*rahbar*) to the homeless wanderer (*qalandar*). In the medieval periods political leaders would sometimes compete to curry favors with Sufi sheikhs,[2] and in the early modern era the authority of the influential Safavid dynasty arose partially out of their claims as Sufi Seyeds, or descendants of the Prophet Muhammad.[3]

To assume a certain political orientation of an individual who espouses mystical thought, in any of its instantiations, is presumptive and misguided. This is especially true in North American and European popular media, where Sufism is frequently posited as the warm and fuzzy branch of Islam, interested only in "introspection" and other forms of nonsocially oriented worship deemed acceptable by neoliberal (read: Protestant) idealizations of religion.[4]

While I hope the other chapters of this book demonstrate how contemporary mystical thought, here unknowing, influences and is influenced by the sociotheological sphere, my goal with this opening chapter is to explore the complexities behind the category of "mysticism" within Iranian intellectual and political history, the legacies of this complex history, and the prevalence of mystical thought outside of Sufi circles. In other words, to explore Sufism in Iran, and Iran in Sufism, or how that which is called "Sufism" has developed in Iran, and in particular how certain political machinations have influenced Sufi practices and formulations, and likewise how the sociopolitical and theological landscape of Iran has been shaped by Sufi groups, especially in the early modern era. I first trace the emergence of *erfan*, and how it came to impinge upon, and in some instances replace, the term "mysticism" (*tasavvuf*/Sufism) in Iran. I then provide an overview of the history of the relationship between some branches of the Nimatul-lahi Sufi Order and the reigning political and theological authorities in Iran since the early modern era, marking how it has varied drastically over time. From there, I briefly look at the position of *erfan* in Iran in the twentieth and twenty-first centuries, including an explication of Ayatollah Khomei-ni's experience with the study of gnosis (*erfan*) while a student and teacher at the religious seminaries in the city of Qom, the advocacy of esoterically inclined hermeneutics by other prominent and up-and-coming clerics op-erating in the seminaries today, and mysticism in the popular imagination as seen through self-help movements and popular fiction. I conclude this last section with an extended description of a typical session (*jalaseh*) of a Nimatullahi Order today. In doing so, I hope to emphasize the point that to assume a certain political stance of a Sufi group—and by this I mean an allegiance to certain political parties or ideologies, that they are always counter to the state or offer a heterodox viewpoint—is grossly misguided. I ask that the four cases that follow this chapter be read with this larger framing chapter in mind.

Sufism versus Mysticism versus *Erfan*: Contested Terms

Before delving into the genealogy of *erfan*, it is important to recognize the vastly disparate responses that people will provide when asked to define the word today. More specifically, their definition of the word may very well reflect their religious affiliation and training. To a literate non-Sufi—that is to say, the overwhelming majority of the population—*erfan* does not mean mystical knowledge, but refers primarily to a distinctly Iranian literary tradition, namely the poetry of a canon of the medieval Persian-speaking poets Hafez, Sa'adi, Rumi, and Ferdowsi, and at times to Iranian traditional music (*musiqiye asil-e Irani*). Thus, to say that you are studying *erfan* means for the majority of Iranians that you are studying literature and/or a literary tradition (*adabiyat*), and almost always something dis-tinctly Iranian. This nationalist bent that is often associated with *erfan* is a phenomenon that demands much further analysis than afforded here, but for now I would only highlight that, outside of Sufi and clerical discourses, the category of *erfan* is not always immediately associated with Sufi or even Shiʻi theologies.

In contrast, if you were to ask a religious seminarian, a member of the clergy, or a more highly educated person to define the term, they would tell you that *erfan* refers to a field of study or is related to a field of study, namely that of Islamic mysticism (*tasavvuf*), which has a distinct history within Shiʻi theosophy and theology. For some, it would also indicate that form of "intuitive" or "esoteric" knowledge of the divine, a form of knowledge championed by prominent twentieth-century Shiʻi thinkers like Allameh Tabatabai, Ayatollah Ruhollah Khomeini, and Mohammad-Taqi Bahjat. This understanding of *tasavvuf* and *erfan* bears striking similarities to that of epistemologies of my interlocutors.

One of the most significant divergences between the theologians and the Sufis, however, relates to the term "Sufism" (*sufigari*). For most of my interlocutors, *erfan*, *tasavvuf*, and *sufigari* are all one and the same, while for many theologians they connote different realities. In other words, while all believe in the importance of esoteric knowledge, in the intuitive knowledge of the divine, as it is sometimes known, a large segment of theologians do not believe that collectives that call themselves Sufi orders (*tariqat*) are concerned with such pursuits, accusing them of focusing upon "idleness," "opium smoking," and "begging" instead. For many members of the clergy, individuals involved with organized Sufism (*sufigari*) either do not understand mysticism or willfully ignore the proper formations, therein casting such people as poseurs or, more violently, charlatans. Intriguingly, to explain this seemingly artificial discrepancy between the terms *erfan*, *tasavvuf*, and *sufigari*, one must look beyond theological debates and into the arena of politics.

The Rise of the Idea of *Erfan* in Early Modern Iran

Having briefly touched upon the contested nature of the definition of *erfan* that exists today, the question now arises as to how and why these contestations surrounding the conceptions came to be.

To understand why, one must look to the period of history when the Iranian plateau first became a Shiʻi stronghold: the early modern period. Contrary to contemporary misconceptions, both Western and Iranian, Shiʻism only became truly widespread in Iran during the Safavid era (AD 1500–1720). It was at this time that the Safavids, *themselves* originally a mystical order with Shi'i leanings (extremist [*ghulluw*] though they may have been in their earliest instantiations),[5] began consolidating religious and political power, the Shi'i becoming the dominant force in the Iranian plateau and the surrounding areas. It was also at the same time that many Sufi orders were either expelled or left the country,[6] as such groups were viewed by the Safavids as unwelcome alternatives to their own designated spiritual authority figures and hence political power as well.[7] The Nimatul-lahi Order left Iran around 1450 CE, and at the invitation of Sultan Ahmad Shah Al Wali Bahmani spent roughly the next three hundred years in exile in Bidar, India, and the surrounding areas.[8]

Given the widespread forced and unforced migration of the vast majority of Sufi orders, one might assume that that would be the end of mystical thought in Iran for the time being. As Ata Anzali has demonstrated, however, this was not to be the case.[9] With the publication of his *"Mysticism" in Iran: The Safavid Roots of a Modern Concept*, Anzali has written the most authoritative interpretation of why, when, and how *erfan* and Sufism (*su-figari*) became distinct concepts.[10] According to Anzali and others, mystical epistemologies were never expelled from Iran entirely, but rather the mystical epistemologies that had been circulating during this era were subsumed under the new Shi'i leadership, so much so that the theology of the Safavid era is often known as "Esoteric Shi'ism."[11] The men writing these esoteric philosophies were all jurists, however, with official posts in the hierocracy; they did not bear the title of "Sufi," and were indeed the respected legal scholars of their time. Moreover, this mystically tinged form of Shi'i scholarship was allowed to thrive due to the patronage of Shah Abbas I (d. 1629), the leader whose very dynastic forebears had driven out many of the organized mystic orders.

This esoteric Shi'ism, also known as Shi'i theosophy, reached its apex with the School of Isfahan,[12] a so-called renaissance of Islamic philosophy that was composed of such famous Shi'i thinkers as Sheikh Bahai (d. AD 1621), Mir Damad (AD 1630), and most notably, Mulla Sadra (d. AD 1640), one of the most famed theologians in all of Iranian history, who is today memorialized in contemporary Iran with streets and squares bearing his name. Mulla Sadra was particularly well versed in the writing of the famed Andalusian Sufi Ibn Arabi, and adopted Ibn Arabi's *insan-i kamel* (perfected man) and *wahdat al-wujud* (unity of existence) as major interests,[13] synthesizing them with other schools of thought, such as those of the Illuminationists (*hikmat-e eshraq*) and Twelver jurisprudence.

What explains this seeming contradiction? In other words, why would the Safavid authorities condone and act as patrons for the mystically oriented works of the School of Isfahan but strongly condemn and quell Sufi orders? The answer lies in the fact that the actual theological orientation of the Sufis was not the primary concern, but rather the fact that organized collectives of the Sufis posed a threat to the sovereignty of the Safavids, a threat that was not entirely unfounded.[14]

To distinguish between the two groups then, what happened was that the category of *erfan* (mystical knowledge) largely replaced that of *sufigari* (Sufism), all the while perpetuating the study and advocacy of many of the same themes. Despite the obvious common grounds, so clear was the bifurcation between *erfan* and *sufigari* in that era that Mulla Sadra himself wrote a treatise against Sufism, wherein he railed against the wandering, drug-taking *darvish* who begged for alms—largely the only self-identified Sufis who remained at the time.

Certainly, this is only a cursory overview of a complex genealogy of the terms *erfan*, *tasavvuf*, and *sufigari*. For our purposes, however, what I wish to emphasize here is that, within the Iranian context, not only does the word mysticism (*tasavvuf*, *erfan*) exist at times as a separate and distinct category from Sufism, but Sufism's critics would contend that Sufism is also distinct from mysticism/*erfan*/*tasavvuf* (a criticism that the Sufis themselves would vehemently deny). This is not to say that Sufism in Iran has been routinely and categorically condemned since the sixteenth-century Safavid era; far from it. Merely that, due to this religio-political maneuver of the Safavids, there has been the opportunity to create sharp distinctions between the categories of *erfan*/*tasavvuf* and *sufigari*, which may not have otherwise existed from a theological standpoint. For this reason, the Shi'ism of Iran shares a long history with mystical knowledge (*erfan*), but not Sufism (*sufigari*).

This politically motivated bifurcation of these theological categories has imparted a legacy that remains today. Namely, while the term *Sufi* or even *sufigari* is far from taboo, and sometimes studied as a topic of inquiry, it has come to mean something much more specific than the far-reaching *erfan*, which is the term known by most literate peoples, even if understood as referring to a specific literary tradition. For while the mystics themselves understand the word Sufism as synonymous with mystical epistemologies/gnosis, for those outside of mystical circles it refers primarily to the fraternities or organizational entities.

Currently, *erfan* is offered as a field of specialization at many religious seminaries (*howzeh*) and secular universities in Iran today. Mysticism then, at least in its *tasavvuf/erfan* form, is understood to be a serious topic of study and, with the exception of a few prominent clerics,[15] is not condemned in and of itself. Indeed, even Ayatollah Mohammad Taghi Mesbah Yazdi, a member of the Assembly of Experts and often purported to be one of the most "hard-line" and conservative clerics, has written on *erfan*.[16] Sufism too, is a topic of inquiry, although usually from a historiographical perspective. It is thus important to remember that the championing of *erfan* does not necessarily equate the condemnation of Sufism, merely its diminishing, and the vulnerability that such diminishing allows.

Indeed, the interest in *tasavvuf/erfan* and the perpetuation of its themes in seminaries and society at large continues undaunted and has continued to attract many students since the time when Shi'ism became the state religion of Iran. In fact, perhaps one of its most famous adherents lived during the twentieth century: Ayatollah Khomeini himself. Beyond Khomeini, figures invested in political Islam, including Mortaza Motahhari and Ali Shariati, have also expressed interest in mysticism, and it is their ideas I turn to now.

The Gnostic as Supreme Leader (*Rahbar*) and Mystical "Political Islam"

Ruhollah Khomeini began his studies in mysticism while a seminary student, initially under the tutelage of Mirza Ali Yazdi (d. AD 1926), who was himself a student of Husayn Sabzavari, the author of *Shahr-i Mazuma*, one of the most foundational texts on gnosis in Shi'ism.[17] Khomeini's primary teacher, however, was Muhammad Ali Shahabadi (d. AD 1950), under whose instruction he studied *erfan* for six years. As Hamid Algar notes, Shahabadi initially denied Khomeini's request to work with him, instructing him to study the more rationally oriented Islamic philosophy (*hekmat*) instead, but Khomeini was so insistent on studying *erfan* that he managed to convince his teacher.[18]

In Alexander Knysh's "'Irfan' Revisited: Khomeini and the Legacy of Islamic Mystical Philosophy,"[19] he conducts a close reading of some of Khomeini's earlier writings on mysticism. Khomeini was an admirer of Mulla Sadra, that early modern "nonmystic," and his work *Kitab al-Asfar* (*Book of Journeys*), which is Sadra's account of the four stages of mystical wayfaring, and tracks the movements and oscillations between self, God, and world. What is noteworthy about this is that the final stage marks the enlightened self, traveling from "man to man, bestowing on his community a new dispensation of spiritual and moral order."[20] Khomeini's studies also highlight his interest in one aspect of the Andalusian Sufi Ibn Arabi's *insan-e kamel* (ideal man), wherein a religious leader leads a community of believers.

In addition to his studies, Khomeini eventually wrote his own mystical treatise, entitled *The Lamp Showing the Right Way to Viceregency and Sainthood* (*Misbah al-hidaya ila al-khilafa wa al-wilaya*) in 1930, in which he remarked upon the supremacy of the gnostics: "In contrast to them [the theologians], the gnostic [*arif*], unveiling the divine one [*elah*] . . . is possessor of both eyes."[21] His interest in Sufism continued after he began his teaching position in the seminary at Qom, and it was for his teaching in mysticism and ethics that he first drew attention.[22] In addition, at the time, and even after he had assumed the position of supreme leader (*rahbar*), Khomeini famously always lived simply, eschewing luxury and living in a modest home until his death, perhaps embracing the ascetic life espoused by certain Sufis.

And while Khomeini's interest in mysticism was eventually overshadowed by his political activism, he never once disavowed his early teachings and writings, nor did he dismiss them as the misguided interests of a young man. In fact, he himself personally granted explicit permission for his supercommentaries and treatises on mysticism to be published in the 1980s after his rise to power.[23] Finally, it is of great significance that Khomeini also made reference to a Nimatullahi Gonabadi *darvish*, Mulla Sultan Ali, during a series of televised lectures on *Surat al-Fatiha*,[24] the opening chapter of the Qur'an. He mentions him during his first lecture, "Everything is a Name of God," when he speaks of "mystics" who wrote well on the chapter, as well as clerics (ulama) who also did a good job, but that none represent a "complete interpretation."[25] In essence, Khomeini uses the examples of these two categories of thinkers—along with several others—to relay the point that a complete interpretation of the Qur'an is nearly impossible, and that even his own interpretation within the lecture series is "based on possibility, not certainty."[26]

Ayatollah Khomeini was also a composer of mystical poetry, which he wrote throughout his life. Ahoo Najafian has provided the first close reading and analysis of Khomeini's mystical poetry, as well as its publication, in her dissertation "Poetic Nation: Iranian Soul and Historical Continuity."[27] In her research, Najafian notes that while the majority of Khomeini's poetry was kept hidden from the public for most of his life, upon his passing his daughter-in-law published his most recent compositions, meaning those that he had written during the last few years of his life.[28] Although there was some initial outcry at the publication, the poetry has been continually published since then, and by none other than the Institute for the Compilation and Publication of the Works of Imam Khomeini, the official institution for publishing Khomeini's written work. The institute has even gone so far as to publish some of his poems online and in translation,[29] with excerpts like the following being made available online:

> I have become imprisoned, O beloved, by the mole on your lip!
> I saw your ailing eyes and became ill through love.
> Open the door of the tavern and let us go there day and night
> For I am sick and tired of the mosque and seminary.

The dramatic professions of love, the relinquishing of the mosque for the tavern: it is easy to see why certain compatriots of Khomeini might feel uncomfortable with such declarations being made public, especially if they are unfamiliar with the mystical tradition or would be concerned that the general public might misconstrue the supreme leader's words. And yet the institute published and continues to publish these words—the objections of any naysayers not enough for the Imam's divan to be hidden from the light of day. Ayatollah Khomeini's exploration of very common mystical themes such as intoxication, imprisonment, all-consuming love, and the rejection of the rational (the seminary, the mosque) in favor of the ecstatic (the tavern) shows not only an awareness of the potentially more "controversial" concepts within the mystical tradition, but an enthusiastic engagement with them. From the information available to us, from his time as a young seminary student to his last years as the most powerful individual within the Iranian nation and an internationally recognized proponent of what is often called "political Islam," Ayatollah Khomeini never saw his interest in mysticism falter in any serious way, nor did he ever view it as contradictory to his theological and political aims.

Ultimately, I have wished to briefly touch upon Khomeini's interest in and embrace of *erfan* to highlight the ways in which mysticism and Iranian Twelver Shi'ism are not only not oppositional to one another, where to declare one the "heterodox" counterpart to the other "orthodoxy" is a gross simplification of matters, but also to demonstrate that they have in fact been deeply intertwined for long stretches of Iranian/proto-Iranian history, and sometimes overlapping in the most unexpected of places.

Mystically Inclined Clerics in Twentieth-Century Iran

Beyond Khomeini, there are a number of key clerical figures and schools of thought within or adjacent to the seminary system who embraced an esoterically inclined form of Shi'ism.

The most famous and perhaps most influential is Allameh Sayyed Mohammad Tabatabai (d. AD 1981). Originally from Tabriz, Tabatabai studied in Najaf under Grand Ayatollah Sheikh Mohammad-Hossein Naini Gharavi and Ayatollah Seyyed Ali Qadi Tabatabai, himself a renowned teacher of mysticism, and from whom he learned about the importance of studying mysticism alongside philosophy and theology.[30] While Allameh Tabatabai is perhaps best known for his massive, twenty-seven volume of Qur'anic exegesis, *Tafsir Al-Mizan*, he made many other contributions in the field of *tafsir* generally, including his twelve-volume analysis of Hafez and on the works of Mulla Sadra.

When he began teaching Mulla Sadra's *Hikmat Al Muta'alyahfi-l-asfar al-'aqliyya al-arba'a* in the Qom Seminary, the classes proved so popular that he felt compelled to make them open to the public.[31] It was then that he received pushback from the powers that be in Qom to not offer public classes on a potentially controversial topic. In response, Tabatabai penned the following letter to Ayatollah Borujerdi, head of the seminary:

> I came from Tabriz to Qum only in order to correct the beliefs of the students on the basis of the truth and to confront the false beliefs of materialists and others. . . . But today every student who comes to Qum comes with a suitcase full of doubts and problems. We must come to the aid of these students and prepare them to confront the materialists on a sound basis by teaching them authentic Islamic philosophy. I will not, therefore, abandon the teaching of the *Asfar*. At the same time, however, since I consider Ayatollah Borujerdi to be the repository of the authority of the *sharīa*, the matter will take on a different aspect if he commands me to abandon the teaching of the *Asfar*.[32]

In other words, he declared that he would continue to teach the material unless Ayatollah Borujerdi commanded him to do so in his position as a religious authority. What I find particularly compelling in his letter is his assertation that "we must come to the aid of these students and prepare them to *confront the materialists on a sound basis* by teaching them authentic Islamic philosophy" (emphasis mine). Here, Tabatabai seems to be making a case that it is not only the imparting of wisdom that he is invested in, but it is important for his students to be educated in such matters in order to be better positioned to wrestle with the forces of materialism. There seems to be an element of a more outward-looking stance adopted here by the esoteric philosopher, one who wished his students to be prepared for potentially hostile forces at play in the world.

And Tabatabai had some students who went on to become hugely influential figures in Iranian history. For while Tabatabai is very well known for his embrace of mysticism (*tasavvuf*), many of his students are less known for embracing such a perspective, despite their deep respect and reverence for him. Indeed, one such student, Mortaza Motahhari, is known much more for his political activism before and immediately after the 1977–79 revolution, especially in English-language scholarship. Upon closer examination, however, it is clear that he never wavered far from his teacher's lessons (despite Allameh Tabatabai's lack of involvement in any revolutionary activities). Here I turn again to the work of Ahoo Najafian. Najafian has shown us how Mortaza Motahhari, a key ideologue of the Iranian Revolution and student, supporter, and later close advisor of Ayatollah Khomeini, was deeply invested in defending *erfan* against its detractors, who claimed it was anti-Islamic. Most notably, he does so by demonstrating the mystical and philosophical underpinnings of the poet Hafez, rallying against those who consider him "just" a literary figure. Beyond simply positing Hafez as mystically oriented, a common if debatable stance to take, according to Najafian it was Motahhari's aim to establish the Sunni Hafez as an esoterically oriented Shi'i above all else. He bases this claim on the idea that certain themes prevalent within Hafez's oeuvre—ambiguity, secrecy, the unseen, paradox, and more—are also key concepts within Shi'i cosmologies. In doing so, Motahhari renders not only Hafez as mystically inclined but posits Shi'ism *itself* to be contingent upon esoteric ideas. Last, Najafian points out how the stakes of this claim are made all the higher by the fact that Motahhari's interpretation of Hafez was inspired, at least in part, as an attempt to reclaim Hafez from nationalist and Marxist readings, understanding him instead as a sort of crypto/proto-Shi'i.

Beyond the extremely high-profile clerics Motahhari and Tabatabai, there are other less famous but still influential figures within the seminary who embrace esoteric Shi'ism. Seyed Amir Asghari's dissertation, "Islamic Philosophy and Sufism in the Contemporary Shia Seminary and their Opponents (1850–present),"[33] provides the most in-depth analysis of the position of mystical thought within the modern Iranian seminary. Asghari uses previously unexplored source material to outline the debates between proponents of teaching mystical thought within the seminary and its detractors. More specifically, he analyzes the works of the "School of Self-Knowledge" (*Maktab Ma'rifat al-Nafs*), a school that advocates for a more esoterically inclined form of Shi'ism to be taught within the seminaries, from the late nineteenth century through the present day, as well as exploring the school's strong ties to two Sufi orders outside the seminary system. Indeed, the School of Self-Knowledge was an institutional version, or perhaps counterpart, to the Zahabiyya Sufi Order, and Asghari suggests that the Zahabiyya Order had its very origins within the seminary. Qutb al-Din Nayrizi and Mulla Ali Nuri, the Mulla Sadra revivalist, are among its famous members. Asghari also offers intellectual biographies of figures like Mulla Husaynquli Shavandi Hamadani and Shaykh Muhammad Bahari (AD 1907), both certified *mojtaheds* trained in *fiqh*, who championed the importance of teaching mystical treatises like divine love and wayfaring (*suluk*). Ultimately, Asghari's work challenges the notion that Sufi thought only developed outside the seminaries.

Such rich and productive debates continue today. In the contemporary era, key figures within the seminary and the university system continue to champion mystical thought, including Ayatollah Hassan Hasanza-deh Amoli (b. AD 1928), Ayatollah Abdollah Javadi Amoli (b. AD 1933), Seyyed Mohammad Husayn Husayni Tihrani (d. AD 1995), Mohammad Hasan Vakili (b. AD 1980), and Sayyid Mohammad Musavi, to name a few. Tihrani was particularly influential in promoting esoterically oriented Shi'ism, establishing the Mashhad seminaries as perhaps *the* place to study Shi'i mysticism within Iran, and his biographies of the Iraqi mystic Sayyid Hashim Haddad (d. AD 1984) and his own teacher Allamah Tabatabai are among the most widely read tomes of Shi'i mysticism.[34] The young *mo-jtahed* Mohammad Hasan Vakili has noted that he decided to attend the Mashhad Seminary because of the legacy of figures like Tihrani,[35] and his recent publication explores the Shi'i inclinations of Ibn Arabi, a favorite subject of Tihrani.[36]

Another Mashhad-based proponent of esoterism, Sayyid Jalal al-Din Ashtiyani (d. 2005), was a student of Allameh Tabatabai and a professor who taught at both the University of Mashhad and the Mashhad Seminary for many years. Ashtiyani was a staunch defender of esoterism, and harshly criticized Sufism's detractors, such as his colleague Mirza Mahdi Isfahani, a member of the antiphilosophy and antimysticism Tafkiki (Separation) School, for failing to properly understand Sufism and lashing out due to an inability to fully comprehend it.[37]

Finally, Ayatollah Abdollah Javadi Amoli is also a compelling figure among the contemporary seminarians, with more than just a passing interest in mystical thought. A former member of the Assembly of Experts, Ayatollah Javadi Amoli has not only held a prominent role in the Qom seminary (*howzeh*) for many years, but also has been highly active in politics, publicly commenting on issues related to Iran's nuclear programs and elections, consulting with the Ministry of the Interior and Ministry of Islamic Culture and Guidance, and acting as a long-standing critic of Iran's banking sector and policies.[38] Alongside this, he has published extensively on *erfan*, with a particular interest in the role of *velayat* as it pertains to mysticism. Javadi Amoli has also spoken on what he views to be the mystical dimension of Khomeini's thinking, which he always refers to as the *erfani* dimension, in talks such as "The Mystical Characteristics of Khomeini."[39] At a meeting with the Society for the Ahlul-Bayt, his institute on the subject of mysticism in 2019, the Ayatollah stated, "The epistemology of true mysticism (*erfan*) is the intuition of essence. There stands no veil between God and creation except for creation itself (شهود حقیقی، عرفان شناسی معرفت اخلق خود مگر نیست حجابی هیچ خلق و خدا بین/است ذات).[40] Such a statement, situated within a conversation on how the true meaning (*mozu*) of mysticism (*erfan*) is the presence of infinite truth, would not be out of place coming from any Sufi sheikh. Indeed, Javadi Amoli goes on to state that with this worldview and understanding of mysticism, "the whole world becomes an *aya*" (*kol-e jahan mishavad ayat*), or a verse of the Qur'an. Here, we see the world as text, and text as world.

I offer this brief overview of these esoterically inclined clerics—some prominent, some up-and-coming—within the seminary and university systems in order to demonstrate the prevalence of mystical thought outside of Sufi orders in Iran today. The Iranian seminary system is a place of enormously rich and complex debates, with creative thinkers and prolific writers producing a theoretically, politically, and philosophically diverse range of materials, and so for those familiar with the recent output it is unsurprising that it contains advocates of mystical thought.[41] These advocates are not without their detractors, of course; there are many who write *against* the role of mysticism as a hermeneutic device or its place within exegesis or "serious" scholarly research. Such debates do not give evidence to a blanket condemnation of mysticism as some sort of "heterodox" aberration, however, but are rather just that: debates, therein demonstrating the seriousness with which esotericism is considered. From Khomeini and Motahhari to Shariati to local groups of self-identified *darvish*, the question of mystical thought, whether in its iterations of *erfan, tasavvuf,* or *sufigari,* is to be found throughout an array of theoretically and politically diverse intellectual circles.

Non-Sufi Mystical Thought in Contemporary Iran

I have previously described mysticism in Iran as a shape-shifter, but it might also be thought of as something like an infiltrator. Outside of the seminaries, universities, Sufi groups, and poetry circles, mystical thought can be found in a wide variety of settings. Niloofar Haeri's nuanced ethnography of middle-class women's prayer circles has shown how their interpretations of Islam have been affected by education—both formal and informal—in Persian poetry.[42] In particular, she highlights how certain concepts taken from the poetry of Rumi, Hafez, and Sa'adi influence the women's understandings of Islam and their relationship to God. These concepts like "the beloved" and "presence of the heart" (*hozur-e del*), very common tropes of mystical thought found within Persian poetry, are what allow the women to feel a particular emotional closeness and intimacy with God, such that the moment of prayer is transformed into a time for close engagement with the divine, rather than the rote and mechanized practice that prayer is often purported to be. As such, these mystical ideas, typically associated with poetic works, then influence the women's interpretation and experience not only of prayer but of religion as a whole. Lastly, Haeri also analyzes the genre of popular literature and essay writing that she categorizes as "simple *erfan*," works expounding upon mystical epistemologies written by nonexperts, typically women. While the category itself is already of interest, Haeri points out that these works of "simple mysticism" are organized in the prayer books (*ketab-e dua*) section of bookstores, indicating that popular mysticism is not considered out of place in the presumably more sober arena of prayer.

In another example of the reach of mystical thought, Alireza Doostdar's exploration of contemporary occult practices in Iran also demonstrates the popularity of debates and discourse surrounding the question of the unseen (*al-ghayb*). In sharp distinction with my interlocutors, who continually stress the *limits* of rational thought (*aql*), Doostdar's interlocutors' focus is the underscoring of the rational and scientific elements of occult practices, as they work to dispel accusations of charlatanism and superstition (*khorafa*) leveled against them. Despite the differing analytical stance of our interlocutors, both this book and Doostdar's demonstrate the intellectual investment in unseen realms; whether it be through spiritualist practices of the occult or Sufi striving toward the Unreal, the otherworldly is of interest. Moreover, Doostdar has highlighted the influence of esoteric ideals among the interlocutors, including a movement called "Cosmic Mysticism" (*erfan-e keyhani*), an Iranian "spiritual-therapeutic movement"[43] that was shaped by a wide array of influences including Western esotericism, Buddhist ideals, self-help gurus like Wayne Dyer, the fiction of Paulo Coelho, radiation therapy, and, if less explicitly, Sufi ideas.[44] For although the Cosmic Mystics do not discuss traditional Sufi concepts (*fana*, wandering) or sources (the writings of sheikhs, poetry, etc.), they are interested in alternative forms of consciousness, the importance of revelation, and of course the unseen— all ideas well within the wheelhouse of many Sufis. As Doostdar astutely points out in an analysis of the writings of Mohammad Taheri, leader of the Cosmic Mystics—himself a *pir*-type figure—what Taheri is essentially arguing for is that "scientific knowledge about the world may be received in the form of revelation or mystical thinking,"[45] and these are ideas that have been prevalent within Iranian thought for centuries, including within Sufi circles. In other words, the Cosmic Mystics are engaged with and pulling from religio-scientific discourses that have long existed within intellectual circles in Iran, and these religio-scientific discourses have long been influenced by and influence Sufi epistemologies.

While I would in no way argue that this spiritual-therapeutic group is a type of "neo-Sufism," not least because the group themselves bristled against accusations of them as wannabe or pseudo-Sufis, and nor do I think such an "are they or aren't they" would be particularly productive or interesting, what I do wish to point out is the investment in esotericism. What I find compelling is that, despite the differences between the New-Ageists, occultists, spiritualists, and so forth, and the Nimatullahi Sufis, they share an affinity for exploring esoteric lines of inquiry, even if the *answers*, or sometimes solutions, they ultimately arrive at are quite different.

The last arena of Sufi infiltration I will mention is that of contemporary poetry. While tracing the presence of mystical ideas within contemporary poetry in Iran is a book-length project in and of itself, I will touch upon one work that has investigated such trends. I have already mentioned Niloofar Haeri's astute analysis of "simple erfan" literature and essay writing. In another recently published work, Fatemeh Shams offers a close examination of contemporary poetry, some state-sponsored and some not, that is explicitly supportive of the ideals, events, and leaders of the Islamic Revolution. The themes and ideas that Shams unpacks in this rich examination of an understudied corpus of contemporary Iranian literature are many, and among them are what she calls "mystic combative poetics."[46] This refers to forms of poetry and poetic writing focused on war—both the Iran-Iraq War of 1980–88 specifically as well as war in general—that use mystical motifs to extol battlefield-worthy virtues such as journeying, sacrifice, and more, so that they might "turn war into a path-of-love (*rah-e eshq*)."[47] For example, Shams observes how the poet Hamid Sabzevari makes reference to the "seven valleys of the quest of love" from Attar's Sufi classic *Conference of the Birds* (*Mantaq-al Tayr*), which is typically understood to be a story a journey of self-discovery and recognition, and a refutation of the idea of ego. Sabzevari instead uses the references to Attar's "quest of love" as a way to shed light on "the hardship and adversities of revolutionary insurgency . . . as an invitation to join the revolutionary crowds."[48] Shams also briefly touches upon the mystical interpretations of death and martyrdom in war poetry, describing how wine and intoxication are equated in certain works with blood and death to formulate a sort of "enchantment of death,"[49] implying death is a heady, enriching, and ultimately desirous event. As Shams's work demonstrates, mysticism holds appeal not only for women's poetry groups and New Age and occultist healers, but also for war-hardened veterans and patriots of the Islamic Republic.

In these sections, I hope to have highlighted recent important scholarship that touches upon the far reach of mystical epistemologies outside of Sufi circles in contemporary Iran, from the seats of revolutionary power and the authority of the seminaries to the living rooms of lay people to the witchy practices of exorcists, all are at least partially familiar with (and some extraordinarily conversant with) mystical concepts and conceits, writings and reflections. In emphasizing these trends, I hope to again impress upon the point that to categorize mysticism as a form of "heterodox" Islam overlooks, in an incredibly egregious fashion, the deep and myriad ways that esoteric ideas have influenced so many facets of Iranian artistic and intellectual output.

With this understanding of the conflicted history of the category of *erfan*, we will turn our attention to the history of the Nimatullahi Order. In this way, we may see how the bifurcations of *erfan* translated into the sociopolitical sphere beyond the Safavid era.

The Nimatullahi Sufi Order was founded by Shah Nimatullah Vali (d. AD 1431) at the turn of the fifteenth century.[50] Born in Aleppo in AD 1330 to a Syrian father and an Iranian mother, he left his hometown while still a youth and spent many years traveling throughout the Muslim world in search of a spiritual teacher. Finally, he encountered Sheikh Abdollah Yafe'i in Mecca, and proceeded to study with him for a period of seven years. Following this period of instruction, Shah Nimatullah began his second round of travels, now in the role of teacher and guide rather than "thirsty seeker."[51] His travels took him through Egypt, Central Asia, and then to Samarkand. He initially wished to cease his travels and stay in Samarkand, but its ruler, Tamerlane, forced him to continue on his journey, not being "appreciative" of his teachings. He continued on. First to Herat, and then ultimately westward to Kerman, in the southwest of Iran. As the story goes, after politely refusing offers of residence bestowed upon him by sultans and great men of learning, he chose to stay in Kerman at the request of an old beggar woman, who served him bread and yogurt and asked him to stay. There he remained for the rest of his long life. Once in Kerman, Shah Nimatullah received hundreds of disciples, who traveled from lands as far as India and Andalusia to study with him. He was a prolific writer, and it was said he wrote three hundred compilations and treatises on scientific, gnostic, and literary works in both Farsi and Arabic. Shah Nimatullah was the composer of his own collection of poetry (divan), and was primarily interested in the works of Ibn Arabi, in particular Ibn-Arabi's *Bezels of Wisdom* (*Fusus al-Hikam*). After living to be over a hundred years old, Shah Nimatullah died in 1430 and was buried in the small town of Mahan, about thirty-five kilometers from Kerman. An elaborate tomb was erected by the ruler Ahmed I Vali in the years immediately following Shah Nimatullah's passing, and today it remains a highly popular pilgrimage site for the Nimatullahi Order.

Following the passing of Shah Nimatullah, his son Shah Khalilullah succeeded him as the order's leader. At this time, as previously discussed, the Safavids were beginning to coalesce their power in Iran, and subsequently to expel or consolidate any potential rival factions. In order to avoid this possible threat, Shah Khalilullah moved the entire order to Bidar, India, at the invitation of the sultan of Bidar, Ahmad Shah Al Wali Bahmani, who had been a follower of Shah Nimatullah. The majority of the order would continue to stay in India for nearly another three hundred years, until the disintegration of the powers of the Safavid dynasty left a power vacuum, as well as the opportunity to return.

A Return: The Nimatullahi in the Qajar Era

The return of the Nimatullahi Order from Bidar to Iran marks the beginning of the current instantiation of the order and the revival of organized Sufism in Iran as a whole. As the Safavid dynasty fell into disarray, its state-approved ulama no longer held exclusivity over the positions of spiritual authority, and what followed was a period of contestation and vying for power among the clergy. Indeed, with the advent of the Qajar dynasty (AD 1785–1925) came a time of weakened centralized state power, resulting in the flourishing of locally based spiritual leaders and jurists throughout Iran, including various Sufi sheikhs. Among them, of course, was the Nimatullahi Order, whose numbers swelled during this time.[52] Indeed, so popular did it prove in certain regions that the governor of Kerman vastly expanded the shrine of Shah Nimatullahi.

This is not to say that there were not challenges involved in their initial return. Most significantly, it was also at this time that the order first declared itself to be a Shi'i order, largely to comply with the reigning Shi'i ulama.[53] Indeed, the return of the Nimatullahi Order to Iran was largely the result of the efforts of three men: Husayn Ali Shah, Majdhub Ali Shah and Mast Ali Shah, who were able to carefully maneuver the theologico-political landscape at the time.

Husayn Ali Shah, in particular, was very strategic in this regard, and extremely mindful about even disclosing his identity as a Sufi. He was in fact a trained jurist, having studied in the seminaries of Isfahan, and wore the robes of his fellow clergy, thereby appearing indistinguishable from the others. His primary goal was to distinguish the Nimatullahi Order from the wandering, "libertine" Nimatullahi *darvish* who had remained in Iran, and in a sense to reestablish their reputation as a "legitimate" and respectable order. His major treatise was a response to a Christian missionary named Henry Martyn, in defense of Shi'i theology.[54] Ultimately, while his philosophical writings were limited, his main legacy was the reintroduction of the Nimatullahi Order to the seminaries of Iran.

His successor, Majdhub Ali Shah, was in contrast a hugely prolific writer who expounded explicitly Sufi ideas with much more conviction, while at the same time arguing that such mystical ideals were resolutely Shi'i as well. Trained in the seminary sciences, Majdhub Ali Shah's greatest contribution was positioning Sufism as a legitimate topic of debate within the seminary systems, holding his own against attacks from vehemently anti-Sufi clerics like Aqa Muhammad Ali Behbehani.[55] In addition to this, it was under his rule that the ranks of the Nimatullahi Order greatly increased, due in large part not only to his scholarship and leadership but also to the decrease in tension between the political authorities and the Sufis as a whole at the time.[56] Indeed, throughout Iran there were Sufis who were now under the protection of local Qajar leaders, even "sharing them" at times with rival jurists or other Sufis.[57]

The final influential *qotb* from that era was known as Mast Ali Shah. Mast Ali Shah differentiated himself from his predecessors in two ways: (1) he was not a jurist, nor had he received much seminary training at all, and (2) he traveled extensively during his life, spending some thirty years in India, Turkey, and the Kurdish regions, speaking with many sheikhs and sages of various religions and creeds.[58] As a result, most of his writings are in fact travelogues (*siyahat name*) rather than treatises.[59] As such, while on the one hand Mast Ali Shah was known for his open-mindedness, given his conversations with disparate groups of people throughout the world, in Iran he was often critical of the Shi'i jurists and "exterior sciences," declaring that any scholar who disregarded "interior Shi'ism," that is, Sufism, was not fit to be a leader on the path.[60] As an outcome of these public declarations, he perhaps unsurprisingly faced much more persecution than his predecessors, given his vocal criticism of the Shi'i authorities.

Ultimately, the late Qajar era marked the time when Sufi orders were in the most direct conversation, and at times heated debate, with the Shi'i ulama. In addition, given the decentralized nature of the Qajar state, there were times Sufis closely aligned with local leaders, as in Kerman and other regions. In one instance, the alliance was such that an order was given the title of "peacock order" or "gnostics of the peacock" (*tavus-ol urafa*),[61] with the peacock being the symbol of the monarchy. Alessandro Cancian has also written that, although the order generally advocated for political quietism, certain early twentieth-century *qotbs* of the Nimatullahi Gonabadi Order encouraged their faithful to consider political activism.[62] Following this era, however, never again would the Sufis be so deeply engaged with both state and clerical power, at least in this explicit a fashion. Finally, as a result of the localized nature of Sufi practice at the time, the Nimatullahi Order fractured into many different subsets, resulting in the dozen or so orders that all claim lineage to it today.

Inside and Outside: The Nimatullahis during the Pahlavi Regime

Following the rise to power of the military commander Reza Shah Pahlavi in the early 1920s and the subsequent centralization of power, many Nimatullahi Sufis largely retreated from openly engaging with political life, as many of their previous benefactors were no longer in power. In addition, Reza Shah's dismantling of the Shi'i clergy's religious institutions undoubtedly proved a motivating factor for the Sufis to step away from engaging in the public sphere in an organized and deliberate fashion. This is not to say that they were not involved and in dialogue with figures of social and political authority, merely that that was done on a much more individualized level. As such, the orders became more self-contained and structured at this time.

For the scope of this project, I will highlight only a few instances that were key to the development of the Nimatullahi Order during the Reza Shah Pahlavi era (1925–41). The first is the reorganization of the system of Sufi practice. Essentially, the Nimatullahis partially drew away from the master-disciple/teacher-student (*pir-morid*) structure at this time, leaving a less formal (*rasmi*) structure in its place. In addition, under the leadership of the *qotb* Saleh Alishah (1891–1966), the order increased in number and reputation, drawing not only more followers but also more patrons to them, as several members of the local aristocracy were also said to have joined. At this time, they were said to number around forty thousand,[63] a huge number. With this increase in funds, they initiated a number of public works projects, especially in the small city of Gonabad, where the order had a large following. These works included the founding of a library, the Ketabkhane-ye Soltani, a hospital, an adult literacy and education program, and the construction of water canals (*qanats*).[64]

This increase in size and public activity did not go unnoticed, attract-ing the attention of none other than the monarch himself. According to my interlocutors, while Reza Shah was not antagonistic to the Sufis ini-tially, he became suspicious after they had grown substantially in popu-larity. The minister of culture, Ali Asghar Hekmat, paid an official visit to the order to ensure that they were not "smoking opium, and bribing judges."[65] Upon receiving reassurance that they were not engaged in il-licit activities, Reza Shah demanded a text outlining the basic tenets of the Nimatullahis.

What resulted was *Saleh's Advice* (*Pand-e Saleh*), which remains to this day one of the foundational texts of the Solantalishahi Gonabadi Nimatul-lahi Order. If you enter any library or bookstore of a Solantalishahi meet-ing place (*khaneqah*) and say that you know nothing of mysticism but wish to learn, this is one of two texts they will hand to you. *Saleh's Advice* has been translated into various languages and, as will be further elaborated upon in chapter 2, is available for free online. It is significant to note, then, that one of the most widely read writings by an Iranian Sufi in the twen-tieth century came into being as a result of the state's inquiry into con-temporary mysticism.

Despite Reza Shah's comparatively lenient view toward mystical orders, there were many intellectual and clerics at this time who denounced Su-fism vehemently, describing it as antithetical to the project of modernism. The most vocal and vociferous of these critics was of course the public intellectual Ahmad Kasravi, who, in his texts entitled simply *Sufism* and *Shi'ism*, decried both modes of Islamic thought and their "evil teachings,"[66] and accused them of promoting factionalism rather than a strong central-ized state. Certain other intellectuals and writers at the time, including Sadeq Hedayet, Ali Dasti, and Tariq Arani, also looked down upon Su-fism, although more for what they called its antisocial behavior and charla-tanism, and considering more the begging *darvish* than organized orders. Within the clerical establishment, Ayatollah Seyyed Hossein Borujerdi was perhaps the most vocal opponent to both Sufism and *erfan*.

At this time, there were of course other Sufi orders active within Iran—including others that claimed Nimatullahi lineage—and a number of these remained more immediately involved with the monarchy, espe-cially during the reign of Mohammad Reza Shah, the son and successor of Reza Shah. In particular, the Safialishahi claimed the interest of Moham-mad Reza Shah's younger brother Ali-Reza, and his twin sister Princess Ashraf was instrumental in the opening of a meeting place (*khaneqah*) for the Zahir od-Dowle Order.[67] Finally, Shahbanou Farah Diba, the empress of Iran, who spent vast amounts of royal funds promoting the arts, literature, and cultural heritage projects throughout the country,[68] funded the Imperial Iranian Academy of Philosophy. This academy was headed by the philosopher Seyyed Hossein Nasr and the famed orientalist Henry Corbin, who championed a Sufi-heavy, quietist form of Shi'i Islam.[69]

Despite these instances of royal interest in mysticism, the Nimatullahi Order remained largely free of royal patronage, and essentially operated as a self-contained entity within the larger civil society, surviving off of the financial contributions of its members, both rich and poor. Indeed, perhaps its greatest influence came in the form of travels by its members to India, Afghanistan, and Pakistan, visiting with other Sufi orders. As such, the order remained outside of the reigning political authorities and disinterested in public debates until late 1968, with the publication of a particular treatise by the current qotb of the order, Reza Ali Shah.

In what was been described to me as a "sudden gesture," Reza Ali Shah began to publicly criticize the government of the Shah in the late 1960s. Most significantly, at the 1968 International Conference on Human Rights in Tehran, which was presided over by the Shah's twin sister, Princess Ashraf, he presented a paper entitled "Religious Perspectives on the Human Rights Declaration." In this paper, he not only criticized the Universal Declaration of Human Rights as failing to meet its goal but in particular criticized its lack of Islamic values, saying the values had been diluted by the "politics of strangers,"[70] the disregard for religious holidays in Iran, the divorce law, the prevalence of indulgence in substances, and, most strikingly, the influence of Westernization or, as was the popular term at the time, "Westoxification" (Gharbzadegi).[71] Needless to say, it was unequivocally the most political and the most oppositional text written by a Nimatullahi Sufi in decades, and placed the order firmly in the position of supporting Khomeini and his compatriots. As the Nimatullahi continued to have sheikhs in their ranks who were also trained jurists, or at least those who had spent time in the seminary, there is no doubt that the order's elders were well aware of the debates that were happening at the time. More significantly, it has been reported that Reza Ali Shah sent Khomeini a congratulatory letter upon his release from prison in 1964,[72] and, as a current sheikh relayed to me, there was a brief meeting between Reza Ali Shah and Khomeini himself in 1978.

Despite Reza Ali Shah's writings on the Universal Declaration of Human Rights and his personal overtures to Khomeini, the Sufis maintain that they have never taken an interest in the political realm. Indeed, when asked about further involvement with the Islamic Revolution, I was given no further information, nor was I able to locate any such documents in my research. Indeed, what was made very clear to me and what I wish to emphasize here is that the various instantiations of the Nimatullahi Order do not possess any interest in politics; neither now, nor in years past.

Sufism in the Islamic Republic

During and immediately following the Islamic Revolution, the Sufis continued to meet throughout Iran, although in more sporadic fashion given the disruption caused by the events of the time. After the establishment of the Islamic Republic, the Nimatullahi Order was able to largely carry out its activities undisturbed, given its ties to Khomeini and the regime. In particular, Khomeini's son Ahmad was said to have strong sympathies for and ties to the order.

The prime example of anti-Sufi activity occurred on the night of November 30, 1979,[73] some eight months after the passing of a referendum establishing an Islamic republic, when the primary Sufi meeting place (*khaneqah*), the Ali Suleiymani Mosque in Tehran, was set on fire in what was perceived to be an act of arson. The mosque was eventually rebuilt, but the Sufis are still reluctant to talk about the incident. Van den Bos expresses encountering a similar sentiment in his research surrounding the incident, noting, "Although I have been unable to ascertain the real course of events, the fact that . . . silence was melancholic in resignation, deliberately not angry, excludes the reading that has the rhetoric of silence, in any power context, as a token of resistance."[74]

There were reports of events in other areas of the country, in particular in Gonabad, where local paramilitary (*basij*) groups had accused the local order of not having pledged allegiance to Khomeini and the government of the Islamic Republic. In actuality, Reza Ali Shah had cemented his ties with Khomeini, and other sheikhs and prominent elders had attempted to further demonstrate their allegiance by attending the funerals and mourning sessions of key members of Khomeini's circle and administration.[75] In addition, the name of the Sufi meeting place, *khaneqah*, was changed to *hosseiniyeh*, or "place of Hossein," referring to the third Shiʻi Imam, thereby making very explicit their status as a Shiʻi order.

Lack of Legal Clarity

Despite these affiliations and attempts at ingratiation, however, the fact remains that within the Islamic Republic there is no official policy toward Sufism or mysticism as a whole, so its practitioners remain neither condemned nor condoned by the state.

The ambiguity of their status is made all the more noteworthy because the Constitution of the Islamic Republic of Iran does in fact lay out specific guidelines regarding the status of religious minorities within Iran in Article 13. In its entirety, it states: "Zoroastrian, Jewish, and Christian Iranians are the only recognized religious minorities, who, within the limits of the law, are free to perform their religious rites and ceremonies, and to act according to their own canon in matters of personal affairs and religious education,"[76] thereby affirming both the recognition of these groups as well as the rights accorded with such standing.[77] The term "only" here is perhaps a bit misleading, as non-Shi'i Ja'fari Muslims are also afforded formal recognition.[78] Specifically, it is laid out in Article 12:

> The official religion of Iran is Islam and the Twelver Ja'fari school, and this principle will remain eternally immutable. Other Islamic schools, including the Hanafi, Shafi'i, Maliki, Hanbali, and Zaydi, are to be accorded full respect, and their followers are free to act in accordance with their own jurisprudence in performing their religious rites. These schools enjoy official status in matters pertaining to religious education, affairs of personal status . . . and related litigation in courts of law. In regions of the country where Muslims following any one of these schools of fiqh constitute the majority, local regulations, within the bounds of the jurisdiction of local councils, are to be in accordance with the respective school of fiqh, without infringing upon the rights of the followers of other schools.[79]

Thus, we see a direction not only to affirm the position of other Islamic schools of thought, but to carry out "local regulations" in compliance with the appropriate jurisprudence (*fiqh*). The other group that might bear comparison is the Baha'is, another group that goes unmentioned in the constitution. Unlike the Sufis, however, the Baha'is have faced consistent oppressive measures since the inception of the Islamic Republic,[80] a fact that is said to be due to their association with British imperialist forces,[81] as well as the members' more "radical" idea of their founder as a form of messianic figure. Moreover, within the founding documents of the Islamic

Republic there exist myriad examples of negative opinions by state officials of the Baha'is, while no such comparative paperwork regarding Sufism is said to exist.[82]

As there exists no litigation currently in place or any active campaign on the part of the Sufis to achieve some form of formal recognition, it would be unfair to say even that they exist in a state of limbo, as such a state suggests a form of waiting and anticipation. To be in limbo implies that there is an end point that should have been reached, but one is instead caught in a space that was always meant to be transitory, and hence the increasing discomfort for those whose stay in it grows increasingly difficult the longer they occupy it. As the experience of the transitory undergoes its unnatural metamorphosis into that of permanence, those in limbo become increasingly uneasy in their experience of waiting, as if watching time being held hostage. In contrast, there is no anticipatory feeling among the Sufis, as theirs is not a problem with an explicit temporal dimension. Indeed, the question of their legal recognition is not even specifically addressed, but is rather evaded.

One might suggest at this point, however, that "evaded" is perhaps too strong a term. In most cities, the Sufi meeting places, the *khanegahs* and *hosseiniyehs*, are not only actively used but their status as part of a *vaghf*, or their status as part of a larger religious endowment, where some sort of charitable donation, most typically land, is made to a religious institute, is still being honored. So, the *vaghf-nameh*, the document of entitlement, or the deed, so to speak, allows the land and the buildings used upon it to remain in Sufi hands, and this is the most striking legal indicator of the position of organized mysticism within Iran.[83] Since the Islamic Revolution, perhaps the biggest obstacle they have faced has come in the form of publication and circulation of texts and sermons. Essentially, when one became too popular, someone from the Ministry of Culture (Ershad) would intervene, bestowing a strongly worded cease-and-desist order in the form of a human messenger.

Over the past five years, however, there has been an unfortunate and noted increase in the harassment of Sufi orders by local governments, primarily in the form of the closure or "discouragement" of large meetings. As such, the Sufis' avowed disinterest in asserting themselves in the sociopolitical sphere has been tested as of late, and has caused, if nothing else, more particular strategizing. I do not delve further into these recent events at the request of my interlocutors.

Instead, at this point I would like to go into more detail about the current routines, rituals, and manners of a Nimatullahi Sufi Order in Iran today. In this way, we might be able to understand the order's operations in greater depth, viewing it not only through the lens of the larger sociopolitical realm but also as its own more self-contained and autonomous entity.

Scene from a Meeting

On holidays the space is always more crowded, as devotees from out of town use the opportunity to come to see the *qotb*, and today is no exception. At 6 a.m., a handful of men and women, those who are more active in the organization, will come and open the doors, give the space a quick cleaning, dusting carpets and setting out a few chairs, and brew tea and arrange dates or pastries to distribute. The crowds begin to gather around 6:45 a.m., with the *qotb* scheduled to speak at 7:30.

The meeting place is a two-story house on a quiet, tree-lined street in an upper-middle-class suburban neighborhood in North Tehran. Originally a residential property, the house has been used by the Sufis for about fifteen years and is still a privately owned property with the deed in the name of one of the prominent families of the order.[84] As people file in, several men stand outside and keep a lookout, for any "government types" (*yeki az dowlat*) or "busybodies" (*fozul*),[85] they say. Upon entering, women are handed a chador, although most are already wearing them. These are not the typical sweeping, black variety, however, but colorful, lightweight, thin cotton sheets in colors from pink to brown, decorated with small polka dots and intricate floral patterns. As is the case with all *mahdaviyes*, the space is gender-segregated, with the women upstairs and the men on the first floor. The *darvish* find seats on the floor, older folks sit in chairs or against the wall, and the rooms fill up quickly.

It's a warm day in early autumn, and the temperature rises as more and more people pack into the space. Sure-footed servers step gingerly between the people, balancing trays, bending down to offer their teas and sweets, navigating the crowded room and forming crooked paths as they weave around the seated faithful. The servers' smiles break the atmosphere of serious anticipation. Most attendees enter quietly, often with a companion or two, although occasionally people will recognize one another, quickly stringing together a number of salutations:

"Salam, how are you? Are you well? God willing everything is well."

No one ever waits for an answer.

A few, however, stand and greet each other with a special handshake, unique to the Sufi order, involving clasping and kissing of the hands. If you wish to submit a question to the *pir* too, you must speak with one of these women who has clearly mastered the aforementioned handshake.

This session (*jalaseh*) will take place in two parts: first, the *pir* will deliver a sermon that will last for twenty or thirty minutes. Following this, he will privately read a number of questions that have been written down on paper. He will then respond to the men's questions, staying downstairs among the men while the women listen to his responses upstairs. The men will then leave and go outside the building, and all the women will come downstairs and the *pir* will respond to their questions.

In order to submit a question, one must write it down and seal it in an envelope. On the outside of the envelope, a particular line of poetry must be written in order for the question to be accepted.[86] In addition, the question must also be written in the proper format, meaning it must be clearly directed to the *pir* and possess the proper honorifics before his name. If the questioner is illiterate, they must speak to one of the helpers before the session. Usually, there are no more than a dozen questions submitted in one session.

But first: the sermon. And now the room is so densely packed that the floor is no longer visible, people perched on windows and standing in the doorway. A stereo system has been set up so that the *pir* speaks into a microphone, amplifying his frail voice and broadcasting to both upstairs and downstairs. The men stand as he enters, but quickly sit down. The women know the sermon is about to begin from the noise coming from downstairs, sounds of shuffling and shifting around, punctuated by cries of "Ya Ali!" and "Ya Hazrat Agha!"[87]

The *pir* begins the sermon. His speech quickly reveals a person of advanced age, with a rasping voice that breaks and is often strained, a sound creased with auditory wrinkles. He occasionally draws long breaths as if coming up for air. Because of its fragility, his voice offers not a stern authoritarianism, but a gentle earnestness, as if he has run a long way to tell us something, and needs to tell us no matter how exhausted. Still, despite the tired quality of his voice, the assured and measured cadence of the speech is undeniable. He speaks extemporaneously, a storyteller of the highest order, weaving together the central themes of his sermon with narratives of sheikhs long gone, excerpts of mystical poetry, and passages (*ayas*) from the Qur'an. The tone is pedagogical and steady, his speech peppered with questions and delivered in simple colloquial language so that all may be able to comprehend. And again the voice, so fragile as to give it an air of vulnerability.

As he speaks, a handful of women begin to cry. While some do so quietly, tears rolling silently down their faces as they rock back and forth, others end up sobbing loudly by the sermon's end, their shoulders shaking up and down as even their bodies are overtaken by grief. This outpouring of deep emotion is typical of Sufi gatherings: Regardless of the content of the sermon, although perhaps more frequently when recounting tragic stories during holidays of mourning, people will begin to cry. Perhaps they are mourning some tragedy in their lives, perhaps they are moved by the words of the *pir*, or even just his presence, perhaps they have gone into *hal*; whatever the reason, it is not unusual to do so.

After the *pir* concludes, everyone recites the *salavat* prayer out loud. There is some shuffling about, and a brief pause of several minutes. Downstairs, he is reading the men's questions, silently, and to himself. After he is done, he begins again.

He still speaks with the microphone so that the women may listen upstairs. The questions are answered in the form of another sermon, the various inquiries and appeals for advice blended into a seamless act of oration,

FIGURE 1.1 Imam Ali birthday (*moludi*) celebration in a *khaneqah*, unnamed for anonymity.

as though reading a monologue. Even though the rest of the *darvish* have not read the questions, it is not difficult to discern the topics that are being addressed by the *pir*'s response. Inquiries about college admittance, performance on exams, health and healing, and even romantic inquiries are all addressed. When he concludes, the names of those whose questions were not addressed are read, and they are instructed to come to a more private meeting to be held later in the week, at a similarly early hour.

Following this, it is the women's turn. The men leave the house. Having all the occupants of the densely crowded upstairs slowly make their way down the narrow staircase, only to refile into the downstairs room, takes time. People both stand and sit, knowing they will spend less time here, and arrange themselves messily. Some women complain about not being able to see, others speak in harsh tones to one another, a third intervenes: "This is not a place for fighting." Crying continues.

The *pir* is seated on a sturdy armchair in the front of the room. His hair is thick and white as snow, he wears a robe (*abeh*) but not a turban (*ammameh*).[88] After the *pir* has finished addressing the women's questions, those whose inquiries went unanswered are directed to come to another meeting. Then he slowly gets up to leave, first leaning forward before pulling himself up.

The women begin to get excited, and reach out to touch him, even as they part ways to clear a path for him. Suddenly people convene quickly around the chair, crowding around, dragging their hands across it as if to feel the presence he has left behind. Others grab bits and pieces he had with him—a tissue is pocketed, as is a napkin and the plastic tea cup. Others roll their eyes at this activity. There are muffled sobs now, others praying furtively under their breath, wishing good health and good fortune for the elderly holy man, watching as he holds his thin cloak around him as he makes his way out, as slowly as he came in. . . .

2 Unknowing of Text, Unknowing of Authority

There were two of them. My sheikhs, that is. But of course, they were not *properly* my sheikhs; as in they were not my spiritual guides, but rather two of my most generous interlocutors. I was fortunate enough to meet a number of sheikhs during my time researching this project, but with these two the meetings were different, in terms of both time spent and the depth of our discussions. And so, they became my sheikhs.

They live in different cities and do not know each other. I will refer to them as Sheikh Noroozi and Sheikh Alizadeh. Both men have their own circle of local, mixed-gender followers with whom they primarily meet to discuss Persian-language poetry, but they also make themselves available to offer advice for whoever wishes to consult with them.

They are examples of leaders of the localized, congregation-like reading circles (*doreh*) that are very popular throughout Iran.[1] Sheikh Noroozi has been convening his *doreh* in his home for about twelve years, and Sheikh Alizadeh has been holding his in a meeting place of one of his devotees for about seven years. More importantly for the purposes of this project, they both identify as *darvish*, even though they are currently not part of any larger order.

Neither of them has any formal religious training, although Sheikh Alizadeh, a civil servant for some forty years, grew up in a devout family, his grandfather and great-grandfather were both clerics, and he memorized the Qur'an as a boy. Sheikh Noroozi is an engineer by training, and received a master's degree in his subfield. In the 1970s, he was initiated into a Sufi order in his city that ceased meeting at the onset of the Iran-Iraq War and never reconvened. The title of "sheikh" was thus not bestowed upon either by a more senior authority figure, but by their followers. Neither remembers exactly when they began to be referred to as such.

Based on extended conversations with both sheikhs, this chapter traces the relationship between text, authority, and hermeneutics. For the Sufis, as for many Muslims, spiritual authority is directly tied to textual authority. Textual authority, in turn, is derived from the ability to provide informed and insightful interpretations of those written materials that provide essential guidance on the cultivation of the soul and transformation of the self. According to Sheikh Noroozi and Sheikh Alizadeh, however, this authority is complicated by their particular understanding of the nature of the text and the limitation of the human intellect in light of the supreme capabilities of the inner heart.

Regarding the former, both sheikhs approach interpretation not as a means to discern answers, but to reveal a further layer of questions that are contained with the text. In doing so, they make apparent to their followers the endlessness of the text, such that each passage, each phrase, and even a single word can contain a multiplicity of ideas and arguments. The Sufis thus adhere to an interpretative framework for understanding poetry that mimics their idea of knowledge as an exercise without limit or finality. And while many, many commentators might share this understanding of poetry, and certainly the Qur'an, as possessing an endless cosmos of ideas, what is unique here is how the sheikhs see this as a limitation on their authority, as if in doing so they affirm the text will always elude human understanding.

Another key idea that impacts their stance as authority figures is the sheikhs' belief in the capabilities of the heart as a guide. What is meant by "heart" is a topic that could fill a thousand pages, and in a way it is terrible to distill it down to shorthand, but for our purposes here I will define the heart as the site of a form of knowledge that cannot be learned from a book or a teacher (solely), but from intimate experience with the divine, through an awareness of non-knowledge. Known by many names, such as the "abode of the light of faith," (*nur al-iman*), the "abode of the light of gnosis," (*nur al-ma'rifat*), and the "secret of divine knowledge," (*sir-e ma'rifat*), to privilege the heart as guide is to privilege (1) each individual's relationship with God, as difficult as it may be to access, over the teachings of an earthly guide; and (2) a form of knowledge that is more experiential than learned. What complicates matters, however, is that the forms of knowledge—learned and experienced—are of course intimately related, such that it is said to be nearly impossible to learn to access this a priori, esoteric knowledge *without* a teacher. It is for this reason (among many others) that there is such reverence for the teacher within the Sufi tradition, a topic that will be discussed later in this chapter. The teacher is no less than the means through which one may become in union with God (*tawhid*). What sets these two sheikhs apart, however, is their *insistence* on their own limitations, an observation that causes melancholy in Sheikh Noroozi and delight in Sheikh Alizadeh.

This chapter explores the relationship between learned knowledge and divine knowledge, between text and authority, and between language and the self. How is each pair constituted and disassembled through one another? How is authority understood for these two sheikhs, and what is the epistemological basis for the perceived limits of their own knowledge? In what way does their hermeneutic stance undo the boundaries of their own authority? Finally, what is the relationship between self, teacher, and the ambiguities of poetic verse, and how might such a relationship lead to more intimate knowledge with the divine, and especially its unknown elements?

Sheikh Noroozi and the Text without End

I had a list of questions, prepared interviewer that I was. These questions varied from person to person of course, but there were a few constants, including the following query I posed to almost all my interlocutors: How does one become a Sufi? While I received a wide variety of responses to this, almost all mentioned at least one simple fact: you must read.

Not a surprising response, given the tradition with which we are dealing, but the significance of reading cannot be emphasized enough. To gain initiation into a Sufi order, to further progress on the mystical path (*tariqa*) to *tawhid*, or simply to become familiar with the topic, you must read. The path to *tawhid*, it seems, is one lined with books.

Which texts must be read? The Qur'an, *Nahj Al-Balaga* (the sermons of Imam Ali), and of course mystical philosophies and poetry—mainly but not exclusively Persian poetry. Ibn Arabi was the favorite non-Persian poet, often read in translation but sometimes in the original Arabic by those who were able. These are works that are not dissimilar to what millions of Iranians read, many on a daily basis, or with which they are at least familiar.

In addition to what must be read, the other question, and of greater interest to us here, is *how* one must read. And so I asked Sheikh Noroozi: What is the best way to read poetry?

He told me, "You must read and re-read. Read and read again. In this way reading is like a form of *zekr* [a meditative act of remembrance, recalling]. I recommend reading it through all at once, then line by line, as slowly as you need, then reading the whole thing in its entirety again. Some people think you should not read it all at once first, because there may be words you don't know and [you] may be confused, but I think the confusion is not something you should try to avoid."

"What is beneficial about the confusion?"

"First of all, for humility. Sometimes we become overly confident when we have been reading for some time. You must never become too comfortable or too prideful when you read in the presence of genius! Second of all, it is better to have a sense of the entire scheme of the poem so that, even unconsciously, you will be able to understand the individual lines [*bayt-ha*] more fully. You will have a better idea of where the line will fit into the poem as a whole."

"What do you mean you might understand 'unconsciously'?"

Here, Sheikh Noroozi smiled: "Your inner heart [*ghalb*] will know the meaning before your intellect [*aql*] does. It contains the unconscious knowledge your mind wishes to obtain."

"Is it better to read in groups, on your own, or with a teacher?"

"All are beneficial."

"Yes, but I thought reading with a teacher is always the best way."

Sheikh Noroozi paused. "It depends on the teacher, it depends on the group. It is highly beneficial to read poems together, highly beneficial, as long as everyone's heart is pure [*ghalb-e pak*]. In other words, that their intentions for reading poetry were true, which in this context means that they were not reading for reasons of ego or any other reason outside of their desire to enrich themselves with the knowledge necessary to become closer to God."

"Because otherwise they might lead you down the wrong path?"

"Precisely. In such instances it is better for one to read on one's own."

"And as for the teacher . . ." he trailed off. "That also depends on the quality of the teacher. Imagine if your teacher was, say, Imam Jafar al-Sadeq [the sixth Shi'i Imam]." Sheikh Noroozi's eyes widened at his own suggestion. "Ah, imagine sitting at the knee of Imam Jafar." He shook his head wistfully, as if even dreaming such a thing was too much to comprehend, to take in. "Then how could you compare reading in a group or by yourself to reading in the presence of Imam-e Kabir?"

Imam Jafar al-Sadeq, it should be noted, died in AD 765, long before most of the great medieval poets had taken up their pens. And so, not only did Sheikh Noroozi imagine himself in the presence of the great Imam, but he brought him literature from the future to read together: collections of verse that, in certain cases, were directly or indirectly influenced by this most esoterically oriented of the Shi'i Imams.[2] If only we had the *tafsir* of Imam Jafar, not only of the Qur'an, but his interpretations of Attar and Hujwiri, his intellectual descendants, how wonderful that would be, per Sheikh Noroozi.

"So, reading alongside a teacher is the best form of reading?"

He paused again.

"I know the right answer is yes, reading with a *pir* is the best way. And I do believe and accept that, for the absolute novice, this is the proper way to learn to read." He said this last sentence emphatically and deliberately, but began his next cautiously: "But, there comes the moment when it is up to the individual person [*fard*] to unveil the text to themselves, to discover the secrets [*sirr*] of the text."

My curiosity was piqued at this observation, and so I asked: "Is it then that someone becomes a sheikh themselves? When they can no longer learn from a teacher?"

"No, no, you don't have to be a sheikh to learn more from your own reading of poetry than reading with a teacher. After being introduced to *what* texts to read—which in any case is not that surprising, many learned people will tell you—and some introduction on the path [*tariqat*], it is your inner heart, your third eye, that is the best teacher. Unless your teacher is a *vali* [saint]."

With this statement, Sheikh Noroozi has given us his take on the centuries-old tradition of the *pir-murid* (teacher-student) relationship that has so often been synonymous with Sufism as a whole.[3] The importance of the role of the teacher within the project of Sufism, and particularly organized Sufism, cannot be underplayed. These were and are relationships that can last for years, decades even; in many cases a student's intellectual world has been often entirely centered and cemented around his master, not to mention his material world as well, as mystics often lived together in lodges (*khaneqah*) in years past.[4] In certain instances people, including the founder of the Nimatullahi Order, Shah Nimatullah Vali, would travel thousands of miles to find the perfect teacher, with whom they might study for years.

Even for those who were not full-time pupils—that is, those not in the intimate relationship of the *pir-murid*—the reverence for their sheikh could approach levels of saint worship, a tendency that persists to some degree in the contemporary era. Accusations of cult-like behavior have sometimes dogged orders due to the zeal with which they have committed to their teacher-sheikhs.[5] While the extent of the devotion is frequently exaggerated—blind and uncritical obedience is advocated by no one—and the pedagogical process between teacher and student often simplified, it is very unusual to see a sheikh's role diminished in favor of a lay person's own initiative. At stake is not only questions of hierarchy, but what constitutes the ideal guide and teacher. Who or what is it that will best direct us, influence us, to that which we seek?

In Sheikh Noroozi's words, it is the "inner heart" (*ghalb-e batin*) and the "third eye" that supersede the pedagogical capabilities of the learned expert. The form of knowledge they are striving to achieve, *ma'rifat*, cannot be learned but only experienced. The typical power dynamic is thus upended, as he advocates for a more elusive teacher to guide one through reading a text, one that is both internal and external to oneself:

"Is it not access to the inner heart that we are seeking in the first place? How can that which we seek be our guide?" I asked.

Sheikh Noroozi smiled. "Ah, see? You have said it yourself! Let that which you seek lead you on your path. What does your inner heart say about the words of [the poet] Jami? Your inner heart and the secrets [*sirr*] of the text are in conversation; listen to these conversations. They are both hidden secrets. In this case you read not with your eyes and intellect, but [with] your unseeing eye."

I found myself pushing back, and I surprised myself with how defensive I was. "But when I read with you, I learn things that I wouldn't have on my own, and I find that . . . the text becomes a living thing, a living text. Don't our reading circles [*doreh*] and your instruction help us gain access to our unseeing eye?"

"Of course, my child, I try to teach them in ways that are helpful to you. There is nothing wrong with imparting information and it is always good for us to read together and I can only pray that I am helping with your increased unveiling of the world. But this is not the same knowledge that is in your heart. Remember what the Qur'an says in Yusef: 'Above every possessor of knowledge there is the One All-Knowing.' Your heart knows more than I ever can, especially when it comes to the poetry of the saints."

"Your heart knows more than I ever can." Sufism is often characterized as hierarchical,[6] and Sheikh Noroozi is indeed professing a ranking of knowledgeability here. But it is himself, and all the learned expertise that he represents and all the mystique of the authority figure, that he positions lower than the "heart" of the lay *darvish*. While affirming that his guidance is beneficial, the wisdom he is able to transfer appears unmatched to what is contained in the knowledge of the heart of the student. So strong is his belief in the inner heart (*ghalb-e batin*), that he summons the Surah Yusef [Joseph], a favorite *surah* (chapter of the Qur'an) of Imam Jafar al-Sadeq, equating the knowledge of the heart with the divine realm. It is the experiential knowledge, that which is most difficult to access and explain, even to oneself (sometimes especially to oneself), that Sheikh Noroozi prioritizes. The one caveat to this idea that one's inner heart is as productive a teacher (if not more) is only when the teacher is a saint, meaning an Imam or perhaps one of the great poets (Mawlana as Hazrat); only they could provide more guidance in textual analysis than the "inner heart." Barring the return of the Hidden Imam, it is highly unlikely that any person currently living will actually encounter any of these saints. Still, in making this exception, he confirms the classic Shi'i hierarchy of the Imams and saints as possessing knowledge outside of the realm of the typical human, even one who is seen as possessing the "light of knowledge."

Barring his affirmation of the spiritual superiority of the Imams, what is even more remarkable is Sheikh Noroozi's insistence that it is "especially" when it comes to the "poetry of the saints" that he is outmatched. It is one thing to suggest that, in a general sense, possession of intuitive knowledge is more powerful than a sheikh's pedagogical skills, that our a priori (if since lost) sense of being one with God is a stronger guiding force than a living human, but it is something else entirely to indicate that, when it comes to learning from and through texts, one's own teacher is outranked by your inner heart.

Contained within Sheikh Noroozi's self-effacing statement is a very particular stance concerning Sufi authority and hermeneutics. As is the case with so many Islamic schools of thought, spiritual authority is derived from textual authority. For certain mystical circles, the heart of the entire project of Sufism is comprised of individuals, often in a group, sitting in physical proximity to a teacher and reading a text under his or her guidance. Textual interpretation is the arena where the authority of the elders is demonstrated, where their familiarity with unpacking obtuse poetics, intellectual debates, and Qur'anic references—among other things—is expressed. While they do offer counsel on a broad array of life matters, for the circles of Sheikh Noroozi and Sheikh Alizadeh, it is their teachers' mastery of literary and philosophical knowledge that draws them near, and we remember the earlier insistence that to become a Sufi one must read. There is no order or group of *darvish* that I encountered in Iran for whom reading and familiarizing themselves with texts and the ideas contained therein was not absolutely paramount to their ethos and objectives. Indeed, texts convey not only important content and ideas but also ways of reading and approaching textuality that challenge our ways of thinking about the world.

In downplaying his capacity as a textual authority, Sheikh Noroozi is thus challenging the efficacy of his spiritual authority as a whole. I would clarify that this does not make him any less legitimate an authority, given that he recognizes the benefits of his reading circles, but instead reconsiders the power of learned expertise vis-à-vis the layperson's intuition and experience in encountering poetic verse. The category of authority is thus thoroughly challenged, its traditional parameters unbound and put it into question, as the unknowability of the text necessitates a requisite unknowing of authority.

After thinking through Sheikh Noroozi's responses, I returned on another occasion with yet more questions, which he again answered with his unending patience and gentleness. This time as we spoke he was running his fingers through his prayer beads (*tasbih*) and I joked I had tired him out with my questions. "You must be calling out for patience with your beads!" I said. He chuckled and replied: "Not at all. It is always nice to speak with thoughtful youth, especially with a soon-to-be doctor. Besides, what else do I have to do? I can go walk in the park with the other old men whenever I want." His tone was grandfatherly and respectful, without the slightest hint of condescension. We returned to my questions.

"Respected Sheikh, why is my inner heart a greater teacher [*pir*] than someone like yourself for understanding texts? I learn so many things during our reading circles." His answer surprised me.

"Because of the nature of the text. And for what we are reading."

A brief pause, and he continued:

These texts themselves are already endless. The thoughts contained with them are absolutely infinite. Each poem is like a gem; you look at it from a different angle and you see light reflected off it in a different way. Each word is a universe, the history of each word is a universe. You could write a thesis on the use of the word *Ey* [a declarative sound, similar in ways to the "O" of English poetry] in Mawlana, you could write an entire library around the word *rend* in Hafez [a notoriously difficult term to translate, the *rend* figure is somewhat akin to a rogue or trickster but one who is at times morally *bi-payan,* or upright]. And then of course there is the entire collection! How does one poem relate to another? Should we think of the Divan as a complete collection or individual fragments [*tik-e tik-e*]? Understanding the poems of the valis [saints] is a task impossible for a single lifetime. In fact, the more you read the more exposed you are to the limitlessness of the text. And so, when I guide you in our readings, I am not looking to give you the proper answers, but appropriate and beneficial questions. To show you their endlessness. There is no one interpretation. Sometimes, I'm not even sure one is better than the other. And so I give you some of my own ideas that inshallah will lead you to your own questions, not my answer. The best guide is the heart.

A hermeneutics described in poetic language: universes, gems, refracted light. Sheikh Noroozi, like many before him, turned to metaphor and simile to best capture the multifaceted and multivalent "nature of the text": poetry begetting poetry. According to the sheikh, these are verses that may be approached from literary, philosophical, and philological vantage points, eluding the capability of any one human to appreciate or comprehend them in their totality. If Ibn Arabi has stated that the nature of reality is unknowable, Sheikh Noroozi seems to indicate that poetry is similarly enigmatic (perhaps suggesting some overlap with Derridean, Heideggerian, and Wittgensteinian thought, but that is a story for another time). Of course, there are echoes here of Qur'anic *tafsir*, where the relationship between the external meaning (*zaher*) and internal meaning (*batin*) can be traced and deduced in myriad ways. Intriguingly, Sheikh Noroozi did not use the word "meaning" (*ma'ani/ma'ana*) at all in his response to me, only "interpretation" (*tafsir*), as if the subjective "interpretation" was more appropriate than the more authoritative "meaning."

And then there is his assertion that "the more you read, the better you understand the limitlessness of the text." In other words, familiarity generates a greater understanding, but an understanding that your task of fully appreciating the poems is an impossible one. This is an idea that I find deeply resonant with broader Sufi theories of *ma'rifat*. The text is in a sense endless, its words able to convey countless ideas that lead to ever deeper philosophical musings the further one goes in one's analysis. In this way, the potential for infinite interpretations of the text mirrors Sufi epistemologies as a knowledge without limit or end. Both forms of unknowing—the unknowing of text and the idea of unknowing more broadly—contest finality, embracing instead the inchoate and still forming.

Moreover, it is his embrace of the idea of the endlessness of the text—both each individual poem as well as the entire collection—that Sheikh Noroozi is using to justify his own perceived limitations as a sheikh. It is due to the "nature of the text," where each poem is capable of generating a series of unending permutations, that he sees the inner heart as the superior guide.

What does it mean to think of a teacher as a provider of questions rather than a purveyor of answers? In some ways, what Sheikh Noroozi is describing is quite similar to how I set up my own seminars with my students; I don't wish to simply recite my opinions at them but push them to come up with their own observations and insights. The primary differences here are that I am a teacher and not a spiritual guide, and what I entreat my students to do is utilize their intellect to tackle the mysteries of the text in front of them, not necessarily their inner heart.

This practice may also be seen in pedagogical situations in the Shi'i seminaries (howzeh) in Iran, where the Socratic method is frequently employed, and the ulama-teacher strives for a form of discussion structured around analyses of highly complex lines of inquiry rather than simply questions followed by answers.[7] How important resolution is, whether it be for a specific question or a broader topic, varies from teacher to teacher, but even for those seminarians who embrace a pedagogical method that emphasizes pure irresolution, it is unusual for them to argue that the complexities of the topic at hand is a reflection on or somehow speaks to the limitation of their own authority.

This would seem to be in contrast to the stance of Sheikh Noroozi, who, in order for his students to access the elusive faculty that is their inner heart, has embraced a particular pedagogical and authorial stance, one where he provides paths and points of inquiries for his students rather than a road map to follow, and emphasizing the capabilities of the inner heart to supersede even his own capabilities as teacher. Authority, while still there, takes on a slightly different color. I am also reminded of his earlier dictum that "confusion is not something you should try to avoid." A state of confusion would seem in line with Sufism's inclination to embrace and even revel in disoriented states. Intoxication (metaphorical or otherwise), whirling, dreaming states; these are all destabilizing phenomena embraced by mystics, experiences that lead to the questioning of the very nature of reality, a questioning that is key to the entire project of Sufism.

And so, Sheikh Noroozi's recommendation that his students accept confusion while reading, and all the frustration and discomfort that accompanies it, supports a hermeneutics that is very much in line with broader Sufi and esoteric Shi'i epistemologies.[8] In other words, it is reflective of a belief in the generative nature of encounters with the abstruse. It is a reveling in the "mysterious" aspect of the mysteries of the divine, with the unknowability of the divine. In other words, interpretation is not only a tactic to uncover a deep meaning or even a better understanding of the material in question, but a way to affirm the boundless nature of the text itself.

Sitting at his dining table, I took all of this in. At first, I could offer no follow-up question or great insight but merely repeat his last assertion, a beat more slowly than Sheikh Noroozi had: "The best guide [murshid] is your heart."

He nodded slowly and continued: "You must turn to your heart. Even though that is the most difficult path and the least clear. That is how these saints wrote, by listening to the inner heart. And so that is the best way to read and understand." It is worth considering another of Sheikh Noroozi's statements: "That is how these saints wrote, by listening to the inner heart. And so that is the best way to read and understand." Here, the reader must follow the example of the writer. As the saints turned inward to compose their poetry, so too must we follow a similar methodology to understand their texts. There is a mirroring between these acts, the act of writing and the act of interpreting, both of them creative, both of them capable of being led by the divine knowledge that resides within them. And, as each takes effort to tap into the world of batin, both lead to the development of the soul.

We continued our conversation.

"Dear Sheikh, I am embarrassed to ask this question, I feel like I should know the answer to this by now but . . . how does one read with the heart?"

"Ah, that is not a simple thing at all! Never be embarrassed."

"I appreciate your patience and guidance."

"Reading with the heart is learned when you advance on the path. The more you do this, the greater your access to seeing with the heart, it is all connected. Ability to see the hidden meaning [batin] in poems and the Qur'an grows along with your heart. Now your question was how is this done, which is an excellent question. For most people it involves lots of familiarizing, but not for all. Usually it helps to study under a teacher, especially in the beginning. But still . . . in some sense, this is a journey that cannot be taught. At least by me." He stopped here, and thought for a moment. He continued: "We have these sessions, and they gather and listen to me, but . . . I should remind them more that they are always their own ultimate guides. At some point the role of the *ostad* is less important, and then not important at all." Another pause. "[Bayazid] Bistami says, 'He who has no master takes Satan as his master,' but ultimately one's own self [*khod-e adam*] must lead themselves. After some time, the moment comes when you must read on your own." Sheikh Noroozi made these comments with a slightly melancholy tone, looking down at his hands. It seemed as though he wanted to say something more, so I waited for him to continue, in quiet anticipation.

He smiled a little now. "Sometimes this business of being a sheikh is something else. I keep God close to give me wisdom, inshallah I am being of help." He said this with a good-natured, even amused, air of resignation. Other learned figures I had encountered often voiced expressions of humility, but those were often stated in a more offhand or perfunctory way, however genuine. And there were still other authority figures who possessed a bone-dry sarcasm, throwing out rhetorical queries and caveats: "But of course, you don't need to listen to me," after offering an opinion, more often than not said as a way of hastening the end of the discussion than as an admission of their own shortcomings. Sheikh Noroozi, on the other hand, could not have been more sincere and accepting of his own limitations.

"Your students say you are a blessing to them! You are a wonderful guide for all." I felt the sudden need to reassure Sheikh Noroozi, even though he did not seem to be fishing for compliments in the least. He nodded politely at my words, but did not seem particularly assuaged.

"They are always too kind, and it is my honor to read with them. But these masterpieces can only be revealed with the inner heart. That is their best guide."

Heavy is the head that wears the crown, or so the saying goes, and humility is a prized virtue in Islam, one often attributed to Imam Ali in his initial deference to Abu Bakr as successor to the Prophet. Sheikh Noroozi's burden, however, seemed to arise not only from the difficulty of the task at hand, but from what he perceived to be its fundamentally impossible nature. He recognizes the necessity of a guide, that embarking upon the journey of Sufism without one is not only unwise but dangerous,[9] but he believes it is ultimately the pupil's inner heart that must lead the way.

His authority then, is one that is fundamentally constricted by an episte-mological conviction that the human teacher must ultimately be super-seded at a juncture or a moment that remains unknown to him.

Sheikh Noroozi's Students

After my discussions with Sheikh Noroozi regarding interpretation and his role as sheikh, I began wondering about how his students viewed his in-struction and guidance. What might it be like to have a teacher so sensitive to his own perceived limitations? How much was it a part of his pedagogy, if at all? And so, after confirming it would be alright to do so, I discussed Sheikh Noroozi's opinion regarding his self-professed "limitations" as sheikh with those who attended his circles.

Perhaps unsurprisingly, they did not share his opinion, although a few were reflective about the nature of pedagogy as a whole. Having witnessed the respect and affection that they held for their sheikh, I attempted to craft my questions carefully, in order to avoid leading questions like, "Sheikh Noroozi downplays his own expertise. What do you think?" Instead, I asked: "I was speaking with Sheikh Noroozi, and he discussed how the inner heart can be a greater guide for his students than he can ever be, es-pecially when it comes to the interpretation of poetry. What do you think about this idea?"

Zainab, a thirty-eight-year-old insurance agent, laughed heartily at my question: "Come on now [*boro baba*]! I wouldn't even know I had an 'inner heart' without the sheikh! How can you learn something new without a teacher? It's because of *him* that I have become interested in these things." I contemplated playing devil's advocate here, arguing that the sheikh would say it was her inner heart that probably led her to seek mysticism in the first place, but I thought that might be overstepping my role as interviewer.

Nahid, a forty-two-year-old homemaker, smiled when I told her of her teacher's deflections. "But see?" she said. "This is exactly what makes him a true *arif*! He has no arrogance at all, despite all of his learning. Some of these other *ruhani* [clergy; interesting that she referred to him as such], all they want to do is find an audience and feel self-important. But not our sheikh, he is much too humble, and that is that proof that makes him a true man of God. He has a pure heart [*ghalb-e pak*]."

Mostafa, a forty-eight-year-old shopkeeper, agreed: "He is only being modest! But then again, maybe he really believes it. A real leader is one who does not want to take on the role or thinks he is not worthy, like Imam Ali."

"In English, we say 'reluctant hero' or 'hesitant hero' (*ghahreman-e bi-mayl* or *ghahreman-e moradad*)." I offered both terms, not sure of the best translation in the moment.

Mostafa laughed. "It's funny to think of Sheikh Noroozi as a hero [*ghahreman*] like Rostam," he noted, referencing the mythical strongman of the epic *Shahnameh*. "But why not? He is a mystical hero [*ghahreman-e darvishi*]! His Zulfiqar [the legendary sword of Imam Ali] is the truth [*haqiqat*]!" Clearly, Mostafa saw his sheikh as following in the tradition of this most beloved of Shiʻi figures.

Nima, who is thirty-four years old and works in gold commodities, reflected on the nature of the role of the guide as a whole: "Of course Sheikh Noroozi is supremely well-informed [*vared*] and has a great skill in teaching others. I have to say, however, that's a very interesting statement [*harf-e jaleb*] he makes. You reach a stage where you develop more without the sheikh than with them, I suppose."

"Can you tell me a bit more about that stage?"

"Well, it's when . . . you realize that have to stand on your own two feet. When the sessions no longer make you think."

"Do you think it is when you feel ready to become a sheikh yourself?"

"No, I don't think you have to become a sheikh necessarily. Not everyone is interested in teaching and working with students. And I think only you can decide when you've reached that stage. It is a station on the path, so it is something between a thought [*fekr*] and a feeling [*hess*]. When you have reached that, or think you have achieved that, that is when you can grow without a teacher."

According to Nima, one can outgrow their own guide, reaching a stage of enlightenment where working with one's master is no longer useful or thought-provoking. What sets Nima's thinking apart from other Shiʻi or Sufi theories of hierarchy is that it is the pupil, and not the master, who determines when they have reached this stage. It is a "realization," "something between a thought and a feeling" that one must obey and listen to rather than a designation from an authority figure. Nima highlighted the difficulty in discerning these moments as well, stating that it is "when you have reached that stage" or when you "*think* you have achieved that" stage (emphasis mine). What is the difference between reaching enlightenment and *thinking* you have reached enlightenment? To trust in such a difference, as Nima does, suggests a belief in enlightenment as an ontological reality, and one that is not necessarily easy to know if you have achieved. (I emphasize again this is his interpretation, and is not necessarily reflective of canonical discourses). What is interesting, however, is that whether you have achieved enlightenment or merely *think* you have, both are instances where, according to Nima, you may remove yourself from the shadow of the teacher.

Nusrat, a fifty-eight-year-old accountant, also mused about the nature of pedagogy in the history of *erfan*. After affirming Sheikh Noroozi's expertise, she noted, "I think certain people might benefit from a teacher more than others. Also, the nature of the relationship can vary so much. For example, isn't Shams always Rumi's teacher? Even after he [Shams] leaves [Rumi]?[10] But in that way, his teacher is also his *beloved*, no? Whereas I don't think Hafez ever thought of his teachers in that way, or his poetry doesn't reflect that at least." She paused for a moment. "But what Rumi and Shams had was so unique. And Shams was perhaps not the typical master."

"Ah, that is very interesting. And in the past, so many traveled for so long to find just the right teacher, no?" I offered. "Shah Nimatullah Vali himself traveled all the way from Damascus to find his master. It is such a special relationship."

"But I still think what Rumi and Shams had was different," Nusrat countered. "Shams came to Rumi, not the other way around. And of course everyone has great affection for their teacher, and the teacher for their students. But that is different from being a *beloved*."

Nusrat is of course correct. In her responses to me, she makes a case for the varied nature of the *pir-murid* relationship and argues that some may benefit from it more than others. She cites perhaps the most famous master-disciple pair in all Sufi literature, if an unconventional one: Rumi and Shams. For Rumi, mysticism begins and ends with Shams; he is muse, teacher, and beloved all in one. His entire spiritual being is inseparable from his love for his master. Then you have Hafez, who, perhaps partially because we have little historical evidence about his early years, has no teacher at all as part of his lore. In highlighting how individuals have disparate experiences with their masters, Nusrat is not devaluing the role of the teacher, but suggests that it is not a universal experience, and much of it is contingent upon the needs of the particular student as well. This speaks to the individuated nature of the mystical path.

I returned to Sheikh Noroozi and told him that his students didn't believe him. He smiled, but seemed unconvinced. "They are only being kind. Clearly, I have much to teach them!" Despite his belief in the limitations of the teacher when compared to the human heart, evidently there were still forms of wisdom he could convey to them.

Sheikh Alizadeh and Poetic Verse as a Form of Exegesis

In Iran, it is very common for people to quote poetry in casual conversation. It is certainly more common for the older generation to do so, but happily, at least for those of us who enjoy linguistic flights of fancy and philosophical musings breaking up the banality of everyday prose, the younger generation is not immune to this tendency. Even so, in a nation of millions who memorize poetry, Sheikh Alizadeh was something else. Not only was his speech absolutely peppered with quotations from dozens of writers, but unlike many people, he did not change his tone into the declaratory sing-song of recitation or even slow down his cadence when inserting lines in the midst of conversation. It was as if he could not distinguish lines of poetic verse from his own thoughts. While impressive, it often produced a humorous or even somewhat jarring listening experience.

His wife, Effat, a woman of great wit, would tease him. "He is so distracted in his thoughts one of these days he's going to start reciting when he's ordering things at the supermarket: "Can I have the *satl-e mast* [yogurt] and 'The sadness of your love has made me wander in deserts/The fleeting illusion [*havaye bakht*] clipped my wings.'"[11] Verses with two phrases (*bayts*) were particularly funny to hear as Sheikh Alizadeh would rush through the two of them without the customary pause in between.

Because I could not identify the writers behind the specific verses myself (save for the odd classic, which I was very proud to be able to recognize), I would always ask Sheikh Alizadeh to name the authors he was citing. So frequently did I ask that the poor fellow started stating the names of his own accord when in my presence, such as: "At dawn a call came from the wine-house/Drunken rogue of the tavern arise arise!/Let us fill with wine one more turn/Before it is destiny that fills our urn. Khayyam," the name falling with a gentle thud at the end like a heavy punctuation mark.

He would often wear the long white tunic (*dashtdashe*) favored by men in the Gulf Arab nations; it not unheard of to wear it in Iran but still a bit atypical, especially for ethnic Persians. Effat Khanum would tease him and say, "Now because he is a *seyed* he must dress like the Arabs!" I arrived one day for breakfast. Sheikh Alizadeh was an early riser, often awakening well before his sunrise prayers.

Over a too-lavish spread of breads, cheeses, jams, boiled eggs, cucumbers, walnuts, and sweet tea, we talked about the interpretation of poetry as a means to achieve *tawhid*. Effat Khanum joined us intermittently, getting up on occasion to answer yet another phone call from a relation or friend or to tend to a domestic matter.

I began: "What is the best way to read poetry?"

"You must read knowing the power that is contained within these pages. Within these writings are holy ideas [*fekr-haye moghadas*]. You must read as a way to varnish the heart. You can read for pleasure [*lezat*] and that is fine, and you can read for knowledge [*elm*], and that is good too, but the *best* way to read is read so that you gain gnosis [*ma'rifat*]." Here, Sheikh Alizadeh was suggesting reading as a practice that can lead to the transformation of the self through the acquisition of *ma'rifat*. Rather than first remarking upon a particular linguistic approach or discussing the proper training required, his first direction regarding best reading practices was to mention the intention and objective of the reader, and recognizing the sacrality and power of the ideas. While the first two are typical of many injunctions concerning reading,[12] the emphasis on the power of poetry is more typical of Sufi circles where, as we have seen, the elevation of the art form of poetry is a central tenet of the epistemology.

"What are some of these holy ideas?" I asked. "Or what is it that makes them holy?" I realized later that he had mentioned that the ideas were holy, but did not go so far as to classify the texts themselves as holy. The reasons why are not difficult to discern, as such a classification could inch toward blasphemy.

"They are holy because they are reflections of the Qur'an through the pools of water that are the eyes of saints!" his voice boomed. "All these ideas are first in the Qur'an and the sayings [Hadith], then they are put into the painterly language by the saints. These are the poets' interpretation of the Book of God, which is the greatest gift God ever gave to us, alongside the Prophet and Ahl-e Bayt."

"So it is a form of *tafsir* of the Qur'an?"

"Yes, a form of *tafsir* of the Qur'an."

Drawing a direct correlation between poetry and the Qur'an, he turns to equally poetic language to describe the composition of verses: there is mirroring and reflecting here, and metaphor; the eyes of the saints become pools of water. In a way it seems as if Sheikh Alizadeh considers poetry as a form of literary exegesis. According to his description, the Qur'an does not operate as a form of inspiration or reference point for the poets, but is the entire source material.

Considering poetic verse as a form of Qur'anic exegesis is unique not only among Shi'i scholars or literary scholars but even among Sufis. Of course, there are innumerable Muslim poets who have been *very* much engaged with and draw inspiration from the Qur'an, everything from referencing specific *ayas* to exploring broader themes contained therein to thinking through revelation and much more. Indeed, although the Qur'an famously notes, "As for the poets, only those are lost in error follow them . . . Except those [poets] who believe and do righteous deeds and remember Allah often and defend [the Muslims] when they have been wrong." (26:224–27).[13] Since the earliest days of Islam, when al-Farabi considered the ethics of poetry and Rabia al-Basra was contemplating her experience with the divine in verse (at least according to Attar), up until the present day, Muslims have been reflecting upon the ideas within the Qur'an, their experiences in reading the text, and more, through the poetic form.[14] Moreover, there is a large corpus of Sufis writing commentaries on the Qur'an (*tafsir*) that, according to some, dates back to the sixth Shi'i Imam, Jafar al-Sadeq, as the first esoterically oriented commentary on the Qur'an and, according to others, especially certain Shi'is, the writings of the first Shi'i Imam, Imam Ali.[15] Indeed, Sufi exegesis is typically considered a genre unto its own,[16] including thinkers like al-Tustari, Maybudi, al-Nabulsi, among many others, which emphasizes aspects like the external (*zaher*) and internal (*batin*) forms of meaning, hierarchies of meanings, and concepts like the heart (*qalb*), spirit (*ruh*), secret (*sirr*), multiple planes of reality (*malakut*), and more.

Thus, there exists a huge corpus of Sufi poetry which examines the Qur'an, as well as a large corpus of Sufi commentaries on the Qur'an (*tafsir*), but Sheikh Alizadeh's categorization of poetry *as* Qur'anic exegesis (*tafsir*) itself is certainly unique, and brings up compelling questions regarding genre. Who decides what literary form Qur'anic exegesis may take? How closely must they hew to the text itself in their commentary? Within a Shi'i context at least, those who may decide upon such matters are the ayatollahs and grand ayatollahs in Qom and Najaf. I think it is safe to say that most spiritual authority figures would distinguish between poetry and commentary; *tafsir* is *tafsir* and poetry is poetry. Even those ayatollahs who carry out *tafsir* and compose poetry, like Ayatollah Khomeini, would be very unlikely to conflate the two.

What Sheikh Alizadeh is suggesting here, then, is a pushing of boundaries and blurring of genres. Moreover, at stake is also the potency of the spiritual authority of the poets; positing them as writers of exegesis as opposed to "simply" poetry, already a highly revered form, increases their role as *murshid*s and, to use Sheikh Alizadeh's word, saints (*vali*). While other Iranian Sufis consider figures like Sa'adi and Attar as saints and key figures in their chains of succession (*silsile*), they do not consider their poetic work exegetical. Writing a commentary on the Qur'an is an endeavor and accomplishment that provides the evidence that one may be considered a spiritual authority in any number of schools of jurisprudence (*fiqh*). In positing their work as such, Sheikh Alizadeh is reconsidering the poets as Qur'anic scholars, bestowing upon them a more traditional basis for spiritual authority, and reaffirming the importance of exegetical work for mystics. In other words, it is a recategorization with consequences for considerations of genre and authority both textual and spiritual, because by considering poetry as exegesis it is giving power to the mystical epistemologies contained within such texts. If non-knowledge challenges the boundaries of self-contained thought, here we see a challenge to the question of genre.

Sheikh Alizadeh's Hermeneutics: Interpretation without End

"What is the best way to interpret poetry?"

"Oh, a thousand ways to interpret! A hundred thousand ways!"

"Of course, you are right, but are there certain techniques or paths [*ra-ha*] you prefer or recommend?"

"Well, first you must understand what interpretation is. Before you asked me, what is the best way to read, then you asked what is the best way to interpret? I am not sure they are different things when you read such poetry. You see, we know that the Qur'an has internal [*batin*] and external [*zaher*] meanings, so that even an unlearned person can understand the external meanings. This is so that all people, even those who are illiterate [*bisavad*] can understand. But! Poetry is all *batin*, there is no *zaher*. Well, maybe a little. The sounds and rhythms of a recited poem are beautiful even for those who don't understand the words, even for those who do not know Farsi. Again, like the Qur'an. But poetry is an interpretation or commentary on the hidden elements of the Qur'an. So, we were talking about interpretation? The best way to interpret is the same way as the best way to read, because to read is to interpret. Anything beyond the most simple reading is interpretation."

"Excuse me if I've misunderstood, the goal seems to be to understand the *batin* of the Qur'an?"

"Ah, almost! The *batin* of the Qur'an *and* the *batin* of the poem! Meaning to find the *batin al-batin*! That is what makes it so fun!" He laughed heartily at this, this search for the secret of the secret. "But there are many things you can do, there is not just one destination or path. But *batin al-batin* is perhaps most important."

Let us start backward to unpack this statement. The idea of a "*batin al-batin*," or "inner secret of the inner secret,"[17] is a common concept within Islamic mysticism and for more esoterically minded scholars. The suggestion is that there exists—in both text and world—a hierarchy and layering of meaning, sedimentary stratums of mystical knowledge that, as one traverses them, going ever deeper, one moves ever closer to achieving union with the divine. It is not enough to ascertain the "secret"; the "secret" is not a totality, but the signaling of the beginning of a journey into ever deeper, ever more esoteric waters. This idea of a hierarchy of knowledge, one that promises ever more layers of meaning, is seen throughout Sufi Qur'anic commentary and in the titles of the esoterically minded treatises beyond Qur'anic commentary, such as Allameh Tabatabai's *The Kernel of the Kernel: Concerning the Wayfaring and Spiritual Journey of the People of Intellect*, or Sheikh Nazim al-Haqqani's *The Secrets Behind the Secrets Behind the Secrets*. As Jamal Elias explains: "Belief in hierarchical levels of existence and meaning constitutes an important aspect of Sufi thought, such that existence and existential truths, texts and divine messages, the human body and the visible world, all are believed to exist on more than one level."[18] Thus, when one is interpreting poetry, according to Sheikh Alizadeh, one is interpreting an interpretation of the more hidden (and hence more potent) meanings within the Qur'an. (As a bit of an aside, it is important to remember that there is a mirroring too of text and world here, as Elias points out that multiple layers of meaning constitute not just the Qur'an or texts but existence itself.)

Then, there is this statement of the sheikh: "Poetry is all *batin*, there is no *zaher*. Well, maybe a little. The sounds and rhythms of a recited poem are beautiful even for those who don't understand the words, even for those who do not know Farsi. Again, like the Qur'an."

Again there is the mirroring of the poetry and the Qur'an, such that the hermeneutics used for the latter may be used for the former as well. If we follow Sheikh Alizadeh's dictum that poetry is an interpretation of the Qur'an, then the writings of the poets are engaged intimately and exclusively with the hidden dimension of the Qur'an which, according to the sheikh and many others, is the more important dimension. Moreover, to state that "poetry is all *batin*" is to suggest that the meaning of a poem can only be ascertained by uncovering its hidden/not-immediately-apparent aspects; there is no surface-level meaning. It is as if the poets wished to honor the esoteric nature of *batin* ideas by maintaining—perhaps even leaning into—its arcane quality through their writings. If poetry is to be considered a form of Qur'anic *tafsir*, then it would appear that its immediate goal is not one of the explication of the text, a means of communicating ideas to readers with clarity, but a form of engagement with sacred material where the style also mirrors the content. In other words, the abstruse nature of poetry is not simply a stylistic choice but the result of reflecting on equally abstruse content.[19] This is not to say that within the genre of Qur'anic *tafsir* there are no writings amongst the millions of pages written that are as elusive as poetic verse or that all are straightforward elucidations for a lay audience. Merely that, in this particular instance at least, Sheikh Alizadeh seems to be highlighting, if not advocating given his enthusiastic explication, such an approach.

Continuing onward, his mention of *zaher* is also interesting here in that he uses it to refer to the aesthetic experience of listening or reading to the Qur'an or a poem. Typically, *zaher* refers to passages in the Qur'an that are more readily apparent. While I do not doubt that he recognizes this aspect of *zaher* too—as he explicitly states, "even an unlearned person can understand the external meanings"—in relation to poetry it is the "sounds" of the poem that he sees as its apparent dimension. The "beautiful" character of poetry—presumably in recited form—while clearly affective and worthy of praise, is thus seen as a less important aspect, as the *batin* is always privileged by mystics.

Finally, there is his statement that "there are many things you can do, there is not just one destination or path! But *batin al-batin* is perhaps most important." He said the first sentence with enthusiasm and a laugh, as if there was nothing more exciting than interpreting a text and searching for meaning in it, and the second with a more matter-of-fact tone and the slightest air of resignation, as if one should not get too carried away. Still, I was curious about these "many things" the sheikh had mentioned.

"What are some of these other things you can do?"

"You can practice recitation, learn to become a master (*ostad*) of [poetry] recitation. You can learn calligraphy, and interpret that way. You can even paint your ideas! There is not only *tafsir*, even if that is the most important. You can discuss your *tafsir* with your friend's *tafsir*. Then you will find something new. That is why we read in groups. If I had any talent at all I would like to express the text artistically but unfortunately I am a fool who only knows how to read."

"Now that is not true."

"Well, I know how to read *and* I have the ability to convince some poor unwitting people (*badbakhha-ye bichare*] that I know what I am talking about!" Sheikh Alizadeh laughed heartily.

"Now you know this isn't true! But these are ways of . . . thinking about the poem, painting and calligraphy, they are also worthwhile endeavors?"

"As long as you are thinking and meditating (*zekr*) over the writings, it is worthwhile. The form and appearance of your thinking is not as important [*Form va shekl-e fekrat mohem nist*]."

What might be called creative and artistic endeavors by others is thus rendered here as an occasion for meditation on a text. There is a *form* to thinking, although it is seen as "unimportant" and secondary to the act of ruminating over the poem. Meaning operates here on synesthetic levels, able to transfer between different aesthetic modes and vehicles of expression. It would appear that in this instance it is indeed the message, and not the medium, that matters.

"You mentioned that *tafsir* is the most important. But does creating a painting inspired by a poem teach you different things from interpreting the words, or . . . working more directly with the words?"

An uncharacteristic pause by the sheikh.

"It's an interesting question."

More time passes.

"It depends on the type of *tafsir*. Let us compare written *tafsir* and, say, a painting. Because the *tafsir* we do in our circles, when I read and teach, is different. That is not as rich as a commentary."

"So, not the spoken *tafsir*, but the written?"

"Yes, the written *tafsir*. We cannot get to the same inner meaning in conversing that we do in writing. So, let us compare [written] commentary and a painting. A commentary uses words to write about words, so perhaps it is more appropriate. But . . . it depends on the commentary. One that is poorly written will not interest you [here he said literally, *bekesh*, 'pulls the reader'], while a very stunning painting might be more illuminating than a poor commentary. . . . It might also depend on the person, different people have different sensibilities. In India and Pakistan they have those beautiful Qawwalis, which I've heard can go on for hours and hours. Perhaps they are more profound than commentaries, I do not know them well enough, or perhaps for the Indians it is more profound just for them."

In comparing different media, Sheikh Alizadeh does not directly address my question asking if the different forms teach different things, but discusses if writing is more effective than painting, noting that "we cannot get to the same inner meaning." Except for his statement that writing allows for more depth of thought than communicating orally, he is hesitant to construct any real hierarchy here. Instead, he notes that the efficacy of these media is dependent upon (1) the quality of the piece, and (2) the "sensibilities" of the person. There is also an interesting "cultural" dimension here, if we can call it that, as he observes that the musical genre of Qawwali may be more "profound" for South Asians. The sheikh allows too that he is not too familiar with Qawwalis, and that "perhaps they are more profound" than commentaries, opening up the possibility yet again that commentaries should not be held up as the most important or most powerful form of critical engagement with poetry, the best way to find the *batin al-batin*, despite his earlier musings that they are the "most important."

"You mentioned that 'using words to write about words' is more beneficial. [I was trying to recall Sheikh Alizadeh's statement in real time but misremembered his exact wording. Rather than 'beneficial' (*mofid*) he actually said 'appropriate' (*monaseb*). Please note my mistake here.] Is it more beneficial for unveiling the secret? What is it that makes it so?"

"This is a very interesting question, I will have to think about it."

I went for another meeting with Sheikh Alizadeh, this time for afternoon tea. His mood was as jocular and jolly as ever. He seemed excited to chat, which made me feel at ease before beginning our discussion, a common occurrence for all visitors who come to his home, I'm sure, given his good-natured joie de vivre. This time, upon his request, I had sent him a list of possible topics and questions in advance. I started with a broad question.

"What kind of knowledge is necessary to best interpret poetry?"

"There are a few areas of knowledge: First, the knowledge of words and phrases. When Hafez speaks of an eyebrow, sometimes it is an actual eyebrow, sometimes it is something else, usually it is both. It is good to know the history of the words too. Each word is a universe unto itself! I would love to write, or get a group of writers, to write a Hafez dictionary. You could make a list of all the terms, find where they are mentioned, in what poems, what his meaning was when using them." Knowledge of terms here seems to indicate a familiarity with how they are used in each poet's repertoire, whether used metonymically, metaphorically, literally, or some combination of all three. Such an awareness would also require an understanding of the larger meaning of the poem itself, it would seem.

"You mean, you could have an encyclopedia or dictionary where each concept is listed? And one of these concepts could be eyebrow, another *rend*, et cetera."

"Yes, exactly! Maybe such a thing exists? I mean, I'm sure someone has written a thesis on Hafez's eyebrows [he laughed] but I don't know [if it was] in the form I am suggesting."

"You should do it!"

He laughed. "Maybe one of these days I will. But that would be a multi-, multivolume project. Anyway, what were we talking about?"

"What kind of knowledge do you need to interpret?"

"Right. Let me see, I wrote this down, otherwise I will get distracted." Sheikh Alizadeh slipped on his glasses and peered down at his paper. "So . . . you need to have a feeling [*hess*] for these words. But you also need to understand grammar and structure, what is metaphor and what is not, you need to have knowledge of the Qur'an, the sayings of the Prophet and the Imams, ideally some Arabic, familiarizing yourself with lots of genres and writers, others' thoughts on the matter, and dream interpretation, and the third eye."

Sheikh Alizadeh is advocating for a *tafsir* that requires a good amount of outside learning and expertise. We discussed the purposes behind each of these types of knowledge, which I summarize here. Knowledge of the Qur'an and Hadith is necessary to recognize references, direct ones within the poetry, as well as the fact that it is always important to read the Qur'an in general. Familiarity with grammar and sentence structure are needed to understand the nuanced meanings of the verses, because "kernels of reality," in his words, can be found when analyzing grammar. Finally, the use of outside sources is also recommended, as the sheikh noted: "For example, what does Attar say about Hallaj? What does Mulla Sadra say about Hallaj?[20] You may understand Attar, Hallaj, and Mulla Sadra differently after reading all of them." Outside sources not only provide their own insight, then, but can be utilized comparatively, such that different topics and ideas might be analyzed through different critical lenses. I will return to the sheikh's idea of "dream interpretation" shortly.

Given the weighty list of recommended types of knowledge that Sheikh Alizadeh prescribed, I noted, "It would seem that it requires many years of study then to properly interpret the writing of the poets, it's something that must not be taken lightly."

"Well, yes . . . yes, it is good to study and become knowledgeable in these subjects. But you shouldn't wait until you have studied for years and years to read *erfan*. That would be a terrible shame. Nietzsche said, 'There are those who are thirty years old and have read all of the books and have not an idea of their own.' It is good to have but not *required*. There is an important difference there. All that is *required* is desire of the heart [*khasten-e del*]; the heart contains the best knowledge."

I was surprised by this, after that long discussion of knowledge required to carry out the best interpretation of Persian poetry. The point about requirement is also significant, as the fact that you do not need to be schooled in jurisprudence, Arabic, and so forth, opens up the possibility of *tafsir* for many; as sacred as poetry is to Sheikh Alizadeh, permission (*ejaze*) to interpret it does not seem to be a concern. There is also the fascinating idea, evidenced by the Nietzsche quote, that one can be *too* learned, where you might be stifled by your own educational training.

"So, it is good to be learned but not necessary."

"Correct."

"And one can read *too* much?" After all I had read about the need for study, all I had heard from my interlocutors about the benefits of reading and textual interpretation, I was mildly shocked by this idea.

"Yes! It is absolutely possible! It depends on the person of course. I think for most people it is impossible to read too much. But some people can read too much, certain people don't want to think for themselves and for these people, yes, it is something they need to be careful of." A warning to read less, for those so inclined, lest they be robbed of their capability for independent thinking, "to think for themselves." Moreover, it is a reminder that it is not the accumulation of knowledge (*elm*) that is the ultimate goal here, but rather the ability to use such training and skills to be able to ascertain the "hidden meaning" of poems, presumably on one's own terms. These are interpretations that must accessed through one's own faculties, constitution, and thoughts.

"Can you speak a little more about dream interpretation? How does one use dream interpretation [*tabir-e khab*] to understand poetry?"

"Ah yes! This is something I have thought a great deal on, and I am not sure it is so popular with other sheikhs. We know of the utmost importance of dream interpretation. What is good enough for the Prophet Joseph is good enough for us! So there are two ways. If you spend some time during your day reading poetry, and then that night you have a dream you think is relevant, you should reconsider your understanding of the poem. Or, if you have a dream that makes you think of a poem or a certain poet, you should then read that poem from the perspective of the dream."

For many Sufis in Iran, dreams operate as a means to communicate with loved ones passed on—or those who have returned to the beloved, as the mystics say—and as a vehicle to receive messages from the Imams or the Ahl-e Bayt [close companions of the Prophet] that provide guidance for life decisions large and small. For Sheikh Alizadeh, dreams function as part of his hermeneutic schema, where the oneiric realm can offer a sort of critical lens into understanding poetry. And it is a critical lens that is seemingly hyperindividualized. Indeed, even if dreams are not considered pure products of one's subconscious, as contemporary psychologists would have us believe, but rather, as Mittermaier has shown us,[21] as a place of interaction between the veiled and unveiled worlds, where external forces can give rise to particular reveries, there is no denying that they are highly individualized events. Long a favorite topic for interpretation unto themselves, dreams are understood here as a tool to better interpret poetic verse.

"Can you give me an example of using a dream to interpret a poem?"

Sheikh Alizadeh seemed uncharacteristically hesitant here.

"Well, it would have to be one of my dreams, because I can't share any of my students,' of course . . . let me think about it."

"Of course."

On a later visit, when I brought up interpretation of poetry through dreams again, Sheikh Alizadeh told me he had thought about it and felt it would be better not to. Instead, he promised that if I had a dream I thought is relevant after reading poetry or that reminded me to think of a poem, I should call him (I was soon to leave his city) and we would discuss it together. "That is okay to write about, because it is your decision."

"How will I know if it's a relevant dream?"

"Only you will know if it's an important dream or nonsense [dari-vari] or unrelated [birapt] dream. I cannot teach you that. You will know."

I felt suddenly a bit nervous, as if I had been granted a great responsibility. How would I know if it was the right dream? I was terribly curious to see how dream-as-critical-lens operated but did not want to provide an example that was somehow . . . not genuine? Inappropriate? I was torn between an opportunity to gather ethnographic information and a desire to respect the intellectual and presumably ethical parameters set in place by the sheikh. Given the gravitas with which Sheikh Alizadeh had approached the topic—needing extra time to consider whether he would share his own dream hermeneutic and ultimately deciding in the negative—it seemed as if such an exercise was not one to be taken lightly. While Sheikh Alizadeh and his group had been exceedingly open, his remark that "it is okay to write about" only my own poem-and-dream and his immediate acknowledgment of the inappropriateness of sharing his students' examples indicated a hesitancy in making them public as well. The sheikh's reassurance did not give me much confidence.

"Thank you, I will try my best to know when and if I have such a dream, one that I can use to understand poetry."

His light-hearted demeanor suddenly returned and he laughed good-naturedly at my nervousness, which I did not realize was so transparent: "Do not look so concerned! It is not so serious as that! You will understand [*Khodat mifahmi*]."

A few weeks later, I was in another city. I had a quiet evening in and watched bootleg DVDs of American TV shows on my laptop and read some poems of Rumi from my favorite collection. That night, I had a dream of open fields. I must admit it was perhaps because I had been reading Rumi immediately before bed, but I felt like it was time to contact Sheikh Alizadeh.

And so I did. I called him that day and we discussed my dream and the poems I had been reading the prior evening. I would like to offer more details here, but a few days after our discussion Sheikh Alizadeh left me a voicemail: "Seema Khanum, I hope you and your family are doing well. Please give them all of my regards. After giving it some thought, I think it may be best that you do not write about your dream interpretation [*tabir*] in your thesis. I fear it is not scholarly enough. I wish you all success and best wishes [*piruz bashid*]."

I called Sheikh Alizadeh on the phone, thinking he had concerns that such a practice was too superstitious (*khorafati*) and not "academic" enough. As it turned out, he was concerned that it was too much of a private (*khosusi*) matter to be made public. "Is it because I am writing it down?" I asked. "Should I not mention understanding poetry and dreams together at all?" "No, no, writing down such things is fine, my students and I take notes about dream interpretation all the time. And I think it is fine to write about it generally [*dar kol*] . . . but, I am not comfortable with publishing it in a book that will be read by many. Even if it is your dream and your thesis." And so, I am respecting Sheikh Alizadeh's wishes and keeping my dream hermeneutic private.

Up until this point, Sheikh Alizadeh had been an extremely enthusiastic and loquacious interlocutor, generously offering his thoughts and wisdom in any way he could. The question of dream interpretation and whether or not to include it in this book was the moment where he hesitated most, his trademark gregariousness replaced with caution and doubt. At issue was not the interpretation of the dream or the transcribing of a vision into language, externalizing and concretizing it, but rendering it public. His responses as to *why* it was not appropriate were more a demurring than an explanation, with a simple reply that "it is better not to [write about it]."

What does this teach us about the dream and dreaming, according to Sheikh Alizadeh? It would appear that the dream is too intimate for public consumption, that something would be lost or, perhaps, exposed, if one were to share with the world their dream and its interpretation, this missive from the unseen realm. The dream should only be discussed and debated by the dreamer and those with whom they are close, and not by someone with whom they share no intimacies at all. In changing his mind about my sharing of even my own dream, in being uncomfortable on *my* behalf, Sheikh Alizadeh demonstrated his belief in the potency of the dream.

Given that we are discussing dreams in the context of poetry I am reminded too of a line by Gaston Bachelard: "The function of poetry is to give back to us the situation of our dreams."[22] Here, the literary realm acts as a means to transport us to the oneiric realm, a world much closer to the divine, the world to which the Sufi longs to return.

Another day, another conversation.

"Does a poem contain multiple meanings or multiple interpretations, and if so are some better than the oth—"

"ONE HUNDRED PERCENT [*sad dar sad*] there are multiple meanings!" I did not even have a chance to finish my question before Sheikh Alizadeh roared back his response with his trademark enthusiasm. "Come now Seema, you know that!"

"There is no singular meaning to a poem. Every time I think I understand a poem, I look again and find something new. And I am just one person! The first time . . . the last time. . . . I have read somewhere that even the name of God, Allah, comes from *alihtu fil-shay*, I am bewildered. Isn't that amazing? It is true, we can never understand God, we must be bewildered, overwhelmed at the very least when we hear his name."

"And one should be . . . bewildered, when reading these poems?"

He continued: "YES! No human can ever know all the meanings at once. It is impossible. You *must* be bewildered at some point. But of course, it is not just bewilderment you feel when you read poetry, it is illumination, it is love, it is divine silence [*khamushi elahe*], and others' stations [*maqamat*] too."

I am reminded here of Sheikh Noroozi's injunction that "confusion is beneficial," that to feel disoriented or perplexed is an admirable and appropriate response to reading poetry, one that demonstrates the acceptance of one's limitations. Sheikh Alizadeh expresses a similar sentiment, although he seems to limit "bewilderment" to one of the stations of reading poetry. On the other hand, he compares the feeling of being overwhelmed when one realizes the limitless number of meanings of the poem to that of being overwhelmed with the concept of God himself. Intriguingly, he also mentions other "stations" that one encounters when reading poetry. The idea of stations on the path, a series of moments or metaphorical "places" that successively mark one's progression toward *tawhid*, or union with the divine, is a widely accepted one within Persian Sufism. Sheikh Alizadeh's suggestion indicates a belief that the process of reading a poem, of interpreting its meanings, mirrors the project of mysticism as a whole.

I turned our conversation to teaching, and pedagogy.

"What are the qualities of a good guide?" This is another question I had sent him in advance.

"The ability to convince others you know what you're talking about" Sheikh Alizadeh declared with authority and then laughed robustly.

"It is all about charlatanism!" His wife Effat Khanum chimed in. Again with the jokes with these two; later I could not help but shake my head and smile, wondering if Sheikh Alizadeh had thought of this joke beforehand. After a bit more prodding, I received a more substantive answer.

"The love and emphasizing [*takid*] of ambiguity/allegory [*mutashabih*]!" He said this assertively, pointing his finger to the sky as he did so. "This is the most important quality for a guide [*murshid*]. Make sure you write that down. Discussing the *mutashabih* verses is what a teacher must do with his students. And the *batin* in these meanings is without end and *should* not end! You will never finish, so as a teacher you must not only be comfortable with this, but you have to have an inclination [*alaghe*] for this task without end. And, and constantly, constantly, constantly remembering that you do not know the best *tafsir* yourself! So, from your student you ask the best questions you can. This will show them their best way [*rah*]. All this is what makes the best guide."

And so, Sheikh Alizadeh has pulled yet again from Qur'anic sciences in his description of poetry. The term *mutashabih* contains a variety of meanings in both Sunni and Shi'i jurisprudence, ranging from "allegory" to "analogy" to "unclear." Typically, Qur'an 3:7 is often cited in discussions of *mutashabih* and its opposite, *mohkam* (direct or clear):

> It is He Who has revealed the Book to you. Some of its verses are absolutely clear and lucid (*mohkam*), and these are the core of the Book. Others are ambiguous (*mutashabih*). Those in whose hearts there is perversity, always go about the part which is ambiguous, seeking mischief and seeking to arrive at its meaning arbitrarily, although none knows their true meaning except Allah. On the contrary, those firmly rooted in knowledge say: "We believe in it; it is all from our Lord alone." No one derives true admonition from anything except those of understanding.[23]

Although here the dangers of ambiguous verses are expressed, especially for those "seeking mischief" who might interpret verses for nefarious purposes, Sheikh Alizadeh takes an alternate route. You must lean into the uncertainty of meanings whose open-endedness, in his words, *should* remain a central point of concern for teachers. Not to unpack them fully, but to remember why they are ambiguous to begin with: to support the limitations of human thought. And so, it is questions, not answers, that a teacher can use to show his students the best path.

"Can you explain the meaning of *mutashabih* a bit more? I thought it meant allegory (*tamsil*)?"

"No, it does not. Maybe when they do Qur'anic exegeses it does, but not with poetry [*shehr*]. But I knew you would ask that! Its definition, I mean. I thought of the words of Rumi [*Mawlana*]: 'Form is the shadow, but meaning is the sun.' You see, meaning is the source and what creates the shadow, so it is more powerful, but you cannot look at it directly, for it will hurt you. But the sun is beautiful, so you want to look at it. So what do you do? You look at both clouds and sun!"

This poetic rendering of *mutashabih*—literally defining it by a line of poetry—is a helpful reminder of what exactly is obscured in all these abstruse verses: meaning. In referring to Mawlana's dictum that "meaning is the sun," Sheikh Alizadeh is not only reasserting the centrality of content over style, but that there is a reason that the wisdoms contained within poetic verse are concealed: direct exposure to them (to continue the sun metaphor) is potentially harmful. Such a sentiment is highly suggestive of other mystical ideas of concealment (*rozpushi*), secrets (*sirr*), and not being exposed to ideas "too soon," lest one become overwhelmed or too shaken.[24] Hence, *mutashabih* operates as a form of cloud cover; not to obscure for obscurity's sake but to shield one from a source too powerful to encounter directly.

"Do the clear/direct (*mohkam*) verses need a teacher less?" I asked this because *mohkam* is the counterpoint to *mutashabih*.

"I don't like the term '*mohkam*' but '*zaher*' [external]."

"Why is that?"

"The external [*zaher*] is a better way for poetry. *Mohkam* is better for the Qur'an. *Zaher* still, it is more like style and form, I think. You need to ask a cleric [*mullah*] for that though, I'm not sure."

"It seems like many of your methods of interpretation seem similar to those in Qur'anic *tafsir*."

Sheikh Alizadeh shrugged off my observation. "Perhaps. But there are a lot of shared ideas between the two, of course, poetry is based on the Qur'an. I need to look at Allameh Tabatabai's al-Mizan [Tabatabai's exegesis of the Qur'an] and his interpretation of Hafez to see the differences. Of course there are many though. I am just a simple neighborhood teacher [*mo'alem*] though. Perhaps I have read too much Qur'anic commentary!" He said this last sentence with a chuckle. Considering he is a man who delights in declarative statements almost as much as he delights in ambiguity, I am intrigued by Sheikh Alizadeh's seeming ambivalence toward his mixed methods of *tafsir*. I tried to discuss his blurring of hermeneutic genres on two other occasions but both times he came across as similarly disinterested, even when I mentioned how his understanding of poetic verse as a mode of Qur'anic interpretation seems to be fairly unique. He restates his inadequacy in his abilities to undertake Qur'anic *tafsir*—unusual in a country where many lay people hold Qur'anic reading circles—although I have a sense he feels so mostly in his role of teacher. In addition, there is his assertion that "poetry is based on the Qur'an," an idea that would certainly support Sheikh Alizadeh's propensity for a shared hermeneutics for both.

Discussions with Students of Sheikh Alizadeh

As I had done with Sheikh Noroozi's students, I also spoke with Sheikh Alizadeh's about how they would describe his pedagogical skills and capabilities as a teacher. While with Sheikh Noroozi's students I was interested in how they might react to his self-professed limitations as a teacher, with

Sheikh Alizadeh's devotees I posed a more open-ended question: "Can you describe the sheikh's teaching? What is some of the advice he gives you?"

My first interlocutor was Ahmad-Reza, a tour guide in his fifties. His response was indicative of discussions I would have with others: "He says always, 'I am humble dust [khak], and always learn with you. He is leading the discussion of whatever text we are reading, but I think he is the most excited to learn of all! You have seen how he is. He is very warm and sociable [Majles rah garm mikonand], so he is a very friendly teacher. He is not intimidating, but seems like we are understanding the poetry together. He asks so many questions, it is like he wants us to lead him. But the batin is difficult, so I think he takes real pleasure in it too."

Two students brought up the same phrase: Kayvan, a thirty-year-old who worked in his cousin's fruit shop, and Mahbubeh, a homemaker in her forties, stated that "he tells us we must be our own guide," again emphasizing Sheikh Alizadeh's understanding of the individuated nature of the path. Mahbubeh said, "He offers the best questions! That's how he teaches us how to read." Kayvan also said, with some amusement, "He always says so many paths, where should we begin? I think he should write something because he has so many ideas, but I'm not sure he will. Maybe he has too many ideas."

Shima, a young woman who held an advanced degree in management but was currently working in a perfume shop, first extolled the sheikh's knowledge of literature more broadly. "He is like a living book [ketab-e zendeh], he is so knowledgeable. It is funny though because he asks so many questions—it's kind of frustrating actually, sometimes I just want to know the answer. But it doesn't make you nervous, like in school when they call on you to answer with the right answer. It makes you think more. So I enjoy it."

Given his emphasis on questioning and the individuated nature of the path, it seems that Sheikh Alizadeh appears to his students as an enthusiastic, approachable, and affable teacher, one whose belief in the endless nature of batin informs his pedagogy alongside his philosophy.

Unknowing of Text, Unknowing of Authority

What is a collection of poetry for a Sufi? What does it provide, and for whom? Where does its power reside, and how might one access it?

According to these Sufis, the reading of poetic verse is something that will transform you, fundamentally and unequivocally. Its alchemical properties are secondary only to those of the Qur'an and the Hadith, the texts with which much Persian poetry is always in conversation. In encountering the ideas contained within, ideas presented in the language of the artist, or "painterly language," as Sheikh Alizadeh says, and reading them with the "open heart" of Sheikh Noroozi, you will travel ever further on the path, progressing into higher stages on your spiritual journey, forever transformed. Such a belief in metamorphosis-through-poetry is not exclusive to these particular Sufis, but it is one that is at the core of the foundation of their broader epistemology.

It is imperative to remember as well that these are "endless texts," as per Sheikh Noroozi, containing a multitude of meanings, both hidden and apparent, and a seemingly infinite number of interpretations. Moreover, the methods by which to appreciate and be affected by the words of the saints are also, if not endless, quite numerous. The actual poems, each *ghazal* and *bayt*, and perhaps in certain instances every word and even every letter, are entryways that lead to a universe of ideas, the collection of poems in turn forming a constellation of infinite meaning. And for Sheikh Alizadeh in particular, for whom Persian poetry is an interpretation of the esoteric aspects (*batin*) of the Qur'an, to interpret is a task without end. Each reading leads to yet another series of questions, ever deeper, ever more profound. With apologies to Paul Ricoeur, sometimes the text *is* an unlimited field of possible constructions.[25] Just as stages of the path of gnosis are graduated, so too are the forms of understanding of the text.

Indeed, many of these meanings—the "deeper" ones, the "hidden" ones, the "inner" ones, the ones of the invisible realm (*batin*)—are able to be ascertained only by those closer to union with God (*tawhid*) as opposed to those in the earlier stages of their spiritual journey. In other words, one's ability to read is in part a reflection of one's spiritual advancement. Remember the early imperative: to become a *darvish* you must read. And so, there is an almost circular exchange of knowledge: the more you read, the more you transform; the more you transform, the better you read, until there exists a blurring here, one between self, world, and text.

Moreover, there is endlessness not only in content, but in method. Literary, philosophical, philological, oneiric, metaphorical, allegorical, historical: these are all modes of critique that are possible, where even the genre is at once utterly clear and yet also a provocation. Can poetry, with its instantly recognizable grammatical structures, also be seen as a form of *tafsir*? What does it mean that there are so many resonances between how these sheikhs and their followers interpret poetry and how other Islamic thinkers—Shi'i, Sufi, even Sunni—might approach Qur'anic exegesis?

For most Iranians, imbuing the reading of poetry with such phenomenological powers also shifts their understanding of poetry as a source of national pride, as the highest literary art form (and for many the highest philosophical art form), into something simultaneously more personal and more powerful. In a sense, it is perhaps not dissimilar to what Kant describes as the differences between beauty and the sublime.[26] For Kant, beauty arises from form, bounded and contained, whereas the sublime is tied to "boundlessness" and formlessness, surpassing all forms of sensory understanding. These works of poetry are viewed by the mystics as similarly uncontained. It is not (only) the perfection of the literary form that they admire, but the philosophical ideas contained within them.

Ultimately, these Sufis adhere to an interpretative framework for the understanding of Persian poetry that mimics their idea of unknowing (ma'rifat) as an exercise without limit or finality. Analysis that leads to more questions than answers, a hermeneutics defined by the possibility for infinite meaning, progressive layers of ideas revealed only as one moves closer to union with God (tawhid) . . . this is what is meant by an unknowing of text.

And so, another question remains: If one embraces such a hermeneutical stance, how is this material taught? As I have tried to elaborate thus far, this stance contains significant ramifications for techniques of pedagogy and spiritual authority.

Throughout my discussions with the sheikhs I noticed at times a sort of deferral of responsibility. In other words, both Sheikh Noroozi and Sheikh Alizadeh are spiritual authority figures who are able and—perhaps more remarkably—willing to designate the limits of their own authority. Before discussing this further, it is important to note that both sheikhs believe that it is imperative that one *begins* the journey of the spiritual path with a guide, one who will point out the appropriate texts and some familiarization with reading techniques that occur in the group meetings. At the introductory stage at least, it is unwise to tread unguided. Beyond reaffirming the necessity of a sheikh, the fact that there is a difference in the capabilities of a teacher for a novice versus the capabilities of a teacher for a more advanced student suggests that there is a real and substantial transformation of the self that occurs.

There are echoes here too of what Shahab Ahmed has called "explorative authority." Ahmed explains: "Whereas the proponent of prescriptive authority views his authority as a license to prescribe to another, the bearer of explorative authority views his authority as a license to *explore* (by) himself.[27]" Ahmed was writing against the tendency he sees in Islamic studies to focus too much on tracing what Muslims deemed "correct," therein downplaying the nonprescriptive, "exploratory" tendencies of Muslim scholars, which he sees as comprising the "historical bulk" of the Islamic discursive tradition. He emphasizes how an ethos of exploration brings forward the ambiguities, vagaries, and intriguing contradictions within Islamic thought, rather than the narrow pathway of prescriptive thought, where things may only be discerned to be "correct" or "not correct." And yet despite this advocacy of centering Muslim scholarship that focuses upon the open-endedness of Islamic thought, just as my interlocutors do here, Ahmed still characterizes this "exploratory reasoning" as a form of *authority*. As he writes: "Exploration is precisely the business of setting out into the unknown, the uncertain, the unexperienced, the unsettled, the new—it is something that not everyone feels able to do (*or* that someone feels that everyone else is able to do)."[28]

In contrast, Sheikh Noroozi and Sheikh Alizadeh emphasize that *all* Muslims, or at least all of their followers, must embrace this experience of encountering the unknown when grappling with mystical epistemologies, not just those who occupy more rarefied intellectual-spirito registers. And while I again should emphasize that the Sufis are clear in their need for a teacher, especially at the beginning of their training, I believe the challenge posed by questioning the authority of the sheikhs is more profound than that posed by Ahmed. Ahmed questions the *form* of authority, not the idea that the notion of authority, when confronted with a type of text or more accurately, a particular hermeneutic stance, can be challenged as a whole. (I would also take some issue with his depiction of the "prescriptive authority" in the works of Talal Asad as being devoid of "exploration," but that is a somewhat separate issue.) As such, while Ahmed would likely be delighted at the hermeneutic stance of my interlocutors, I believe their attitudes toward textual authority/nonauthority pushes beyond the "explorative" and into the undoing of the category as a whole.

Moreover, both Sheikh Noroozi and Sheikh Alizadeh seem to be in agreement that, at some point, however difficult to determine, a guide will outlast their purpose. For Sheikh Noroozi, this is the moment he defers to his student's "inner heart" as a better teacher than he, and when Sheikh Alizadeh insists that the "desire of the heart" (*khastan-e del*) dictate his students' textual analyses. In extolling the limits of their own pedagogy, the sheikhs reaffirm the individualized nature of the project of Sufism. It is only through accessing this most interiorized form of knowledge, this a priori knowledge that has been lost, that the individual can best interpret the text before them. Just as intimate knowledge of the divine cannot be directly taught, so too can the inner meaning (*batin*) of the text not be transmitted via another.

The singular nature of the path is also seen in the sheikhs' desire to guide their students to find the appropriate *questions*, rather than provide them with the most accurate *answers* for a text, especially with the students of Sheikh Noroozi. In doing so, his role as instructor is one who suggests further modes of inquiry, other conundrums to mull over, pushing them to think further on unexplored epistemological terrain rather than offering information to then think through. This element of their pedagogy I consider less a deferral of authority but rather a reimagining of the master as the ultimate provider of questions than the source of all knowledge.

Finally, in my conversations with the sheikhs I noticed an affective dimension too: Sheikh Noroozi seemed a bit melancholy in describing his limitations as a teacher, especially as he described the possibilities for learning at the feet of the sixth Shi'i Imam, Imam Jafar al-Sadeq. It seems that for Sheikh Noroozi the "inner heart" might be a better guide than he, but not better than one of the Holy Imams, therein reaffirming their position as exalted ones as well as his own lesser one. One's own "inner heart," one's own intuitive cognition, is thus merely a substitute or stand-in guide for these beloved Imams. Given that it is currently the age of the Larger Occultation, where the last of the Shi'i Imams is in hiding, waiting to return on Judgement Day, Sheikh Noroozi's melancholy is understandable. In the end, he is a poor substitute for a spiritual authority unequivocally greater than he, a sentiment harkening back to the time immediately after the occultation of the Last Imam, where no one seemed eager to assume any spiritual authority after the age of the Imams.

In contrast to Sheikh Noroozi's melancholy is Sheikh Alizadeh's seeming delight at the spiritual path's inability to be chartered and communicated. The infinite layers of meaning, the highly individuated process of interpretation, the insurmountable ambiguity of poetic language: all of these puzzles he recounted with great pleasure. For Sheikh Alizadeh, all these hermeneutic stances are what lead to the "unteachability" of the text, and are also what he views as their source of greatest enjoyment (*khoshi*). As he has taught his pupils, he is a teacher who delights in not knowing the answer. His inability to do so is not a reflection of a lack of knowledge on his part, but an affirmation that texts of infinite meaning allow opportunities for engagement without end. Ambiguity in poetry hence allows for more possibilities for readers, even if it means their guide has to take a more circuitous route by which to teach them. This is what is meant as an unknowing of authority. It is not a total refutation of the classic spiritual guide (*murshid*), but a reconfiguration of their capabilities and responsibilities in light of these groups' mystical epistemologies.

3 Unknowing of Self, Unknowing of Body

Reach for the cup and make us all drunk, for no one has become
happy unless they are hidden from themselves/When you have
concealed yourself from yourself/Flee the world quickly! Do not
turn to face/Back toward yourself—beware, beware!

RUMI, *DIVAN-I SHAMS*

All things in creation suffer annihilation and there remains the
face of the Lord in its majesty and bounty.

SURAH AL-RAHMAN, QUR'AN 55:27

Upon arrival, it is already very crowded. We locate spots on the floor,
silently and gingerly stepping around the men and women already
seated. Those who come after us hover around the doorway, spilling
out into the next room. No matter. They'll still be able to hear things
from there.

Entering the room, one first notices that the walls are as crowded
as the floor. From the carpet to the ceiling, the sides of the room
are a veritable display case of instruments—long-necked sitars and
slim *neys*, round and delicate *daf* drums and even a sturdily mounted,
heavy-looking *santur*—and calligraphic works large and small, relay-
ing *surahs* from the Qur'an and *ghazals* from the medieval canon,
their thick, black ink appearing even more emphatic against deep
gold inlays. The two largest works are invocations: *Ya Hazrat Mawlana,*

ya Hazrat Ali, invocations of the saints whose names have been called up an endless number of times, in a limitless array of situations and circumstances. And there is more: strings of prayer beads (*tasbih*) of various colors, glass and plastic, pinned at various intervals; a cowhide, brown and white, stretched to full length; two old cloaks (*abeh*) like the clergy wear, but that were worn by most men in Iran in the early part of the twentieth century; more sinister objects as well, chains and *dast-bi*, the objects used for self-flagellation in the Ashura ceremonies. There are also photographs: candid snapshots and formal portraits of several Iranian Sufi *qotbs* and sheikhs of various orders, sheikhs from both within Iran and those who lived abroad, accompanied by a good number of photographs and sketches of the *ostad*, or master-teacher, who works in this space.

The *ostad* himself sits at the front of the room, on the floor like everyone else, slowly leafing through a large volume of poetry, his gaze cast downward. Several other enormous tomes are placed around him.

The rest of the room sits quietly. A few whispered exchanges occur between neighbors, but generally all are silent. Their silence communicates both their readiness and their expectation.

Not long after, the *ostad* clears his throat and begins.

He starts with Rumi, reading through the lines and then in the same breath offering his interpretation (*tafsir*). He speaks slowly and deliberately, taking pains to provide emphasis where he deems necessary, holding his gaze out to his listeners: Do they understand this point? He discusses literary allusions and contesting views, metaphors and rhythms, asks questions to no one in particular and sometimes offers answers, and then re-reads the lines (*bayt*) before continuing onward. He moves through the tomes, reading the words aloud, then speaking aloud their meaning, or at least a possibility of their meaning, in a tone both pedagogical and animated, his own eloquence a respectful response to the beautifully crafted phrases, his cadence going up and down like the swirling calligraphy on the page.

And the people listen. Mainly intently, it would seem. Men and women—the youngest seems to be a boy of about fifteen, the oldest a wiry octogenarian with a thick white beard—sit with serious countenances, some with gazes downward, others with gazes upward. A few look at the *ostad* with a strangely impassive, almost knowing glance. Some are crying. . . .

Until the *ostad* concludes his readings, and slowly brings out his *kamonche*, resting it across his lap. He plays at the instrument, tuning and tightening the strings, until slowly the notes he plucks from the strings begin to resemble a melody, phrases moving in and out, improvised always. A frame drum (*daf*) player joins him, softly, playing from the back of the room. The phrases are mournful and contemplative, the punctuations of the *daf* acting more as emphasis, a friend verbally agreeing with you, than rhythmic pacesetter. The sing-song phrases continue, until suddenly you realize the melody has become more focused, more assertive, no longer sliding back into silence or starting over again. The musical phrases are still improvised but always driving forward now, always moving forward at a steady pace. The *daf* too has grown less intermittent, following along in the manner of a sturdy companion. The steady pace continues, until one begins to realize the sounds of the *kamoncheh* are increasing in volume, increasing in tempo, when suddenly you realize they have reached a rollicking pace, the emphasis coming on the beginning of each measure, forming a repetitive and hypnotic phrasing, one after the other, clear and relentless, once and again, once and again, as if each measure is the first, and you cannot escape. Long mournful notes emerge sporadically, their duration all the more pointed as they are ultimately swept away by the quick ones that succeed them. The singing notes of the stringed instrument reach up and out, but the first note in the phrase is still the most important. It continues in this way until it all becomes about that one note, the ones that follow simply trailing in its wake, allowing you to prepare yourself before the onslaught returns.

And then suddenly the *kamoncheh* has fallen away, the *ostad* having put down his stringed instrument and taken up another *daf* drum to join his accompanist performing from the back of the room, who never ceases to play. The *ostad* quickly joins him and they move now, in unison, the auditory pattern arriving from both the front and the back of the room, flat palms hitting the stretched material, rolling fingers forming a staccato beat, hard caresses along the frames' edges making a whooshing sound to join the hard percussions. Faster and faster the notes come, the players moving their whole bodies now, shoulders rising, pushing themselves forward while seated, rocking back and forth. The rolling sounds continue forward. All is rhythm now, impact and speed.

The old man with the wiry beard rocks his head forward and back, forward and back, raising his hands from above his knees as if in danger of losing his balance, half jumping up from his position on bended knees; several women bury their heads in their hands, their sobbing filling the space; other heads sway slowly sideways, tilted first one way then the other, the listeners close their eyes, perhaps to shut out all the other senses, to inundate themselves with sound and sound alone. Others move, up and forward, back and down, or side to side, their bodies demanding recognition, with movement as affirmation.

The rhythms continue. We are lost somehow, pulses quickened and for no other reason than the sound emitted by the players before us, our circulatory system responding to the pulses of the drums, disoriented in the wake of an external rhythm.

"Hu!"

Breathe deeply in the wake of fast pulsations, I had been told, so you may keep your calm.

Louder and louder, until an abrupt and dramatic stop.

. . .

The room returns the silence of the drums, as bodies relax and soften, and people sit wordlessly for a minute longer. Quietly, slowly, some more slowly than others, we begin to disperse. I catch the eye of my friend Noosha, a student in her midtwenties, across the room, and she smiles widely as we meet, the lines of people slowly swarming into a mass around the door. "So, how was it?" I ask. "Did you go into a state [raft-i to hal]?" I find myself asking the question somewhat shyly, I think because, having spoken to Noosha before, I knew she chooses her words very carefully and does not like to think of herself as one of those—in her words—"crazy" (divooneh) Sufis, something that "going into a state" (hal) might suggest. This time, however, it seemed she had no such reservations. "Oh, it was really great [kheili ali-bud]," she replied. "I was in another world [to ye alam-e dige budam] during fana, I have enough energy for the whole week now."

A moment in the Real to fuel a week in the Unreal. The musico-poetic gathering described here is called a zekr ritual or ceremony. The word zekr means "remembrance," or "recognition," arising out of the trilateral root "to remember." Through music and listening, poetry and contemplation, the zekr offers an opportunity for the individual to remember God so fully and completely that the self is totally subsumed in the divine. This active extinguishing of the self is called fana, as Noosha describes experiencing above.

Within Islamic mysticism the self is typically understood to be a burden, or an obstacle. It is a hindrance that impedes one's ability to achieve union with God. Bayazid Bistami (d. AD 874), whom some scholars designate as one of the earlier thinkers to reflect on fana,[1] describes the need to remove the self with the following: "I saw the Real most high in a dream and asked, 'What is the path you like?' He said 'Say farewell to yourself, and you have attained me.'"[2] In other words, if one wishes to be united with God (*tawhid*), it means that the self is so full of remembrance of God, so consumed with His presence, that there is no room for the self as we typically know it. As such, subjectivity must undergo a radical transformation in order to approach the divine register. This is the goal of the *zekr* ritual, to achieve the loss of self that is necessary in order to become united with God, to unknow the self in light of the experience with the divine.

The idea is as abstruse as it is ubiquitous within mystical literatures. While the musings, directives, and explorations surrounding *fana* in the mystical literatures are deeply complex and highly worthy of further exploration, my focus here is how lay Sufis articulated their understanding and—where relevant—their experiences of *fana*. For some collectives with whom I worked, *fana* was acknowledged as an important concept but did not occupy their attention the way other mystical conceits did. It was not until I worked with the group in this chapter, these most musically inclined of my interlocutors, that it came to the forefront in our conversations.

In the first part of this chapter, I explore lay Sufis' experiences of the *zekr* and *fana*, annihilation of the self. What I found is that the mystics' experiences tend to fall into two broad categories. The first group articulates their understandings of *fana* in a way that is redolent of the thoughts and writings of the classical literatures, meaning that the extinguishing of the self is expressed in largely theological terms, like the quieting of the lower soul (*nafs-e ammara*) and the turn to nonexistence. The second group, in contrast, describes their experience of *fana* as the loss of a much more socialized self, interpreting the loss of self as the loss of what might be called identity politics or the self in society. In the final part of this section, I compare these Sufis' desire to extinguish and destabilize subjectivity in light of earlier calls by Iranian intellectuals like Jalal Al-e Ahmad and Ali Shariati to "return to the self."

In the second half of this chapter, I examine the relationship between *fana*, listening, and the body. I explore contemporary Sufi aesthetic theories that expound upon the relationship between intentional listening and the transformation of the self specifically, understanding the ways that bodily and sensorial engagement might invoke a momentary alternative to the Foucauldian body. In this way we might consider the *zekr* as an aesthetic phenomenon as well, one where the listening act emerges as a mode of critical engagement for the destabilization of subjectivity.

In both sections, we see instances of an unknowing of self and body, an advocacy for the unraveling of subjectivity and of bounded bodies in favor of more opaque existential and ontological registers. To unknow the self is to allow for the formulation of a radical subjectivity/nonsubjectivity, which is necessary to become closer to the divine, a formulation made all the more difficult by the fact it cannot be an act of pure volition. Union with God cannot be achieved through the liberal autonomous self alone; at some point such forms of subjectivities become a hindrance and must be subsequently challenged and ultimately abandoned. Providing guidance in this difficult endeavor is the experiential knowledge gathered from the body, a body untethered.

The Nur Street Collective

The *zekr* ceremony described in the opening of this chapter took place in a residential neighborhood on Nur Street. The collective is largely the result of the organizational efforts of an individual I will call Irfan Ahmad and a few of his friends. These organizers were in their late twenties to late thirties, many married and some with young families, all had gone to college, and some had graduate degrees. The large space on Nur Street in which they held these gatherings was a private residence that belonged to an aunt of one the organizers, although I never met the aunt myself. Using private residences for large gatherings for devotional practices—Qur'anic study groups, ceremonies for mourning saints, luncheons for saints' birthdays—is quite common in Iran, as Niloofar Haeri and Azam Torab have written.[3] People may reorganize their homes to host such an event, shuffling furniture around to create space for guests to sit on the floor, and very wealthy families or groups of families may devote a basement or part of an apartment building for such purposes or even purchase a space for such uses.

The Nur Street space was only different from these other domestic devotional enclaves in that it was marked by extensive decor that was explicitly Sufi: from the portraits of various high spiritual leaders (*qotbs*), the mystic's begging bowl (*kashkul*),[4] the calligraphic works praising "Hazrat" Rumi (*hazrat* is an iteration of *hozur* or "presence," but often used to refer to saints)—these were all visual signifiers that any Iranian would recognize as adorning a place designated for (or at least sympathetic to) mystical practice. In fact, the decor was much more elaborate than what I saw in most long-established Sufi places of worship (*khaneqah*). Only certain shrines I encountered, with their many lamps, flowers, portraits, photographs, and votive gifts donated by the faithful, could compare to the elaborate wall coverings of the Nur Street space.

These aesthetic decisions are also significant in light of the fact that, out of all the Sufi collectives with whom I worked, the one described in this chapter was the least cohesive. The *zekr* gatherings happened once or twice a month on Fridays or Thursday evenings, were open to all, and were made known to people through word of mouth and/or SMS, this occurring before the age of Telegram or WhatsApp group messaging. People did not chat among themselves before the poetry discussion and dispersed immediately after the *zekr* concluded. Some individuals were regular devotees, and others came or were brought by friends a single time. The attendees' mystical activities outside the *zekr* gatherings varied wildly, with some being members or even sheikhs of other Sufi collectives, and others just devotees of the live music and poetry. The only other activity Irfan Ahmad and his friends organized in this space was a poetry group, forming some sort of core collective that also attended the *zekr* regularly. Private or group music lessons were sometimes held in the space as well.

Glancing around the room at the photos of *qotbs* from disparate Iranian Sufi orders, past and present, I asked this core group if they identified as being part of or affiliated with any particular order, or if there were any mystical authority figures of the moment or the recent past to whom they were most drawn. I was unsurprised when they seemed unmoved by the question; from their decorating scheme alone it did not look as if they favored one or the other. "They all have something to teach us," one of the founding members told me. "They are all Shi'i, they all write in Persian, they all follow Shah Nimatullah Vali." Someone else noted: "They are all important, respected sheikhs, we read anything we find interesting." And so, authority was clearly recognized here—someone had made the effort here to procure or print out a photo of a *qotb*, frame it, and hang it upon the wall—but no individual had been identified as *the* single authority. These elders and their writings all existed as equally respected sources, therein upending the Sufi tradition of devotion to one single, saint-like figure. This is an important characteristic of this group, as it belies the typical notion of mystics' steadfast devotion to a single authority figure, oftentimes characterized as "saint worship," in favor of a more self-directed form of study as well as a more complex relationship to authority figures, a notion I have explored in more detail elsewhere.

Finally, considering the loose ties between the individuals who attended the *zekr*, I am very grateful to Irfan for introducing me to people as someone they could trust, as there were not too many opportunities to get to know them otherwise. It is through his generosity, of time and of spirit, that much of the research for this chapter was possible.

Written Definitions of *Fana*, Past and Present

> I summoned the self to the Lord: it did not answer, and I abandoned it and went to the presence alone.
>
> JUNAYD, THROUGH ATTAR, *EARLY ISLAMIC MYSTICISM* (1996)

Before delving into the discussions and interviews with my interlocutors, I would like to spend some time exploring *fana* and the *zekr* ritual as delineated by authority figures of the classical and contemporary eras. In this way, we might be able to better understand the ways my interlocutors' experiences and articulations of *fana* and *zekr* converge or diverge from these more authoritative accounts.

As a reminder, the goal of Nimatullahi Sufism is *tawhid*, or union with God. This union is not a simple coming together of individual and divine, however, but requires a much more substantial transfiguration on the part of the human. Indeed, in order to (re)unite with the divine, one must discard no less than human consciousness itself. If one is to travel from the Unreal to the Real, to enter into the realm of divine ontologies, they must first remove the basest parts, or attributes (*sefat*) of their consciousness in order to allow room for divine consciousness. This form of base human consciousness is often translated as the "self" or "lower self" (*nafs-e ammara*). As Bayazid Bistami has written: "O Lord, how long will there be a me and a you between me and you? Take out the me, so my me will be in you, so I will be nothing."[5]

Even by Sufi standards of abstruseness, *fana* is a particularly thorny concept, and the questions embedded within its very formulation are many: How can one actively discard their own self? What remains in place of the self once it is removed? Does there remain any vestige of the individual's consciousness, or have they been subsumed entirely by the divine? To better understand *fana*, I'll outline here some definitions based on the writings of prominent thinkers of Islamic esotericism as well as twentieth-century Iranian sheikhs. Although this is a poor exploration of a complex and nuanced idea, my objective is to establish something approximating "canonical" definitions in order to have something with which to compare my interlocutors' definitions as we explore their understanding of the un-knowing of self.

To begin, *fana* is typically seen as an active process, one that requires much contemplation (*ta'amogh*) and discipline. In his Qur'anic exegesis *Kashf al-Asrar*, the sheikh Maybudi (d. AD 1514) makes frequent mention of "killing" or "subduing" the self (*nafs*), but also that one can achieve a higher form of self (*nafs-e mutammin*) through contemplation and medita-tion.[6] Iranian sheikhs of the twentieth and twenty-first centuries use simi-lar language in their definitions of *fana*. Javad Nurbakhsh describes it in perhaps the simplest terms: "*Fana* is the . . . contemplat[ion] of the being of the Divine, thus annihila[ting] his own being. . . . [One's] inward state is annihilated in the Divine."[7]

Thus, we have the removal of "being," and the "inward state" through the act of contemplation of the divine. The removal of the "inward state" is particularly intriguing, as it would seem that it is exactly this "inward" register that would be responsible for the act of contemplation. By being "annihilated in the Divine," however, the "inward state" has now simply become indistinguishable from that of God. Seyed Mustafa Azmayesh de-scribes the process through simile:

> In other words, consider your true self as being like crystal sugar (*nabat*).
> Nabat cannot crystallize without first being dissolved into water. So for crystallization to occur, the sugar has to be dissolved in the water. The water is the reality, the intervention of the Master, in order to allow this process to occur. . . . This process of dissolution is called *fana* in Sufism, which means annihilation. In appearance the sugar is completely dissolved, but only when it has disappeared completely it can crystallize.[8]

Describing *fana* as an almost chemical reaction, Azmayesh highlights here the way in which it functions as a process and mode of becoming, with hints of engagement with the material world, with the "water" being an "interven-tion" of God. Such utilization of the physical world will be seen in Azmayesh's writings on music and listening later on as well. Through both the medieval and contemporary examples, we see how this transformation of subjectivity, this unknowing of self, at some point involves a process of activation.

The obliteration of the self into God, this closeness with the divine that we have discussed thus far, might also seem to suggest something poten-tially blasphemous: the individual essentially becoming divine themselves. Indeed, if one is obliterated into God, might that not mean they become God-like themselves? This is an accusation that has plagued mystics for centuries, most famously in the case of Mansur al-Hallaj and his ecstatic cries of "I am truth" (*ana al-haqq*) or Bistami's notorious cries of "I am He" (*Ana howa*) and "Glory unto Me! How great is my majesty!" (*Sobhani! Ma a'zama sa'ni!*). Even today, the case of Hallaj in particular remains polarizing, especially given the outsize influence of his legacy.[9]

Most Hallaj sympathizers, however, are quick to point out the distinction between achieving *fana* and "becoming God-like." In his short treatise *Ketab al-Fana*, Junayd (d. AD 810) provides clarity on the issue. I use here the translation by A. H. Abdel-Kader:

> When a man goes forth from his own qualities and enters into the qualities of God, he goes forth from his own will, which is a gift to him from God, and enters into the Will of God . . . *those who have erred in this doctrine have failed to observe that the qualities of God are not God.* To make God identical with His qualities is to be guilty of infidelity.[10]

Junayd offers here yet another definition of *fana*, and one made by many others:[11] that becoming "annihilated into the divine" means gaining divine attributes (*sefat*) specifically. In other words, the loss of self is the loss of base attributes (ego, envy, stinginess) in favor of divine attributes (unity, compassion, spiritual largesse). This is the definition that I saw a number of my interlocutors adhere to or allude to most frequently. Perhaps one could say that, by this definition, *fana* here is an existential transformation into becoming godly, rather than godlike. Finally, it is worth noting that for Junayd *fana* is also an active process, as he "goes forth from his own will, which is a gift to him from God."

Fana is also articulated by many thinkers as becoming nothing, or becoming nonexistent. To return to Bistami: "O Lord, how long will there be a me and a you between me and you? Take out the me, so my me will be in you, so I will be nothing."[12] This embrace of self-as-nothing not only avoids the accusation of *fana* as a means to "become God," but also reaffirms the world of the Truth—the divine realm—as that which is Unreal. The prominent twentieth-century Shi'ite cleric Allameh Sayyed Mohammad Tabatabai has also discussed the merits of nonexistence quite extensively, exploring such themes in his *Risalat-e Wilayat*.[13] Here, to lose the self means not that one has been replaced by the divine, merely that the distinction between the person and the divine has been collapsed. There is a subtle but key distinction there: In this way, the annihilation of the self is perhaps better understood as the removal of the boundary, or as is more commonly known, the veil, which separates the two.

Finally, it is also imperative to remember that it is only the rare Sufi master, one most "advanced on the path," who actually is said to *achieve* this state. Indeed, despite the clear delineation of the objective of the *zekr*, only a few are able to reach such rarefied planes of experience. The rest of humanity is only capable of partial success, which is itself a specific state, one where *awareness* of the annihilation and some level of base consciousness remain. The Sufi, then, is caught between consciousness and unconsciousness, the tangible and the intangible: this is what we will later call the realm of bodily knowledge. However, at this point it is crucial to remember that, during the *zekr* ritual, some element of consciousness for these particular Sufis remains, even as it is constantly put into question. For the overwhelming majority of people, the complete and total unknowing of self is never fully achieved, and hence some element of consciousness is present. But what remains, a form of alternative consciousness based on a destabilized self, is distinct enough from the consciousness of the fully stable and known self.

In this brief overview of canonical and contemporary written definitions of *fana*, we have seen the embrace of a transformation of consciousness in this existential and subsequent ontological restructuring. Whether *fana* is understood as a form of dissolution into the divine or a complete negation of being, it is clear that in any articulation of *fana* a radical reconfiguration of subjectivity must occur.

Fana and the Disappearance of the Unreal

With this understanding in place, let us now look at the ways in which *fana* is articulated by lay Sufis, meaning those who have limited to no "training" or education in mystical epistemologies. How widely do they deviate, if at all? Given the abstruseness of the idea and the diversity of the individuals of this group—in terms of age, socioeconomic background, education, and gender—it is perhaps not surprising that I received a wide range of responses to my inquiries.

To reiterate, I found two major forms of articulations of *fana*. The first group described the extinguishing of the self in terms of a loss of what might be called sociopolitical identity and/or material conditions. The lessening of the self meant that they were freed from the concerns of being a person-in-the-world, unencumbered by very serious material concerns such as unemployment, financial problems, or family issues, therein freed from the difficulties of life in the Unreal. In doing so, this group is less interested in a refutation of the self as a whole and more interested in a distancing or liberation form a certain *type* of self. This articulation of *fana* seems to me decidedly distinct from the forms of unknowing of the self discussed thus far; the investment here is on the removal of those attributes that anchor oneself in a certain position within the Unreal, so that closeness with God requires less an annihilation of subjectivity in and of itself and more a quieting of the Unreal world.

The second group spoke of the experience of *fana* in language that more closely mirrored classic discourses of the phenomenon, where extinguishing of the self indicated a squashing of the lower soul (*nafs-e ammara*). This second group also utilized more typical theological terminology to describe the experience, making little mention of the Unreal world or how the *zekr* was a release from matters of the trials and tribulations of the everyday. In the following sections, I will explore these two articulations in greater detail as well as how each fits into the broader Iranian sociotheological milieu.

Sara and Setare, two recent college graduates who had been good friends since middle school, usually attended the *zekrs* together. They had been introduced to the gatherings by a third friend, who sometimes accompanied them as well. Setare had also started attending the poetry groups held at Nur Street, and had long been an avid reader of the medieval poet Hafez. She had an easygoing, affable air about her. When I asked what it was about Hafez that interested her, she shrugged her shoulders and said, "Hafez is a genius. It is beauty, it's wisdom, what's not to like? [*Chizi nist keh adam dust nadasht-e bashe*]" The merits of Hafez as self-evident as the beauty of a sunrise.

Sara was more animated, and voluble. I turned the conversation to the *zekr* gatherings, and I asked them both what they saw as the objective of the ritual.

"To become close with God," Sara replied. "I feel so close to God during the *zekr*." Setare agreed and added: "I become very aware of God. This is what the *zekr* should do, make you remember what is important, and that is God."

"Yes, exactly," Sara reaffirmed. "During the *zekr*, when I am close to God, I feel a sense of calm [*aramesh*]." She elaborated further:

I don't have to worry about things, like things that [are] bothering me or occupying my thoughts, like getting a job. It's tough for everyone but

I think especially tough for women, you know? There are so many more qualified women than men! I feel like sometimes they will hire men over women because they think that "oh, she will go and get pregnant" or "he needs to support a family." Anyway, this has been on my mind a lot as I'm looking for a job and then during the *zekr* and for some time after, I have none of these worries. Maybe that is off topic [she says with a laugh], I don't know. Anyway, I don't have these problems women have to deal with during the *zekr*.

The trials and tribulations of the quotidian realm—here the gendered nature of job searches—fall away during the *zekr* ritual. Her experience of the ritual was so tied to this dilemma in her life that Sara's entire discussion of the *zekr* focused around this pressing issue. She did not discuss the sounds of the music, the content of the poetry, but the injustice she feels that she may be encountering as a woman. In addition, Sara's remark that her response was "off topic" reflects a certain self-awareness that perhaps what she is expounding on is atypical of a discussion surrounding *zekr*, but not enough to backtrack on her earlier statements.

After agreeing that women face unfair biases in the workplace, in Iran and also the world over, I turned the conversation to the topic of *fana*, the extinguishing of the self. Again, I posed a broad question: How would you describe *fana*? Have you experienced it? If so, can you tell me a little about it?

The more gregarious Sara responded first: "Oh, you are asking some really tough questions [*soal-e sakhte sakht*] now! *Fana* is really mysterious." She paused for a moment. "I think it is related to *zekr*. *Fana* means I'm not thinking about myself, that I need to get a job, because I'm not even important. My job is not important. Only God is important."

I turned to Setare, who seemed to be mulling over the question.

"Setare, what do you think?"

"Well, I agree with Sara. When you are with God there are none of these types of concerns. You *cannot* have any of these concerns because you are with God."

"What type of concerns?" I asked.

"The things that preoccupy us in this day and age [*ruzegar*]: money, how we appear to others—"

"Traffic!" Sara added with a laugh. Given the often-heavy traffic in Iranian cities—where people schedule their days in ways to avoid peak rush hour time—this is not an insignificant complaint to have.

"Well, yes, even traffic," Setare concurred. "How much time do we spend talking, no, *complaining* about traffic? When we go into the state [*hal*] of *fana*, none of this matters. We are with our beloved, merciful God." For Setare, *fana* presents an opportunity for the self to be wrested away from the heaviness of the ordinary, from the trials and tribulations of the everyday, and into the arms of the beloved. And while the idea that the extinguished self is one disengaged from the Unreal is highly prevalent within mystical thought, it is Setare's and Sara's particular articulation of the Unreal that is noteworthy. For them, *fana* indicates, first and foremost, a destabilization of the social self.

I received numerous iterations of this same assertion: that to remember God is an affirmation of that which is significant in life, namely the love of God and the presence of God, and not all that which is insignificant yet occupies most of our time and energies. When questioned as to what exactly was being referred to as these "insignificant" things and occurrences, people responded by giving examples that included actions as imperative as finding a job to feelings as petty as envy at a friend's new car. They would give examples of "insignificant" or "less worthy" things such as "worrying about school," "getting good exam scores,"[14] "making money," "traffic," or alternately, "the stresses of traffic," "worrying about what others think, what the neighbors think," "worrying about elections," "the things I have to get to for the day," and "dealing with my annoying coworkers," among other concerns. Another category within this group of insignificant things was the negative emotions such as "jealousy" and "unhappiness" or not being satisfied with one's material possessions or finances. While these certainly constitute a broad array of examples, what is imperative to observe here is that they are all contrasted with and presented as seemingly disparate from the realm of God. We see an amalgamation of experiences and feelings that might be categorized as the dilemmas of the everyday as presented as counter to the divine register. Following this, to remember during the *zekr* ritual necessitates a certain distancing from these experiences and emotions, to redirect one's focus from long- and short-term "practical" goals to the recognition of the presence of the metaphysical register.

In some cases, this opportunity to distance oneself from the Unreal that the *zekr* offers also allows from a break from geopolitics. Minoo, a *zekr* attendee in her late twenties, described *fana* as a form of momentary relief from worrying about a possible military strike against Iran: "When you go into *fana*, you leave this world. This country with all its problems; I stop . . .

being, and just . . . go into the heart of God.[15] I feel a sense of gentleness in my body. I don't have fears of someone attacking the country." In this remarkable statement, Minoo explains how she experiences *zekr* as a form of escape, leaving a world where she and her loved ones have a target on their back, a target that is perpetually going in and out of focus depending on the whims, moods, and election cycles of politicians a world away. *Zekr* and the extinguished self are here a negation of the Unreal, one characterized as a realm full of precariousness. Indeed, Minoo's description of the Unreal is less a "prison of the self" as explicated by the classical literatures but a place (a plane?) full of vulnerability and powerlessness that exists as a result of geopolitical tensions and domestic problems of the nation-state ("this country with its problems"). In other words, it is not a distancing or separation from the beloved (i.e., God) that causes anguish, or even weak human traits such as envy and ego, it is the current sociopolitical situation that is identified as the primary source of pain.

And still . . . is it not the distancing from God that causes humanity to seek power in the first place, is it not the blindness induced by inhabiting the Unreal, of being preoccupied with "that which is not important," as my interlocutors told me, that is ultimately underlying all of the ills of the world? This is a fair assessment and interpretation, but I fear that would be putting words into her mouth. Upon reflecting on my notes some weeks later, I thought to go back and ask Minoo exactly this question. In the end, I chose not to; I did not wish to be the ethnographer with the leading questions.

My immediate response to Minoo's statement was as follows: "So, when you are close with God, when you see the realm of the Real, you are not worried about these political issues between Iran and the rest of the world."

Minoo continued: "Exactly. *Fana* is a type of freedom [*azadi*]."

"What type of freedom?"

"When I feel this gentleness in my body during *zekr*, it frees me from depression [*afsordegi*] and stress. When you are lost in God, there is no stress! He is all merciful, I remember it is up to him, even if I don't understand. So I don't worry about these threats against Iran." For Minoo, the extinguished self is one that is free from worry, free from fear. A simultaneous affirmation and overturn of the primacy of the socio-material world, the annihilation of the self here is understood to be one where the self is left intact, and certain social characteristics have been removed instead. While there is a contestation of things as they are, it is less an unknowing of selfhood and more a rejection of the status quo as articulated through mystical terminologies.

What I have hoped to demonstrate in this section is the intriguing shift in contemporary interpretations of the *zekr* ritual and *fana*. Namely, this articulation of the annihilation of the self as a loss of social identities is a drastic departure from descriptions of the same phenomenon made by spiritual authorities, both contemporary and canonical. The self has been reimagined as a coalescence of a series of essentialized categories determined by the larger power structures in which it resides. Obviously, neither in Iran nor elsewhere is this mode of thinking anything particularly new. What is noteworthy, however, is that this form of discourse has entered interpretations within the confines of what might be called a mystical experience. The removal of those human elements/attributes (as articulated by the classical literature) has been transformed into a removal from the discourses of power.

Moving onward, I would now like to look at the experience of *fana* as articulated by some other members of the Nur Street Collective, who expressed their "version of events" somewhat differently. For these others, the talk of rupture, escape and, most importantly, the sociopolitical realm was exchanged for discussions of transformation and nonexistence (*naboodi*). More specifically, they would explain their experiences through the poetico-theological language found in the canonical texts discussed earlier in the chapter. Their explorations of *fana* and *zekr* do not utilize the language of social identities or make mention of geopolitics, but instead revolve around what might be called more "abstract" registers. The question then arises: How do understandings of the self between the two groups compare? And finally, how do these contrasting visions of *fana* fit into broader notions of subjecthood within Iranian modernity today? To answer these questions, I turn first to discussions with those interlocutors whose interpretations align more closely with the canonical literature.

Fana as Appearance of the Real

Abdullah Khan was one of the oldest individuals who attended the Nur Street *zekr*s. He had the facial hair of Sufis of a bygone era, with a prodigiously full beard and curled mustache, now gone white with age. He had grown up in a nearby village and had little formal education, but as a young man had briefly studied at the foot of a Sufi master (*pir*), one who was capable of miraculous things: "My *pir* could fly," Abdullah Khan said, "I saw it with my own eyes. One day he visited Imam Ali on one of his night flights, and after that he could make the blind see. Other ailments too, but he was a specialist in vision." Abdullah Khan was so moved by this man that he wished to devote his life to study under him, which in those days, and for this particular group, meant becoming a student (*murid*) and going to live in the Sufi meeting place (*khaneqah*) full-time, but his father told him that Sufis (*darvish-ha*) don't amount to anything, and that he should get married and start a family. Even now, decades later, Abdullah Khan shook his head wistfully as he recalled the directives of his father: "I could not bear to disobey him, so I did just that. But I shouldn't bemoan the past, I have a wonderful wife and children instead." He was now retired and lived in a modest home with his wife Kolsoom. They had grown children, grandchildren, and one great-grandchild. Despite the family life he had chosen, he retained a keen interest in mysticism (*tasavvuf*) his entire life. "I wasn't able to become a student (*taleb*), but still, in my heart, I have always been a *darvish*."

And the *zekr* for him was an integral part.

"In those days we had no radio, no television. If we wanted to listen to music we had to play it ourselves! There was a boy who played the *daf*, and we would gather and say *zekr*! How wonderful it was [*Che ghadr aali bood*]!"[16]

"I wanted to speak a little about the remembrance of God [*zekr-e khoda*]," I said. Abdullah Khan gave me a skeptical look: "Well, what do you want to know? The remembrance of God is the remembrance of God."

"Well—" I started.

"See, you can't *think* about it so much. You have to feel it [*hess*] to really understand *zekr*; if you must think, you must think with your *heart*. The answer is already there, in your heart. If! If! If you can access it. You said your field is anthropology, no?"

In Persian, anthropology is translated as *ensan-shenasi*, with the word "*ensan*" typically understood as "human," so it can read as "the knowing of humans."

"But the thing is . . . you can never *know* humans, right? Never! Only God knows! And of course, we don't know what God knows either. This is what we must remember too when we remember God. We are lost in him and remember that which is in our hearts. You must remember with every single cell of your body! Not only during the *zekr* ceremony [*marasem*], but when you do your prayers, when you go buy bread, always!" Here *zekr* is understood as an occurrence that can and should happen at the most quotidian moments; it is not a phenomenon that is relegated to the time and place of the ceremony at all. Such thinking is in line with many injunctions in Islamic—not just Sufi—thought that the remembrance of God must be a constant activity in one's life. Still, there is a contrast here with the language of rupture that other interlocutors used to describe the *zekr* ceremony.

On another visit, Abdullah Khan related a story about how he sometimes would hold a silent *zekr* by himself. "When the children were young, many years ago, we would sleep on the roof in the summer, before we had this air conditioning. Sometimes that was when I would have wonderful *zekr*, under the stars, I would be in another world. It would *become* another world."

To "be in another world" versus "it would become another world." Making a distinction as subtle as it is powerful, Abdullah Khan spoke the statements with barely a pause between them, self-correcting almost immediately. The former assertion indicates an ontological relocation of the individual; the latter, a broader ontological shift, one of an entire plane of existence. His words evoke the power of the transformative effective of meditation (*fekr va zekr*), a practice of mystics from time immemorial. I wondered then what the necessity of the *zekr* ritual was, and particularly its music, if such experiences could be had by oneself, with only the calm of the night sky as guidance.

"Is this different from reciting prayers [*du'a*]?" I asked. "The silent *zekr*?" A silent *zekr* usually involves individuals repeating a prayer or phrase or word to themselves in their head.

"Yes, of course! *Zekr* requires more concentration [*tamarkoz*]. I don't say prayers the same way." I will leave our discussions of the role of music for later in this chapter.

I asked about his thoughts on *fana*. He paused for a bit, stroking his beard: "*Fana* is nonexistence; it is the creation of nothing. So that you might then be filled with something. That something is *baqa*. Do you know *baqa*?" I did, but asked him to explain it so I could understand his interpretation. "*Baqa* is the other half of *fana*. You enter into *baqa*. You are no longer yourself; you don't exist!"

"What happens to *you* then? Do you feel [*hess*] anything? Do you think again?"

"What happens? I don't exist!" He paused. "Sometimes I feel [figuratively] intoxicated [*mast*], I am in the tavern of ruin." "Tavern of ruin" is a very common phrase used in Persian poetry, alternately interpreted as experiencing a darkness of the soul, a heightened emotional state, or a moment of transformation, among other things.

I wondered later if my question of the use of "feeling" was too lead-ing. "I am ruined in the ruins [*dar kharabat kharab-am*]." Here, Abdullah Khan invoked a phrase that is common within Persian poetry that means, crudely translated: "I am drunk or ecstatic [i.e., ruined] in the house of drink or the tavern [the ruins]."

"Do you remember it?"

"Of course! If only I could have that mindset all the time!"

His conviction was palpable, infectious even. His responses to my questions took the form of advice and directive, a style that is not at all unusual for an older person answering the queries of a younger person in Iran, regardless of content or gender. Throughout our discussions, he described *zekr* and *fana* as forms of transformations of subjectivity, of an intoxicated and/or nonexistent self. Absent was any mention at all of the socio-material realm. If I wished to understand experiences of con-temporary Iran vis-à-vis my conversation with Abdullah Khan, I would be hard-pressed to say I learned anything. And yet, perhaps that is exactly the point. Unlike the experience of *fana* for Setare, Sara, and Minoo, the socio-material world is irrelevant for Abdullah Khan when he is in a state (*hal*). He speaks instead of nonexistence, of the tavern of ruin. There is not calmness (*aramesh*) here, as my other interlocutors spoke of, but a frenzied intoxication (*masti*). The fact that he advises that we all must at-tempt to invoke such a state during quotidian moments like buying bread speaks to a belief in theories of immanence, not transcendence. Ultimately, Abdullah Khan's views on *fana* reflect not only a different interpretation of the annihilation of self, but a different understanding of the structuring of the world. For him, the socio-material world is, in fact, something that can fade into the background/disappear during *fana* rather than give shape to the experience as a whole.

I also spent time with another individual who had similar views con-cerning *zekr* and *fana* as Abdullah Khan. Cyrus was in his twenties and held a graduate degree in psychology but was working in his uncle's flower shop while he contemplated pursuing a PhD. I had a few conversations with him, and each time we met in a park, where he asked his fiancée Zohreh to join us so that "I might be more comfortable," meaning he feared that I, as an unmarried woman, might feel uncomfortable meeting with a man alone in public. (While I'm sure Cyrus, who was unfailingly polite even by exacting Iranian standards of politesse, was indeed concerned for my comfort level, I soon realized that our conversations were also a way for him and his fiancée to be together outside of the umbrella of the family. I was more than happy to be the cover for these sweet reunions; it was the least an anthropologist could do.) Unlike many of the other young Sufis I encountered, he had some more familiarity with mysticism due to some relatives he had who were also Sufis (*darvish*). When I asked if his relatives also attended the gatherings at Nur Street I received a curt but polite "No," which made me hesitant to ask any further about them.

Cyrus described *zekr* to me as the following: "The goal of remembrance is the remembrance of God. Of course, God is always with us, but when we remember, we become more aware of His presence." For Cyrus, *zekr* operates as a catalyst to remind one of the omnipresence of metaphysics: an activation of memory that results in the affirmation of the idea of an a priori supreme being: that which was always there. The guarantee of the unseen companion, one who, in the eyes of the faithful, is there to guide and protect, never wavering.

His fiancée Zohreh, who did not attend the *zekr*, interjected here: "But shouldn't we always be remembering God? In all the moments of the day? It shouldn't be just during the *zekr*!"

"Of course, it definitely shouldn't be. We need to be doing it all the time, that is of course ideal. But I would be lying if I said if I am remembering God as fiercely as I do during the *zekr* all other hours of the day. I try not to be in the prison of the *nafs*, I try to see with my third eye as much as possible, but I cannot do it. This is my shortcoming. During the *zekr*, though, I am reminded of what is possible when I *do* remember God with my entire being."

Zohreh seemed both charmed and unconvinced. "Well, it seems a bit like cheating to me," she said with a laugh.

"Well, excuse me if I am not as pure of heart as you, madam!" Cyrus replied, also with a laugh. "You see Seema, I have a saintly fiancée!"

"How lucky you are!" I concurred. "You should be really thankful, you know." After a bit more gentle ribbing at Cyrus's expense, I returned to the matter at hand: "Now, you just remember God with your entire being? What does that mean?"

"It means that you're able to remember God, to call His name." A pause. "When you forget yourself, it's like your lower soul [*nafs-e amarra*] is no longer blocking your ears from the hearing truth [*haqiqat*]. All the lesser attributes [*sefat*] are wiped away so I can become closer to union with God [*tawhid*]. Now, I do not think *all* my attributes are wiped away, nor that I am completely lost in God, but . . . maybe a little closer."

I asked him too about the "prison of the *nafs*" (*zendan-e nafs*). This is another relatively common phrase used in the mystical literatures, describing the self as a form of prison from which one must break free.

"The prison of the *nafs* is . . . see, it is the tragedy of being in the veiled world. We have the ability to see beyond, or at least a little bit," he said with a laugh. "It is a prison that we have made for ourselves by not remembering God. We are trapped by this type of consciousness. Of course, we will only be reunited with God in death. But . . . I am closest to being the type of person I want to be in *fana*." He seems contemplative, almost a little melancholy.

"Separation from the beloved . . . it's really difficult, no?" Zohreh teased him again. "How hard it all is! Now, I am not God of course but I can be your beloved too!"

"You see, Seema? What I have to put up with?" Cyrus laughed.

Despite phrasing it in the form of gentle mocking, Zohreh's statement about "the beloved" reveals her familiarity with mystical thought, as Cyrus was referring to the separation from God that all humans are said to experience while inhabiting the Unreal. Like Abdullah Khan, Cyrus's understanding of *fana* speaks to a type of transformation of the self rather than a break from the socio-material world. His demeanor and the language he uses, "the prison of the soul," is more melancholy than the ecstatic enthusiasm of Abdullah Khan, but both are classic descriptors of what happens when one recognizes their distance from God (in the case of Cyrus) or when they become closer to the divine (as Abdullah Khan does). Both are reflecting upon the unknowability of God, positioning themselves in that moment and place where the limitations of human thought are revealed, which in this instance is through the recognition of the limits of the contained self. It is only when the "prison of the soul" is no more, when subjectivity becomes dissolved through *fana*, when they are in "nonexistence," that they are able to become closer to God. If *ma'rifat* is the contestation of the finality of thought, then the unknowing of the self for Cyrus and Abdullah and certain other interlocutors is the contestation of the bounded self.

Lastly, I think it fair to say that the socio-material realm is of concern for neither during their *zekr* rituals. When the self is extinguished, when the self becomes an unknown entity, it is a moment when the socio-material world is not overturned or destroyed but rendered irrelevant. And to render something irrelevant is perhaps even more powerful than labeling it something to be overcome. In other words, the opposite of love is not hate, but indifference. The veiled world is not escaped, but dissolved into the unveiled world entirely.

Return to Self versus the Disappearance of the Self

At this point I would like to take a moment to pull back from this Sufi community and to turn our attention to broader intellectual trends in Iran, for these destabilized selves have been seen before in Iranian discourses. Indeed, outside of mystical traditions, the questioning of the self as an entity has come up throughout the twentieth century (if we are to restrict ourselves to the modern era). There are of course the obvious parallels in the writings of esoterically minded Shi'i clerics like Allameh Tabatabai, who has a not insubstantial number of writings on nonexistence and nonexistent selves. And while parsing through the differences between the vicissitudes of subjecthood as articulated by Shi'i clerics and lay Sufi Shi'is is certainly worthwhile, what I wish to focus upon here are destabilized subjectivities as expressed in the writings of some other Iranian intellectuals slightly further afield from the realm of the ulama.

In his highly influential essay "Westoxification" [Gharbzadegi],[17] Jalal Al-e Ahmad writes of the *bi-simayi* or "facelessness" of Iranian youth. In his view, young people have become unmoored from their own religious and cultural touchstones, replacing them with an attraction to the machinations of the West without understanding the reasons behind their attractions. This uncritical unmooring results in a generation of "empty selves," who have lost "any sense of self-hood." Al-e Ahmad uses the language of ephemerality to explain the status of these lost souls, describing them as "faces on the water," and "particles suspended in the air," phrases that would not seem out of place in Sufi discourses on destabilized subjectivity.

Of course, these "empty Iranian selves" of Al-e Ahmad are seen as failures—failures of the nation state, of the ruling classes, as well as the shortcomings of the intellectual capacities of the individual. In contrast, Sufis who are "emptied" of selfhood are seen as advanced, having achieved something that could, crudely, resemble a "success" on the path toward *tawhid*. Al-e Ahmad mourns a "faceless" generation devoid of authenticity (*bi-esalat*). The Sufis see annihilated selves as finally freed from the shackles of the Unreal in favor of moving into the Real. The "Real" is an imperfect antonym to "inauthenticity" but it is clear that there are contrasting views of emptied selves at play here.

As Vahdat and others have pointed out, Al-e Ahmad saved his harshest criticism (of which there were many) for the secular intelligentsia.[18] That said, it was not the idea of secular intellectualism that he saw as the broader dilemma. In fact, he considered an increase in intellectualism and general critical thinking as the solution to these lost selves. A lost subjecthood is thus seen as something that needs to be restored, fully and wholly, rather than as an opportunity for an existential transformation as per the Sufis.

Another prominent Iranian intellectual, Ali Shariati, also explored the idea of lost subjecthood in a number of writings on the theme of "return to the self."[19] Considered to be one of the preeminent ideologues of the Iranian Revolution, it is difficult to overestimate Shariati's influence on twentieth-century Iranian thought.[20] Most well known for advocating a revolutionary sensibility based on Shi'i history and theology shot through with socialist ideologies, Shariati espoused an idea of "return" that is a more nuanced and complex version of Al-e Ahmad's. Like Al-e Ahmad, Shariati views Iranian subjectivity as having been eroded to nothing in the face of colonial violence. A return to self, he argues, would entail a "return to culture" and "a recognition of our self as we are."[21] Selfhood is in a sense in need of a restoration, one that is based upon the culture and religion of a people that was always already there.

While they agree about the need to wrest Iranian subjectivity from the influence of colonial powers and the existential toll that such influence takes, Shariati and Al-e Ahmad diverge in terms of the temporal dimensions of their proposals. For Al-e Ahmad, the problem of the "faceless selves" involves a restoring of ties to the past; it is thus less a transformation of the self than it is a reestablishing of something lost. Shariati's understanding of lost selves vis-à-vis the past is a bit more complicated.

Arash Davari has eloquently explored Shariati's anticolonial strategies in light of his conversations with Frantz Fanon alongside his discussion of martyrdom (shahadat), which may also be considered a form of annihilation of the self. The comparison is of course complicated, however, by ideas of sacrifice, where the annihilating of the self in the context of martyrdom occurs for the collective good rather than for the individual. And yet both, according to Shariati, involve a broader transformation of the self. Here I quote Shariati's writing cited by Davari. In Shariati's words, a martyr [shahid] is

> no longer a human, a person, an individual. He is thought. He was an individual who sacrificed himself in the pursuit of his thought and as a result has been transformed into thought itself. For this reason, we do not recognize Husayn as a particular person who is the son of Ali. Husayn is a name that signifies Islam, justice, charismatic leadership, and tawhid. . . . As a result, he has become an absolute sanctity himself. All that remains of

him is a name. His substance is no longer an individual. He has become a source and *maktab* [school of thought]—meaning he has become tantamount to a *maktab*.[22]

There is a transformative element to this extinguishment of self; there is another form of nothingness here. More significantly, as Davari explains, Shariati sees the ability to carry out martyrdom as dependent upon the individual's capability (1) to recognize the need for martyrdom, and (2) to see themselves as *capable* of such an act. Davari writes: "Shariati's conception of *shahadat* constitutes a direct call to the masses to act as readers of themselves and thus to 'return' to who they are in the now."[23] This "return" is less a restoration of a break with the past as suggested by Al-e Ahmad, and more one that requires a self-recognition/recognition of an a priori self. This is deeply resonant with mystical understandings of knowledge of the divine as already being present within the heart of the individual, it is only a matter of how they might access what was there all along.

This brings us to the temporal aspect of Shariati's argument. Davari writes: "Instead of imagining a return to a historically factual past, [Shariati and Fanon] argued for a 'return' to a self that exists immediately in the present but is yet to be realized."[24] The self that needs to be restored exists in a state of latency, neither past nor fully future but wholly present. In this way, the return is a restoration or fulfillment of a potential that is already there. In her exploration of the relationship between the ideas of Shariati and Walter Benjamin, Mina Khanlarzadeh offers thoughts on Shariati's ideas of futurity,[25] writing that for Shariati "the future resides, rather, at the heart of the present in the form of a messianic longing for a more egalitarian future that is not far from the present."[26] In other words, the future is already here, or perhaps *almost* already here (and the almost is key), existing in an intimate, affective relationship with the present, with both future and present comprising and forming one another simultaneously. Given this complex temporal matrix with which he approaches the idea of "return," it is clear that Shariati's understanding of formulations of the self and "return to the self" is not as straightforward as one might assume.

And so, one might ask what would Shariati think of these Sufis, and their thoughts on subjectivity? Behrooz Ghamari-Tabrizi has investigated Shariati's thoughts on Sufism, both in its order-based, "organized" formulation as well as mystical thought itself, examining what attracted him to mysticism as well as what repelled him from it. Ghamari-Tabrizi writes how Shariati undertook exercises in solitary isolation as a young man, composing "desert contemplations" (*khaviriyyat*), and identifying with Sufi saints like Rumi and Hallaj. Later in his life, however, he expressed frustration at the tendency of Sufi orders to seemingly ignore the injustices of the world around them. And yet Shariati never disparaged mystical epistemologies themselves, Ghamari-Tabrizi describes: "He rejected an organizational logic in Sufism, not its embrace in the plurality of mystical experiences."[27] I have also written about Shariati's mystical predilections,[28] especially the ethos of becoming and transformation that permeates all his work; whether it is referring to a transformation or a "return" or the upending of the unjust status quo of society, his work is overflowing with ideas of "development," "evolution," "growth," "perfection," and many other calls to *change*. In this regard, Shariati shares an affinity with the mystics, as both he and they are committed to an existence that is predicated upon the fact that only with radical change, and all the labor that accompanies it—spiritual, intellectual, physical—a change that must occur on what Shariati calls the "existential" level, can one fulfill one's true potential in life.

And yet still, it is clear there are differences between the stance of my interlocutors and those of Shariati. For while Shariati sees the transformation of the self and society as related to one another,[29] my interlocutors expressed a much more ambivalent or indifferent stance toward the role of society as it relates to their experiences of *fana* (even though I surmise most of the Sufis would propose that undergoing *zekr*, working toward *tawhid*, would generally be a "good" thing for society).

And so, after such a long fight for a restoration of the collective Iranian psyche, where so many people struggled and died so that Iranians may be free to be themselves, to be their whole selves . . . what would Al-e Ahmad and Shariati make of these Sufis extolling the virtues of annihilated selves? Would they shake their heads at individuals praising *fana*'s ability to transport themselves away from the sociopolitical world of contemporary Iran or others who bypass any talk of "profane"/worldly matters altogether?

If this ethnography took place in 1971, for example, when most intellectuals viewed any apolitical activities contemptuously or at least dismissively, they might have viewed the Nur Street Collective with some derision. Perhaps they would have seen them as irresponsible, ignoring the suffering of the masses and assaults against Iranian identity and autonomy, indulging instead in esoteric practices that have no real impact on the sociopolitical world. Certainly, many of the clergy in Iran were accused of such a mindset at the time, viewed as having their heads buried in the proverbial sand, obsessed with arcane rules concerning purity rituals while the world burned.

Forty years after the revolution, the fear of colonial influence is not what it was. It is still present, of course, especially in the form of fear of military invasion, and the power of empire is experienced every day under the international sanctions imposed by the United States. But the imperialist powers' abilities to corrupt the soul or psyche of the nation or its youth is no longer a priority of many Iranian intellectuals, leftists or otherwise.[30] Even as Iranians grapple with their difficult relationship with the United States and their allies, and as Iranian government officials frequently invoke legacies of colonialism and foreign interference, the situation is undeniably different now than in the era of Mohammad Reza Pahlavi, the erstwhile ally of the United States (however complicated his allyship was). There is of course a healthy discourse on what it means to be Iranian today, about the identity of the nation, what it stands for, and so forth, but I would argue that the Iranian self is no longer regarded by members of the intelligentsia as under existential threat from outsiders in the same as it was in the prerevolutionary era, and thus Shariati's and Al-e Ahmad's concerns are not exactly applicable in the way they once were. It is in this way that the activities of the Nur Street Collective might be viewed as a postrevolutionary phenomenon. Perhaps it is only when the self is whole that it may be erased at all.

Sufi Aesthetic Theories: Unknowing of Body

> Therefore Sufism is not a religion, nor a sect,
> only music, rhythm, the inner vibration.
> SEYED MUSTAFA AZMAYESH, *MORVARID-E SUFI-GARI* (2008)

> I live by tangible experience and not by logical explanation. . . .
> There all possibilities are exhausted; the "possible" slips away
> and the impossible prevails.
> GEORGES BATAILLE, "THE TORMENT" (1998)

"You must listen with *every single cell* within your body! You must *remember God* with every single cell within your body!" Abdullah Khan told me this with such fervor, his eyes widening and his index finger pointed skyward, that I was almost taken aback by the intensity of it all. He was a passionate man in general, but this discussion of the body seemed particularly urgent, as he *insisted* on this type of bodily listening.

"You must look inside your heart. It is the *heart* that knows. Not the mind. God is in the heart and body [*badan*]."

"The body as well?" I inquired. The heart as the abode of the divine was a common enough refrain but the role of the body was much more contested.

"Yes, of course! The heart is in the body, so the way to the heart is through the body. You see there are layers. First the mind, concentration [*tamarkoz*] and things like that, then the body, breathing [*nafas-keshidan*] and listening [*sama*], and moving [*tekun khordan*], *then* the heart. Each one is a layer, until you are living in the world of the heart [*alam-e del*], you reach the knowledge of the heart. I'm pretty sure there are other layers but that is enough for students [*taleban*] like us."

Layers upon layers. In Abdullah Khan's statement there emerges a clear hierarchy of faculties: mind, body, heart. These faculties—the rational, the sensorial-epistemological, and what may be called the cultivated instinctual—constitute the ideal progression by which to achieve *tawhid*.

While there is much to be said about this progression, or the idea of progression or stages in general, what I would like to focus on here is the second stage: listening and the body, and what type of unknowing/non-knowledge they might engender. Indeed, all my interlocutors insisted on the importance of music and listening within *fana*. Although there are certain groups of Sufis in Iran, most notably the Soltanalishahi Order, who do not utilize music at all, the *zekr* of the Nur Street Collective always incorporated some sort of musical element. And it was this musical component that they saw as vital to engaging the body in ways that might otherwise not be possible. A number of the organizers of the group, including Irfan Ahmad, had spent some time reading materials that discussed theories of listening and music. These included the writings of mystical premodern thinkers like al-Ghazzali and Hujwiri, the contemporary Sufi sheikh and expat Seyed Mustafa Azmayesh, the University of Tehran professor Nasrollah Pourjavady, as well as the British neurologist Oliver Sacks and his book *Musicophilia*.

This section hence examines what might it entail to understand the *zekr* as a sensorial and corporeal experience, and how mystical epistemologies might simultaneously influence and be influenced by these aesthetic encounters. In order to pursue this inquiry, it will ultimately be necessary to posit the *zekr* at that strangest of junctures: the instance between the material and immaterial divide.

In this section, I will address the following questions: What is the role of music in the transformation of the self? Why is sound necessary to dislodge subjectivity, and what specific qualities does the auditory possess to carry out such a lofty task? In other words, how is the destabilization of subjectivity achieved vis-à-vis sound, that defining characteristic of the *zekr* ceremony? And how are listening practices and the body implicated in this process of *fana*, if at all?

As a starting point into this exploration of the convergence of the material and metaphysical realms, let us begin more specifically, with the aestheticization of the verbal/vocal: that which is uttered, rather than those aspects of the ritual that may be construed as more traditionally "musical." Indeed, if our goal here is to disentangle and isolate the sensorial dimension, the physical surface of things, the physical sound of the words articulated aloud must surely be held accountable.

Voice, Utterance, and Comprehensibility

"Hu!"

If there is a word that is most closely aligned with contemporary mystical practice, it is this breathy and assertive monosyllable. Short for Allah-hu, one of the ninety-nine names of God, when spoken aloud, especially in the declarative form, the long "o" sound of "Hu" draws out a long breath from the speaker, deep from the chest. This is not unintentional, as the primary organizer of the Nur Street Collective, Irfan Ahmad, told me: "It is absolutely necessary to engage the body [*badan*] during the *zekr*, otherwise you are just listening passively. When we say "Hu!," that causes us to breathe more deeply and engage the body more, you have to engage with your whole body during the *zekr*."

Other frequently voiced phrases include "Ya Ali," "Ya Ali Madad," ["Ali help me"], or "Ya Hussein," "Ya Fatima." (These utterances of the names of Imams are absolutely not exclusive to Sufis but invoked endlessly by many Iranians. At this very moment that you read these words I would wager that someone, somewhere in Iran is saying "Ya Hussein!," either because the spirit moves them or because of more quotidian matters such as lifting a heavy box.) I appreciated the individualized takes on these standard phrases as well. One friend of mine took pleasure not only in inserting

"Hu" in more casual conversation, but would also say out loud numbers of spiritual significance—numbers used in textual and decorative materials, but not usually used as invocations—peppering her dialogue with "Hu 121,"[31] sometimes causing her friends to roll their eyes at her playful exuberance.

Within the *zekr* ritual, "Hu" is the most frequently invoked phrase by far. Sometimes it is repeated over and over by all assembled, forming a rhythmic invocation that ties together all present in a way that only group chanting might do. Other times it is individuals who will speak a single "Hu" at random moments during the ceremony, sometimes loudly, sometimes under their breath, so that the music is punctuated by these spontaneous declarations, popping up here and there as if enthusiastic songbirds had infiltrated the space.

Irfan tended to use group chants with smaller groups of people, finding that such vocalizations tend to get unwieldy in large gatherings such as the one described in the beginning of this chapter. "Those *zekr*s are open to anyone, so you have people who are totally unfamiliar with mysticism [*tasavvuf*] and it can get to be a big mess [*gharashmish*]."

"They can't keep the rhythm?" I asked.

"No, they probably can, but they might get confused or maybe even intimidated. 'Oh what are these crazy *darvishes* doing,'" he said. "It's better that we keep the vocalizations to those who know a bit more, so we don't have to be distracted or worried about the new folks, and just focus on the *zekr*."

We also spoke about remembrance and repetition. Equally important as the invocation of the phrases is the repetition of them, namely to fulfill the following two purposes: (1) to conjure the act of constant remembrance, recollection, and mindfulness, a phenomenon that I will discuss later; and (2) to experience the words in such a way that they become an entry point into an alternative form of consciousness and the experience of the divine. Upon immersing oneself in a ceaseless repetition of words, simultaneously speaking them and hearing them, receiving them and producing them, it becomes more and more difficult to treat them as self-contained signs as they move ever closer to reappropriating themselves as empty signifiers. It is perhaps not the word or phrases themselves that are so important, but the repetition therein that is imperative to the task at hand. Thus, as vocalization becomes a mode of repetition, these words *lose their meaning and become sounds*, as al-Ghazzali writes: "Rather, [the Sufi's] song itself does not reside in the literal meaning of the verse . . . for they are affected by listening to the sound of the hautboy, even though it has no meaning. It is for this reason that those persons who do not know Arabic are affected by listening to Arabic verses."[32] Hence, it is the experiential element of the affect of the speaking-act, conveyed by its sound, that emerges here as the ultimate goal of this listening, rather than the linguistic meaning of the words themselves. Herein lies the radical potential of the poetico-experiential invocation, one that suspends itself in the reverie of language and song, thereby activating the auditory imagination of the divine.

More importantly, however, this transference does not occur passively, whereupon the listener is made to surrender to some form of sacred music, but rather is characterized as a supremely active reflection, such that the listener must demand their critical faculties to fully engage with these intricate sounds, as al-Ghazzali suggests: "It may also be that one understands something of the Arabic verses that are not in their meaning, but what one imagines them to be."[33] In other words, the knowledge or meaning that may be generated from the reception of the verses is not dependent upon their predetermined, dogmatic definition, but rather the listening subject's imagined interpretation of them.[34] Furthermore, this statement should be not seen as an advocacy or an instance of logocentrism—again, the sign remains arbitrary—but rather that it is the very arbitrariness contained within language that is significant; these words are no longer words, but a spell. Through the process of repetition, through the emphasis of arbitrary sound over sense, the immediacy of meaning is destabilized through the imagination's ability to undermine the very totality of meaning itself. It is not understanding that is important here but, as I will attempt to further explain, the experiential as a means to come into contact with the incomprehensibility of the divine.

The subversive potential in this observation is seemingly enormous; "meaning" has become synonymous with "the imagined," various modes of desire may contaminate things, and an ordinary listener has been granted the role of interpreter. It this invocation of the projection of desire and interpretation that al-Ghazzali finds so appealing within the zekr ritual, remarking that it is only within these spaces that such modes of spiritual engagement are possible. As he writes: "For each person there is a condition which is eager to hear a verse suited to his own state . . . it is not proper that you interpret the Qur'an according to your own whim and alter the meaning of the Qur'an."[35] At the same time, even as he advocates what may be perceived as a slightly heretical exercise, he warns consistently of the risks this critical listener faces: the ever-present potential for indulging carnal desire,[36] and the chance of arrogant interpretation,[37] as he writes: "the danger of music to one's love of God Most High is tremendous."[38] It seems, then, that this act of recollection is not one for the faint of heart, but rather for those of a select constitution, those able to withstand the temptation to deviate.

Aesthetic Exposure, Revelation, and Concealment

Having addressed the use of vocalization in the *zekr* ritual, what I have hoped to impress upon the reader thus far is that the significance of the material nature of both these disparate phenomena is not that they provide an empirical manifestation of metaphysical meaning, but something quite dissimilar. Ultimately, it is the remembrance of that *incomprehensibility* of the divine that is actualized through listening, a radical form of immanence acutely experienced but never fully comprehended. Through an encounter with the aesthetic, knowledge of the divine becomes manifest as a mode of experience, and not as an instance of reason. Hence, listening emerges as a catalyst by which to undergo experience, whereupon knowing (reason) evolves into a form of nonknowing (experience). Similarly, put in less poetic language by Nurbakhsh: "*sama* means the 'realization and discovery of mystical states which is necessarily accompanied by the loss of the faculties of retention and judgement in one's internal consciousness.'"[39] Consequently, as we will explore in further detail, remembrance within *zekr* manifests itself as a form of "realization," whereby a new form of epistemological awareness allows one to "discover" the divine through a process of forgetting and unknowing.

Indeed, as al-Ghazzali notes, understanding is only the first "station" within listening; more important is the state of ecstasy (*wajd*) that is unveiling: "Know that there are three stations in music: first, understanding; second, ecstasy; and third, motion."[40] Thus, in music, knowledge is apprehended by the ecstatic, definitive comprehension overtaken by the elusiveness of the divine, until all cognitive modes are caught up in a volatile interplay between knowing and not-knowing, awareness and unawareness. Further elaborating upon the ecstatic phase, al-Ghazzali writes:

> Those sublime states which begin to attach to them from the invisible world because of the music are called "Ecstasy." It may [have] happened that their hearts become as cleansed and purified as silver which is placed in fire. That

music throws the fire into the heart and removes its tarnishings. It may be that that which is attained through music is not to be attained with much self-discipline. And music activates that mystery of the relationship which is between a human being and the world of spirits until it becomes possible for him to receive everything from that world so that he becomes unaware of all that there is in this world. His limbs may also falter and he may become unconscious.[41]

Here then emerges al-Ghazzali's philosophical positioning of music as a mode of perceptive and cognitive transformation, one wherein aesthetic experience is used to reveal the "mystery" of God, demarcated here as a state of "ecstasy." Indeed, the state of *wajd* materializes "because of the music," such that the auditory is posited as a mode of "activation," the auditory intermediary to the divine event. Furthermore, the invocations of "cleansing," "burning," and "purification" clearly indicate that some process of transformation is at work here, a physical alteration demanded of the listener so that they are prepared "to receive." Finally, by noting the ambiguity of the relationship between "the human" and "the spirit world," as well as stressing the power of materiality within the knowing/unknowing act—that is "until it becomes possible for him to receive everything from the world so that he becomes unaware of all that there is in the world"—it may be argued that al-Ghazzali is putting forth a theory of immanence. Everything is put into effect by the listening act, just as the auditory metaphysical event impresses itself upon everything in turn. In other words, what first happens is that listening to music sets the condition for a form of hyper immediacy with the world, and that this new awareness somehow engenders an erasure of that surrounding reality. This would evoke that "first station" of music, understanding, though reinscribed in a convoluted procedure of "unawareness." However, as the *zekr* continues and the vocalizations of remembrance are uttered again and again, the disparate kinesthetic elements begin to be experienced in such a way as to reflect the immaterial nature of the divine experience, as well as the immaterial nature of perception.

Again, this is not simply the manifestation of belief, the metaphysics of aesthetic presence, but rather a form of exposure to the experiential nonknowledge of the divine. Undoubtedly, by altering the perception of time, the voice, and (as we will soon see) the body through the listening act, it is ultimately the *affect* of the aesthetic experience that proves most potent in provoking this interface between thought and unawareness. Thus, it is the transfigurative affect of the sensory engagement that escapes rational empiricism, and moves metaphysics instead to the realm of the unknown.

Within the confines of sensoriality, then, we find the most immediate way to embrace experience over reason, until the listening subject is irrevocably transformed. To this end, al-Ghazzali stresses nonunderstanding in service of the metamorphosis of self and world: "The listening to music of this person is not in the way of understanding sublime reality; rather, when the music touches him, that state of nonexistence and one-ness is renewed; he becomes completely absent from himself and unaware of this world."[42] Hence, what might be obtained from this statement is that a becoming transpires here, that a vital transformation has taken place, rather than the absorption of knowledge.

At the same time, however, al-Ghazzali has invoked a classic dilemma of aesthetic theory: Where does the material, sensorial aspect of aesthetic experience begin, and the cognitive engagement of it end? In other words, who or what is responsible for the induction of this state: is it the music that lulls this listener into nonunderstanding, or is it the listener whose critical imposition upon the auditory ultimately provokes this enterprise? In the end, for al-Ghazzali and various others, this is a transformation that can only take place under certain conditions; namely, that of a listener who approaches *zekr* with the correct intentionality. Indeed, it is only with the proper ethical framework in mind that one may fulfill the act of remembrance that defines the *zekr*. . . .

Eternal Beginnings: Remembrance, Forgetting, and Repetition

As stated earlier, *zekr* is characterized above all else as an act of remembrance, oftentimes characterized as being "mindful" of God. Thus, at this point I would like to investigate the way in which *hal* and ecstasy might allow for such activations of memory. Moreover, I would like to see how an encounter with the occasion of the enigma of the divine might invite such an instance of remembrance, and how the experience of "unknowing" might aid in such an endeavor.

To begin with, I would posit that this instance of conscious remembrance is felt so acutely mainly because it is arises out of an a priori moment of forgetting. In other words, just as there exists a constant interplay between an awareness and unawareness of the physical realm while attempting to enter *hal*, so too is the act of remembrance similarly entangled with the movements of forgetting. Just as the immanent encounter is revealed only after the material world is concealed, so too is the willful form of recollection possible only once something has been forgotten.

In describing the particular stance of a Nimatullahi *tariqa*, Richard Netton describes reminiscence as a form of inverse forgetting: "One of the features of *zekr* is that it represents anamnesis, the 'unforgetting' of that which, in our deepest core, we already know."[43] In this way, it may be argued that in order to remember what was already known, what was already felt, and perhaps even what was predetermined, one needs to "forget" in order to reexperience and remember the unattainable union. It is the very unknowability made manifest in the *zekr* ritual that lends itself to the act of remembrance, for when the listener is confronted with this volatile epistemology of awareness/unawareness, one must constantly reassert oneself within *hal* in order to remain focused. This is a ceaseless, willful form of recollection; to constantly forget so that one might remember all over again. To remember the love of God is essentially only the first movement of total recollection, as a conscious remembrance would consistently undermine the unknowability present within ecstasy. Schimmel quotes the writings of Abu Nasr al-Sarraj: "'True *zekr* is that you forget your *zekr*.' . . . Since even the word or thought 'O God!' implies the consciousness of subject and object, the last mystery of recollection is complete silence."[44] This "mystery of recollection" is thus effectuated by a constant entangling between remembering and forgetting, a continual interplay characterized first and foremost by repetition. More precisely, in order to re-create and relive the exact moment of the conscious activation of memory, without lingering for too long on the security of this instant, the moment must reconstitute itself again and again. Within the space of performance, linear and nonlinear temporalities exist hand in hand.[45] Executed by the endless cycle of repetition, the beginning becomes indistinguishable from the end, until all that remains is a dialectical interplay of initiation and conclusion. And yet, how then might such a ritual reach a sort of definitive conclusion—are *hal* and *wajd* not considered as a means unto *fana*, a state of total and seemingly definitive annihilation? In short, I would posit that this apparent contradiction is reconciled by the intimation that *fana* (at least as it is interpreted here) is a *hal ahwal* characterized by instability; a state of destabilization that would apparently defy logocentrism[46] in favor of the ambiguous interplay of immanence,[47] whereupon the finite is rendered infinite, and vice versa.

Furthermore, this phenomenon is underscored by the fact that the existential and metaphysical dimensions of remembrance within *zekr* are made manifest in its stylistic aesthetics, or as Shannon writes: "However, closure in the *zekr* is never final. The *qafla* [*closure, or lock*], like musical closure, marks a temporary pause before the opening of another section or of another *zekr*, if it is the *qafla* of the last section. The end of the *zekr* itself is not marked with any sort of finality."[48] Indeed, the cyclical and repetitive nature of the *daf* drum is highly evocative of the constant vacillation between the conscious and unconscious states. Hence, what is apparent here is that the existential and the aesthetic are inextricably intertwined, as an encounter with the divine unknown is instantiated through an existential engagement with sensorial experience.

Finally, it should also be noted that this articulation (internal as well as external) of mindfulness is one driven most prominently by a willful desire to encounter this nonunderstanding. The endurance required is not typified with what might be conceived as an exceedingly frustrating phenomenon, one typified by Sisyphean impossibility and indeterminacy; it is the drive to persist in this quest for remembrance that ultimately defines the *zekr* ritual—it is only out of love that one would persist. Consequently, it is for this reason that Schimmel makes the following ostensibly innocuous observation: "*Zekr* is the first step in the way of love; for when somebody loves someone, he likes to repeat his name and constantly remember him."[49]

Auditory Bodies: *Sama* as Mimesis

Having thus far observed the *zekr* ritual in light of questions of subjectivity and aesthetics, let us now turn our attention to exploring the relationship between *sama* and the body, with specific attention given to the role of motion, transfiguration, and mimesis.

Recently, there has been much written regarding the concept of embodied practice within contemporary Islam and the postcolonial context,[50] as well within more generally situated studies of ritual practice and the body.[51] As such, using Talal Asad's conviction that "abstract ideas are not opposed to bodily practices" as a starting point,[52] I would contend that this argument might be slightly altered in the instance of mysticism.[53] More specifically, given the immanent potential contained within all things material—including the body—within Sufism, it would be somewhat limiting to simply understand *zekr* as an instance of "practice," meaning a routinized habit or exercise possessing a similarly prescribed objective, instantiated within a carefully prescribed context. This is not to suggest, however, that various incarnations of the *zekr* rituals across the disparate *tariqas* do not suggest or demand specific postures or even ritualized movements of their practitioners (far from it). The distinction I would make is that these "abstract ideas" arise out of a sensorial, bodily practice, rather than being implemented within them. For example, the Naqshbandiyya Sufis decree the following bodily engagement: "The Sufi must keep the tongue pressed against the roof of his mouth, his lips and teeth firmly shut, and hold his breath. Then starting with the word *la*, he makes it ascend from the navel to the brain. When it has arrived at the brain the *ilaha* to the right shoulder and the *illa'llah* to the left side, driving it forcefully into the pineal heart through which it circulates to all the rest of the body."[54] Because of the elusiveness of the objective of *zekr*, as well as the experiential characteristics that it entails, it would seem that to depict it as simply a manifestation of a practice might limit or reduce its existentially transformative potential.

Thus, we might instead understand the role of the material body within *zekr* as a space of metaphysical mimesis,[55] and thereby implicate it as a vehicle for encountering the mystery of metaphysics. To begin to explain this idea, we might first look to one of most basic tenets of the *zekr*: Once the critical listener is engaged, the swaying body begins to essentially mimic the rhythms and dynamics of the music involved. From here, we look to understand what Seyed Mustafa Azmayesh calls the "inner music" or, as he suggests quite literally, the sounds of the heartbeat: "The Sufi seekers are intensely interested in the inner music in their body, the inner vibration coming from the source of their hearts. They try to listen to their heart, and try to hear their heart beat. This heartbeat reminds them of something of their origin."[56] The purpose, then, of the instrumental music is not to act as a spiritual guide in and of itself, but as a means to reveal the internal percussions of the body: "Every rhythm, every melody is like a bridge to the heartbeat. When you play a certain rhythm for two minutes your mental and spiritual state changes."[57] As such, it is for this reason that the *zekr* mainly utilizes the percussive music of the *daf* (hollow drum) as its sole instrumentation: the staccato beat of the drum mimics the percussive beat of the heart, and it is to the batteries of this latter sound that people dictate their movements: "On the path [of *erfan*] we work on this transformation by certain music, certain rhythms and the inner music."[58] Therefore, listening to this type of music is able to make one conscious of these otherwise unconscious bodily rhythms, therein offering what we might see here as a strange form of reverse or auto mimesis. In other words, through contact with a foreign substance (this instrumental music), the rhythm of the body's movements mimics the rhythm of its own heartbeat: an externalization of what was there all along.

Furthermore, it should be noted that this revelation-through-mimicry is of course certainly not a stable phenomenon nor one that comes easily, as the participants need to reenact these motions again and again, incessantly repeating the bodily gestures, as this newfound awareness continually slips back into unawareness the moment it comes into fruition, caught in a dynamic and volatile exchange. What emerges here, then, is a form of knowledge characterized as much by consciousness as it is by unconsciousness, a phenomenon brought into fruition by the unhinged experience of this auditory body. For it is this very destabilization that makes one's relationship to the body all the more visceral, transferring a metaphysics of the body for a heightened corporeality, offering an instance of what Michael Taussig calls "the bodily unconscious," where "the self becomes part of that which is seen, not a sovereign transcendent . . . [and] thought [is] more like poetry."[59] Offering an instant of corporeal poetics, here is understood the unknowing of the body, a realm outside the confines of pure reason, as Azmayesh writes: "The most fundamental solution of the problem lies in the inner vibration of the music. The *Daf* is a bridge between hearts, outside of geography or history. The rhythm united the heartbeat of two or more people to become one rhythm with the hearts of thousands. We are invited to reason, but at a certain point the thinking stops."[60] In other words, the listener is mimicking not the music itself, but *that which is heard* through the body. As we have seen, however, this listening act is not a passive mode of reception, but a critical transmission of an encounter with the divine mystery. As such, the body is not mimicking any supreme being, but rather replicates the listening act itself. Here, then, what emerges is a phenomenon that one may call the auditory body: through the aesthetic encounter, the subjective body begins to converge with the listening act. Indeed, if we understand mimesis to be, as Taussig writes, "a stunning instance of imitation blending so intimately with contact that it becomes impossible to separate image from substance in the power of the final effect,"[61] then we see how this sensorial "contact" positions itself not simply as a mode of reception, but a vehicle for transformation. Indeed, as the listening subject begins to disappear into the listening act, the Foucauldian social body of the everyday may be transformed—if only fleetingly—into the auditory body.

Ultimately, however, the goal is to need no music at all, but to develop such sensitivity in one's listening ability that even listening to silence becomes revelatory and all forms of hearing are emblematic of *sama*. Turning again to Azmayesh: "If we put it differently, we can say that Sufism is based on silence and listening to the inner music. The goal of the seeker is to become one, to unite with this inner music."[62] For certain, it is for this reason that silence is given such importance within Sufi poetry and thought, so much so that Rumi alternatively signed his writings as "Silence" or "The Silent One" (*Khamushi*). In looking toward the relationship between listening, the body, and silence, the objective then is to be able to be aware of this body when there is no music present at all. As such, this goal is similarly investigated by American composer John Cage, as he offers a similar proposition regarding the inaudible sounds of the body in the following iconic statement:

> It was at Harvard not quite forty years ago that I went into an anechoic [totally silent] chamber not expecting in that silent room to hear two sounds: one high, my nervous system in operation, one low, my blood in circulation. The reason I did not expect to hear those two sounds was that they were set into vibration without any intention on my part. That experience gave my life direction, the exploration of non-intention. No one else was doing that. I would do it for us. I did not know immediately what I was doing, nor, after all these years, have I found out much. I compose music. Yes, but how? I gave up making choices. In their place I put the asking of questions.[63]

When faced with nothingness, as silence and sound collapse into one, another form of experiential knowledge emerges. At first glance at this passage, what results from the audition of silence, as with the audition of percussive music, is the hearing of the body, a revelation of one's own vital—breathing and circulating—consciousness. While this form of "non-intentional" listening might appear to be at first antithetical to the willful body movements activated by listening to music previously described, the goal is to re-create this experience where the two modes of listening overlap. In other words, what Cage is proposing here is the intentional generation of nonintention, described as the composition of "the asking of questions," with special focus given to the role of the body. In silence then, we are able to see the more idealized form of an unknowing of the body, wherein one is freed from the need for sensorial experience as impetus to experiential knowledge, and operates instead through what might alternately be called instinct, as Azmayesh explains: "During your journey in the darkness you are being guided by your heartbeat, your sixth sense."[64] Between the provinces of knowing and forgetting, between the material and the metaphysical, the body and the soul, the event of the instantiation of *fana* culminates as a new existential composition for the participant, interfacing silence and sound, ecstasy and exhaustion.

4 Unknowing of Memory

> When the disaster comes upon us, it does not come. The disaster
> is its imminence, but since the future, as we conceive of it in
> the order of lived time, belongs to the disaster, the disaster
> has always already withdrawn or dissuaded it; there is no
> future for the disaster, just as there is no time or space for its
> accomplishment.
>
> MAURICE BLANCHOT, *THE WRITING OF THE DISASTER* (1982)

> True *zekr* is that you forget your *zekr*.
>
> ABU NASR AL-SARRAJ, IN SHAH-KAZEMI, *JUSTICE AND*
> *REMEMBRANCE* (2006)

Meeting

On late Friday afternoons, the Sufis gather at their meeting place
(*hosseiniyeh* or *tekiyeh*)[1] on the eastern side of Takhteh-Foulad Cemetery as dusk falls.[2] The people file in slowly but steadily, the men
off in one section, the women heading into another, polite greetings
and chatter filling the old spaces. Now is not the time for deep conversation, however, as there is business at hand, the call to prayer
quickly approaching as the sky darkens. Shoes are slipped off at the
door, placed in plastic bags and quickly stashed on wooden shelves,
in handbags, or in other vessels. The people speak in hushed tones as
they pad into the rooms. Carpets, thin and dusty but still providing

a welcome cushion, line the floor as the faithful sit cross-legged on the ground, a few chairs in the back for the elderly and infirm.

They have come here for Friday prayers, and to pay respects to the great sheikh and poet Nasser Ali. He was unusual among the spiritual leaders (*qotbs*) of the order to be buried not at the pilgrimage site of Beydokht in Gonabad, in the northeast of the country, but in centrally located Isfahan, and so it is here that the members of the present order are lucky enough to meet in the presence of such a great spirit.

"It was wonderful," Simin would later recall. "I really felt like he was there with us, and he watched over us specifically since God had chosen for him to stay with us for eternity. We were so lucky to have him there."

The call to prayer from a nearby mosque sounds (the shrine is prohibited from broadcasting anything from a loudspeaker or anything louder than from a portable stereo, as per the municipal government's demands), and everyone rises to their feet. A sheikh begins the prayers, his voice clear though unamplified, his accented Arabic practiced and confident, and all followers pursue. Mouths take the shape of well-worn words, bodies fall into the familiar movements, patterns, and actions as practiced and polished as sea stone. Once the sunset prayers are complete, there may be some short remarks, or the reading of some classical poetry, but now is not the time for sermons.

As the faithful file out, the line moves slowly as people pause at the entrance to bend down to put on their shoes and then quickly shuffle out to make room for the others, mothers slipping sandals onto the feet of fidgeting children, others rustling through plastic bags and cubbyholes, where an occasional mismatched pair may emerge; the sky is still lit, though the light is fading fast. Another week's prayers done, the whole meeting has lasted about forty minutes. A holiday or special occasion notwithstanding, the building will stand empty until next week, when all will gather for Friday prayers again.

On late Friday afternoons, the Sufis gather on the eastern side of Takhteh-Foulad as dusk falls. Exchanging polite greetings, they have come for sundown prayers. They are all carrying the small carpets, the *jah namaz* used to provide a transportable prayer place, unfurling them onto the concrete as they take their spots on the empty lot. There is still rubble along the sides of the vacated lot, the high walls of another section of the cemetery complex coming to an abrupt end, having sustained some damage when the shrine was demolished. The grave, however, was left intact.

The Sufis had resisted the demolition of Takhteh-Foulad for nearly seven months before it was razed to the ground in the early morning hours of February 18, 2009.

In late autumn of 2008, a sign had been posted on the door by the municipal government (*shahrdari*) that the building was in disrepair and was to be destroyed as part of the city's beautification initiative. Several members went to *shahrdari* offices to inquire further on the matter, but the only information they were given was another printout of the sign on the door. The decision had already been made, they were informed, and it was final. When they asked to whom they might appeal, the city official told them simply: "Why should it matter who made the decision? It was already decided upon, wasn't it? Don't waste your time, and now you are wasting mine."

Distraught, the Sufis gathered to decide what should be done about the matter.

"Two hundred years, two hundred years this building has stood here in this very spot, and now it is to be destroyed!"

"Why would they do such a thing? We weren't even using loudspeakers!"

"This is truly a sin. Leave it to these fools, they are even destroying graves and disturbing the dead."

They decided upon the following tactic: they would appeal once more to the municipal government, promising to never use the shrine again if only it would be left alone. This was a risky move, as it was essentially calling out the city for what the Sufis suspected were the real motivations behind the demolition: the site was being used as a meeting place by a group that did not have official permission to do so.[3]

A letter was drafted and several senior men returned to the *shahrdari* to ask to whom they might submit the letter. The same low-level bureaucrat they had seen before took it from them, barely raising his gaze from the files he was going through.

After receiving no response to their letter, including several follow-up efforts to see if anyone had actually read their plea at all, their worst suspicions were confirmed. The city was still planning to go ahead with its plans. A new tactic would be necessary.

And so it was decided that they would resist the change with direct opposition, with their physical presence, their physical being. A sentry would be posted at all times at the shrine, day and night, and if there were any signs of construction vehicles or other vehicles of destruction, they would alert other members via mobile phone to gather immediately at the shrine and protest the demolition. Surely, they reasoned, if the building was full of people, they wouldn't dare raze the shrine? They will probably arrest us, some argued. Let them, at the very least it will slow down the demolition, and besides, is there anything else left we could do? Perhaps there will be too many of us and they will hesitate a bit before proceeding with their actions.

And so names and numbers were taken of volunteers, both men and women (women would stand guard during the daytime only), for guardians of the shrine. Day and night they stood sentry, mobile phones fully charged and at the ready, keeping an eye out for any construction vehicles or anyone who carried himself with an official air (that unsettling and unpleasant attitude of supreme confidence and detachment—it is easy to carry yourself so when you feel there is no consequence to your actions; such is the danger of the bureaucrat). But for months, there was nothing. People began to wonder if the municipal government's warning was just that, an empty warning, an empty threat, although such decrees usually had some sort of substance to them. It was more a matter of when rather than if. In Iran things take so long to get done, they joked, we even have to wait for unwanted actions (the politics of dread). And so they waited.

They waited until winter's turn, when a person could no longer stand the cold during the darkest hours, when the old stone building stood empty from ten in the evening until sunrise prayers. Still, the Sufis stood guard during the day, they stood the best they could. Until someone who had a relative in the city government heard a rumor that the building was to be destroyed that very night. That night, a group of about fifteen Sufis arrived and vowed to stay until morning, wrapped under layers of clothing and clutching thermoses of hot tea. A tense evening came and passed, and some of the members went home as the clock inched passed midnight. Surely, the danger had passed for this night. Still, a group of five remained.

Not long after the others had gone, however, the remaining *darvish*, sitting on the ground, huddled under blankets, dozing in and out of consciousness, heard someone shouting orders. The whirring, beeping noise of construction vehicles arose. Before they knew what was happening, several members of the security forces entered the *hosseiniyeh* and the men were pulled to their feet: "You are illegally occupying this building and are hereby under arrest." Before they even arrested them, however, the first thing they did, the Sufis would say, was force them to give up their cell phones. They were taken to the police station and kept overnight in a "detention room" but then were released in the morning.

As the five sentries were being taken away by the authorities, in the early morning hours of February 18, 2009, a city-commissioned bulldozer came into Takhteh-Foulad and razed the building to the ground. The vehicle was accompanied by a large group, somewhere between one hundred and two hundred individuals, police officers, security personnel, and plainclothes agents, most likely members of the paramilitary group the Basij, who had joined in the event of a fight breaking out. But there was no one there. Only some two-hundred-year-old bricks, dusty lights, and an old grave. The neighboring library was also destroyed, the yellowing volumes of poetry and exegesis torn to pieces in the rubble. When it was gone, perhaps they were surprised by the large field of rubble left in its wake: things always take up more space when they are in pieces.

And yet something stopped the authorities from destroying the grave itself. Perhaps they felt it unnecessary, since they were already removing the meeting place, leaving the Sufis with no place to gather, and that had always been the real objective. Or perhaps something felt wrong, perhaps something stirred in them, that to destroy the final resting place of the dead would reap consequences beyond this life. Perhaps it was never part of their orders at all; but whatever the reason, though the building was gone . . . the grave remained.

And that was all that was needed.

The Steel Throne

Takhteh-Foulad, or Steel Throne, is a series of large, interconnected open-air cemeteries within the city of Isfahan. It is divided into different spaces by gates and walls that bifurcate it into distinct segments, with each section having its own name: the Mausoleum of Baba Rokn-Al Din, the Garden of the Martyrs (Golestan-e Shohada), the Mausoleum of Mir Fendereski. By all accounts it is the second largest Shi'ite cemetery in the world, following only that in Najaf, Iraq, home to the resting place of Imam Ali and hence among the holiest sites in Shi'ite Islam. The city describes it as a "complex" or "necropolis" in English. Some of the cemeteries are surrounded by high walls and others have fences. If you were to enter from one of its many entry points, you would most likely encounter rows of beige tombstones laid flat, as is the custom, Persian and Arabic calligraphy etched in the stone, facing skyward, with large, gazebo-like tombs and towers distributed throughout the graves for especially important figures. Small

FIGURE 4.1 Takhteh-Foulad Cemetery, Seyed al-Araghaen *tekiyeh*, where the author's grand-father is buried.

FIGURE 4.2 Takhteh-Foulad Cemetery, Seyed al-Araghaen *tekiyeh*.

buildings and towers line the perimeters, most containing more graves, some with framed black and white photos of the deceased hanging on the wall. There are also some larger mausoleums that contain paintings of scenes from Islamic and Shi'ite history: the battle of Karbala, the Prophet's night journey to heaven. A number of small museums are also scattered throughout Takhteh-Foulad, including the Museum of Stone, a small museum that commemorates the Iran-Iraq War, and a Journalism Museum that is largely a collection of early and mid-twentieth-century newspapers.

With some of the oldest buildings dating back some eight hundred years, it continued to be the primary burial ground in Isfahan, alongside such cemeteries as the Abbakhshan and Sonbolan, for hundreds of years until the Bagh-e Rezvan Cemetery was established after the Islamic Revolution. Throughout this time, most scholars, artists, spiritual leaders, and other local dignitaries were buried in Takhteh-Foulad. According to the Takhteh-Foulad Cultural, Historic and Religious Organization, there are 2,400 such "luminaries" contained within, as well as fifty-eight tombs. From about roughly 1981, however, the cemetery was closed to all other new burials until a new graveyard, the Golestan-e Shohada, or Garden of the Martyrs, was created to bury the soldiers who died in the war. Today the war martyrs' cemetery also is home to a handful of Iranian soldiers who died fighting ISIS in Syria. With the exception of these more recent burials, there were few buried in Takhteh-Foulad after the martyr-soldiers of the 1980s.

Despite the general moratorium on burials, Takhteh-Foulad remains an active site, with certain sections seeing far more activity than others. The Garden of the Martyrs is the most active, receiving school groups on class trips and holding tours, and of course many parents and family members come to pay respects to the martyrs of the war. Art history students visit the rich frescoes at every mausoleum. And even among the sleepier *teki-yehs* there are visitors. In some sites, people will visit the graves of local saint figures, with requests for suitable marriage prospects for their sons and daughters being a common ask, or simply to visit more distantly passed relatives. My own maternal grandfather was among the last of the nonmartyr burials, having passed away in 1981, and so my family and I have consistently visited the *tekiyeh* of Seyed al-Araghaen since then, bringing with us large plastic bottles we have filled with water to wash the dusty grave as is the common practice. Unlike the busy Garden of the Martyrs *te-kiyeh*, we were often the only people there save for the occasional presence of a kindly groundskeeper, with most of grandfather's "neighbors" having been interred much earlier. And of course there were the Sufi visitors. The tomb of Nasser Ali was unsurprisingly busiest on Thursday evenings and on Fridays, when people would gather together, but individuals might stop by on their own during the week as schedules allowed and the spirit moved them. It was a pillar of the community, a corner of the sprawling necropolis that is Takhteh-Foulad that was theirs alone.

Amnesia and Active Forgetting

Given the importance of the tomb of Nasser Ali, one would expect the mystics to commemorate the site, and I think it is fair to say they did but, in doing so, they adopted not only a unique method of commemoration but a different understanding of the site itself. Indeed, rather than mourn the destruction of their meeting place outright, when questioned about the incident, the members assumed a rather curious position. Namely, the denial that this meeting place ever existed, that this destruction had in fact not taken place, and that any and all memories of the old building must be dismissed. There was only the grave and that was all that was needed. In other words, in their desire to not place too much importance on the physical space itself, the practitioners distanced themselves from even this forced removal of the space. So resolved were they in their desire to dispute the memory of this building, in fact, that several of them essentially refused to speak plainly regarding the matter. Ultimately, what is being embraced here is an instance of a decisive refutation of memory, a forgetting so purposeful that the material may be rendered immaterial.

What has willed this vanishing act, however, cannot be called simply an instance of forgetting. There are too many streaks of passivity that run throughout pure forgetting, too much of an offhanded carelessness that characterizes its treatment of the past. To forget something, even if it is forever caught up in the unconscious dialectics of memory, is to disregard it, to devalue it.

And herein lies the contradiction within the project of a desire to forget, of a need to forget, or what might be called a mode of active forgetting. If forgetting implies a passive dismissal, how might such an occurrence be transformed when something is forgotten precisely because it is valued? And, because it is valued, must therefore be consciously, willfully forgotten? Or, to put it another way, how does one remember to forget, to unknow a memory?

To answer this question I would posit that perhaps forgetting is the wrong phenomenon of remembrance altogether here. Perhaps the objective here is not one of forgetting, but more an instance of amnesia. For when we consider amnesia, we consider a phenomenon that is characterized by awareness; the amnesiac is aware that they remember nothing. Amnesia is characterized by the realization of an absence, it is the emergence of a now dispossessed memory of an absent time and place. Thus, not dissimilar to the ideas of Nietzsche and Benjamin,[4] just as we see memory emerging as a device against history as an objective and legitimate totality, here we see the disappearance of memory possessing similarly reconstructive capabilities. And so the order strives not simply to forget, but to induce an amnesiac state.

As a consequence, it is in this way that the subject's role within the construction, or in this case, negation of the past, is given the utmost importance. The individual act of remembrance is afforded the capacity to subvert any claims of "historical reality." Similarly, given the subject's conscious and active desire to undermine the past as a totality, it is in this way that the amnesia would distance itself from the phenomenon of repression, even considering this particular instance of a site of trauma. Repression involves the unconscious aftermath of trauma, imposed upon the subject by the source of disturbance. This self-induced amnesia is a conscious activity, whereupon the subject imposes upon the ontology of the original trauma. Hence, just to clarify once again, the ultimate objective of a willful amnesia is an awareness of a forgotten past, an awareness that implicates itself just as heavily.

The amnesiac encounter would imply a hyperconsciousness or a hypersensitivity to the gap in memory, to the evacuated space where a memory should exist. One realizes that there exists a gap in their memory. Now I would note that whether this goal, this mental state, is ever achieved is a question of an entirely different sort, but at the very least, there is a willingness here to invoke an instance of willful amnesia, even if it ultimately proves an impossible task. On the other hand, it is to this very impossibility that we may return . . . unknowingly.

In this chapter, I investigate the Sufis' reaction to the destruction and the decision to "remember to forget" the site. In particular, I argue how this contestation of memory is tied to broader mystical theories of remembrance/forgetting, some of which lie in theoretical underpinnings of the *zekr* ritual, and the consequences that such a refutation holds for understandings of the Real and the Unreal. From here, I explore the ways in which this technique of commemoration exhibits both similarities and differences to the Islamic Republic's own exercises in the construction of public memory, especially as it relates to their investment in legacies of the Iran-Iraq War. In doing so, I will touch upon the convergences and divergences between Nimatullahi Sufi theories of remembrance and those of Ja'fari (Twelver) Shi'ism, the official form of Shi'ism of the Islamic Republic. I conclude the chapter by reflecting upon what it means to demand such malleability from the Unreal—our profane world—through this dismantling of a memory, where a community may undermine the ontological status of an object, and one that has been targeted by hostile forces. In doing so, we might better understand the epistemologies involved in such an endeavor, where the application of unknowing (*ma'rifat*) has allowed for no less than the questioning of what is real and what is not.

Sanitized Shrines

Before discussing the impetus to "remember to forget" in more detail, I would first take a moment to consider the actions of the city authority (*shahrdari*). My evidence here is scarcer than I would like it to be, as the typical avenues of investigation were unavailable to me. Still, I will offer the information I was able to gather, especially that which pertains to broader developments happening at Takhteh-Foulad at the time. And developments were happening to be sure.

In 2006, the Organization of Islamic Countries selected Isfahan as the cultural capital of the Islamic world. In light of this development, the Takhteh-Foulad Cultural Organization was formed in affiliation with the Isfahan Municipal government (*shahrdari*), with Hossein Hamidi-Esfahani as the manager (as well as donor), the vocal support of Dr. Saghaian Nezhad, the mayor of Isfahan, and with an office space on Chahar Bagh-e Bala in the south near Darvaze Shiraz, essentially a prime piece of real estate in the heart of the commercial district. And the cemetery was first given the official title "Majmooye Tarikhi, Farhangi, va Mazhabi-e Takhteh-Foulad," or "The Historic, Cultural, and Religious Center of Takhteh-Foulad."[5] The purpose of this organization was noted as the following: "carrying out extensive projects-works at maintenance and renovation as well as cultural, research, and educational levels. These include publishing books, leaflets, and brochures; holding conferences and education workshops; organizing galleries and exhibitions on photos, stone artifacts, and journals; guiding tourists; and making films about the lives of the departed dignitaries."[6] In addition, in March 2009, the center published a book that had been commissioned in English, describing the lives of many of the dignitaries contained within Takhteh-Foulad, and their very extensive website notes that more than 150 foreign dignitaries have visited the site.

Given the sudden influx of preservation projects and promotional efforts, it might then seem strange that, in February 2009, one month prior to the publication of this English-language text, the *hosseiniyeh* was destroyed in the early morning hours. What might have prompted such a drastic and irreversible act of demolition right when the municipal government was beginning to bring attention to the cemetery for the first time in decades? Rather than proving a contradictory act, such "alterations" were exactly in line with the construction of the new image and reality that the authorities wished Takhteh-Foulad to assume. In other words, by razing to the ground a shrine that was still being actively worshipped—meaning attracting a sizeable group of visitors on a regular basis—the municipal government made the decision to halt such visitations as resolutely as possible.[7] The existence of the mystics' gathering spot and the attention it received from the *darvish* each week was not in line with the image of Takhteh-Foulad that the municipal government wanted to project: that of a dormant and long-abandoned site, of use only for scholars and tourists, "historical" in the sense of inactivity. And certainly not a location where a religious group—one, though Shi'i, was certainly distinct from the religion of the state—came to gather at a shrine, to reaffirm their community and make use of public space. Remember the official reason given was that of "beautification of the neighborhood" (*zibayi-ye mahal*), or some mode of alteration to render an entity aesthetically pleasing to a particular set of standards. Here, these standards demanded the eviction of a Sufi order whose regular visits and presence inserted them into the landscape of Takhteh-Foulad, a presence deemed unacceptable.

Indeed, the restriction of the Sufis' activities and the desire to hide them from public view is emblematic of a larger effort by the Iranian government, particularly the national government, to homogenize and sanitize Shi'i practice. For despite the claims of autonomy from outside influence of the Islamic Republic, the government assumes great care in the image that it presents to the world, taking pains to set forth not only a cohesive image, but one that remains dignified and measured; a Protestant Shi'ism, if you will. More specifically, this entails the banning of "folk" practices such as exorcism and trance, and the "discouragement" of fortune-telling.[8] Perhaps most tellingly, Ayatollah Khamenei, the supreme leader, issued a decree (*fatwa*) banning the ceremonial mourning practice known as *zanjeer-zani*, a ritual where practitioners self-flagellate with blades and other weaponry, practiced during the Ashura holiday, a day commemorating the martyrdom of Imam Hossein. Ayatollah Khamenei banned the practice, a violent and often shocking spectacle where blood covers the streets almost as much as it does the bodies of the faithful, with the declaration that: "The eyes of the world are sewn upon us" (*chesm-e donya ru mah dookhteh ast*), an ominous warning to remain cognizant of Iran's role as an exceptional state in the world, one constantly under the threat of invasion and attack. Thus, by discouraging such "folkloric" activities, deemed too extreme or too unguided by proper authorities, the Islamic Republic attempts not only to maintain its grasp over all "spiritual activities," but to present a unified and sober image to the larger world, thereby acknowledging and reaffirming the "eye" or the gaze of the world, and most notably the imperial powers, of which it has long claimed to be free.

Disparate Recollections

Given the actions of the authorities to sanitize the "wrong" forms of worship at Takhteh-Foulad, it is perhaps all the more striking that the Sufis decided to "remember to forget" as they did, to refute the finality of the memory of the tomb of Nasser Ali. At this point, I would like to consider this decision more closely, and particularly how they articulated their responses to me when questioned about the incident. First and foremost, I would emphasize the deeply complex nature of their response, as it is imperative to note that the individual accounts of the memories of the *tekiyeh* at Takhteh-Foulad and the destruction that transpired there vary greatly. For despite the order's seemingly "official stance" on the matter, the diversity of responses I received reflects not only the difficulty in predicting individual reactions, but the tenuous foundation on which the constructions of this willed amnesia is based. Indeed, such a tenuous foundation suggests the need for constant maintenance of such a stance, and the ways in which retaining this position remains an active process.

It must also be made clear that in many instances the amount of information made available to me was directly related to the nature of my personal relationship with the interlocutor. In other words, I noted a correlation—

to use a word favored by social scientists—between how close I was to my interviewee personally, our level of intimacy and the extent of our friendship, and the ways in which they discussed the tomb of Nasser Ali.

There were those who not only gave straightforward accounts of what transpired but interspersed their narratives with personal memories as well. To all my interlocutors I posed a simple query: "What happened at Takhteh-Foulad?" These interviews took place in autumn of 2010.

Sepideh was one of the first people I spoke to and she recounted the tale in intimate fashion: "Oh, it was terrible. We used to always meet in Takhteh-Foulad, for prayers and sermons. On holidays we would have our silent *zekr* there. Now it's no longer there. I was so upset when it happened."

Fati, an older and very devout woman who passed along any gift you gave her to those she deemed less fortunate, and another Sufi whom I knew well, expressed anger in contrast to Sepideh's despair: "What happened? They won't let us live in peace. If it is not their *masjid* it is no one's. We weren't bothering anyone, and they still wouldn't leave us alone."

Amir Hussain assumed yet another affective stance when discussing the destruction, one of heavy resignation: "You know, it was only good that you weren't there. It was too sad. They tried so hard to stop it, and still they destroyed it." His double use of "they"—expressed in the Persian not as a pronoun itself but as the suffix of the verb—implicates both Sufis and the authorities in the events that transpired at the tomb of Nasser Ali, a naming without naming.

In these statements we see acknowledgments made, and accusations. There are clear actors and agents, a before and after, an "us" and a "them." Shame was ascribed onto the authorities for their actions, a direct imposition of the local government onto the Sufis' practice. Remorse and a sense of loss are expressed at the destruction of the meeting place, a linear and tragically clichéd narrative of the political powers that be limiting the practices of a local community.

These same interlocutors also described the actions that were taken after the destruction. Again, I turned to Sepideh: "We had a session. Several of the sheikhs came and spoke to us, that we shouldn't be upset, that we didn't need it [the building]. We tried but now must remember *tawhid* [union with the divine] instead. They told us we should remember to forget." Here we see the important injunction relayed by the sheikh: "remember to forget." Hajji Mahmoud, an older fellow who had been visiting

Takhteh-Foulad his entire life, and continues to visit other shrines in the complex, relayed a similar sentiment: "Hazrat Agha (a sheikh) told us to forget the building, the grave was still there, to remember God in all places, to look for him everywhere. . . . Forget the building had even been there." Finally, Fati provided a bit more information on the sheikhs' theological reasoning behind their decisions, or at least what was conveyed to their followers: "They spoke of the invisible and the unseen. The grave remained, and we might pray everywhere. Try and forget the building. . . . They are very wise, and so I have." There is a fascinating juxtaposition here, a privileging of both the material (the grave) and the immaterial (the unseen, the invisible, forget the building). This speaks to broader Sufi theories of materiality, particularly those who espouse the idea that not all materiality is created equal, where some forms can be seen as distractions from the "Real" and other forms—particularly auditory forms, as we have seen— are considered as conduits to closeness with God (*tawhid*).

More broadly, from these anecdotes it is clear that a strategy had been adopted by the spiritual authorities, one that was hence adopted by their practitioners. It was a position based not on commemoration but on forgetting, a remembrance to forget, to "try and forget." Throughout my discussion with this group, the meeting following the incident was clearly recognized.

Glaringly absent here, however, are discussions with the sheikhs themselves. They did not wish to discuss the incident at Takhteh-Foulad, but said it was fine for me to write about it in light of their followers' statements. Given the sensitive nature of what transpired, this is all I will say on the matter in regards to the sheikhs.

Evasion and Forgetting

Let us return to my conversations with the lay *darvishes*. In contrast to the discussions with interlocutors with whom I shared a certain intimacy and friendship, others were much more evasive in their responses to queries about Takhteh-Foulad. Here, my ethnography relies just as strongly on silences, ellipses, and meaningful glances as on verbal articulation. There were those who acknowledged the destruction but clearly did not wish to discuss it, dismissing my questions with a wave of the hand and, in one or two cases, with raised eyebrows and a knowing look. "Don't worry about what happened there," I was told. In response to my query, "What happened at Takhteh-Foulad?" (*"Chi pish amad dar Takhteh-Foulad?"*), I received the following answers:

> "In Takhteh-Foulad? We had some problems there, but it wasn't important."

> "We used to meet there, but not anymore."

> "Yes, we used to go there but it's not important to go there anymore."

Here, there is either a recognition that some misfortune occurred or at the very least an acknowledgment that Takhteh-Foulad once acted as a meeting place. Still, the answers were vague and brief, with a tone that could convey a dismissiveness, a reassuring air ("don't worry about it"), or slight irritation ("it's not important"). There was the feeling that much was being left unsaid, the feeling that there was an imperative to forget.

And still there were yet more responses, from interlocutors to whom I was not personally close but who were not evasive at all but in fact quite direct—direct in that they stated they had no knowledge of that which I was speaking of at all. There was no knowing glance with this latter group, not even an exasperated wave of the hand. Instead there was a quiet confidence in their response, which was sometimes paired with an air of confusion since what I spoke of did not seem to register with them. The responses were typically short and always direct, as demonstrated by the following statements from four individuals:

> "No, you must be mistaken. There was no tomb there."

> "We have many places to meet."

> "There was never any building in Takhteh-Foulad."

> "I'm sorry, I don't know of what you speak."

I must admit these were among the strangest and most uncomfortable moments of fieldwork I encountered, these polite responses that initially left me quite perplexed, sometimes causing an abrupt stop in the conversation. The first of these direct refutations I encountered was particularly confusing, and made me question my own understanding of the event. Was I mistaken? Was there another name used for the site of which I was unaware? Was I referring to the wrong *tekiyeh*? They had transformed the memory of the event for themselves with such conviction (or at least it was conveyed to me in such a way) that my own understanding of the event began to falter, began to become unknown.

Ultimately what we are witnessing here is a direct refutation that anything transpired, an unwillingness to note the building ever existed at all, and/or the questioning of the validity of my inquiry. For this group of individuals, their responses reflected the highest form of willful amnesia, the active and conscious erasure of the memory at hand.

Willed Amnesia and Material Form

With the differences between my interlocutors' recounts of the event established, let us turn our attention now to the physical, material space at hand (at least before it was negated). To reiterate the order's stance, it was asserted that this building should be "forgotten" (*bayad faramushesh bokonim*), or rather that they "should forget it." The building thus was deemed irrelevant for its larger purposes, easily replaced and therefore easily forgotten. At the same time, however, if it was regarded as "just a building" why then was such an effort taken in order to disremember this structure?

The Sufis' ability to undermine and negate the "sacredness" of this house, to deny its past as a site of *zekr* ritual, exposes the fact that the material building can be transformed, or at the very least the memory of this material space might be altered. Through this negation, the very ontology of the building is transfigured; first, into an immaterial memory, whereupon the significance of its prior use value is subverted in favor of remembering it as "just a building," just a physical space, if admitting its previous existence at all. We might remember here too that unknowing is always a generative event. Concluding this act of transformation/denial of space through memory, however, is the denial of the memory itself. Here, then, physical space is rendered meaningless, insignificant to the point that even its memory is denied. In other words, through this act of willful amnesia, through the negation of a sacred space, the ontological status of the building has been transformed from a metaphysical presence into a material absence. This is a material absence rather than simply a metaphysical one, in that it is the subject who has instigated this transformation, it is the subject and not the divine who has challenged the existence of this space.

And so, having discussed this willful forgetting and the transformative capabilities it entails, let us broaden the argument a bit further. More specifically, I am wondering here how this temporal phenomenon might extend itself into a broader epistemological question. In other words, is there room for knowledge within this amnesia, and if so what kind? For when you have such a purposeful refutation of the memory of this *tekiyeh*, it would be assumed that by refusing memory, you are subsequently refusing knowledge. Nevertheless, having established this disappearance of the Sufi *tekiyeh* as not simply a passive forgetting or a repression in response to trauma, but as a complex form of willful amnesia, so too might we suggest that the knowledge of such an event is similarly complicated. Certainly, it would be too simple to say that they merely do not possess any memory of the building or any knowledge of the building, but rather that they know *what happened*, they possess a knowledge of what Maurice Blanchot would call the disaster. Thus, through this amnesia, the Sufis are formulating a mode of non-knowledge, of unknowing, an awareness through the unaware. And so, in the end, a question emerges out of this disappeared space: What are the epistemological implications of this willful amnesia? And how might they be tied to the unknowability of the divine?

First, we may consider amnesia to be characterized not simply as the loss of memory, but as that moment of realization that there has been a loss. In other words, amnesia comes into being the moment where one becomes cognizant that there is a gap in memory, as opposed to the moment of vanishing itself. Hence, I would suggest that amnesia as we are dealing with it here is defined as an epistemological phenomenon first, one determined by, as we have seen, cognizance, realization, a conscious awareness, and so on, and a historical phenomenon second. As such, if amnesia is the absence of memory made present, a willful amnesia is the awareness of the absence of memory made present.

Having considered this, let us look a bit more closely at this awareness of absence, and how awareness may distinguish itself from and simultaneously align itself with remembrance. Indeed, complicating this problem of the amnesiac's knowledge of the absence from the outset is the fact that this absence is not a pure absence, it is not simply a void. To better understand this, let us return to the Sufi context, in this case how the *zekr* ritual might help us in better analyzing the question of the void.

Shi'i Strategies of Remembrance

If we pan the camera further back, extending beyond the self-enclosed community of the Sufis and their immediate practice, the larger milieu of contemporary Iran comes into view, and the question then immediately arises: How are we to understand these practices of active forgetting, of willful amnesia, in such a setting as the Islamic Republic, a system of government whose founding/establishment, concretization, and continued existence is so intimately tied to ideas of remembrance? Where, from its earliest assumptions of power, the ominous command to "remember," ostensibly to remain ever mindful of the constant threat by both the imperial powers and the Sunni-secular army of Saddam Hussein, was synonymous with a declaration of allegiance to the state, a rallying cry to both the theological (here, Shi'i) and postcolonial foundations on which this new nation was based. And the memories invoked by the state were of a very specific nature: the remembrance of the Iran-Iraq War, and all those who perished, the reasons behind their sacrifice, and the way that these memories must remain active in the realm of the present. Thus, when the state commands its citizens to remember, it often speaks to a very specific incident: the Iran-Iraq War, or as it is known in Iran, the war of "the Holy Defense."

Beginning in September 1980 with the surprise air attack of Saddam's forces and ending in a UN-brokered ceasefire in August 1988, the war's casualties have been estimated at half a million soldiers and civilians, with the oil-rich region of Khuzestan in the southwest being particularly devastated. And while nearly thirty-four years have passed since the ceasefire, the material and semantic presence of the war within Iran, through memorialization practices alone, remains undeniable. Much has been written of the various manifestations of commemoration in Iran, especially in visual cultural studies, including works by Pamela Karimi on the legacy of Iran's famous war murals, Pedram Partovi and Roxanne Varzi on the impact of the cinema of the "sacred defense," Pedram Khosronejad on the proliferation of war museums and other forms of visual culture, and Amir Moosavi on the theorizations and maintenance of martyrdom within Iranian literature, to name but a few, and it is this scholarship upon which I am relying here.[9] To name but a few instantiations of remembrance of the Iran-Iraq War and its martyrs: In every city, street names and major thoroughfares invoke the names of the martyred dead; various national holidays celebrate and commemorate the beginning, end, and particular moments of the war; banners, each adorned with the solemn visage of a different uniformed young man, are hung on street lamps; vast billboards and murals painted on the sides of buildings depict scenes of soldiers in the foreground, a benevolent-looking Ayatollah appearing in the background; war museums and statues are found in a diverse array of cities, large and small, throughout Iran, the largest and most extensive in Tehran; and there exists an entire industry and subgenre of "war films," complete with state-sponsored conferences and film festivals. Furthermore, the powerful government agency and lobby group of the Martyr's Co-operation continues to provide tax breaks, college scholarships, and other financial and governmental support for the widows and families of war martyrs, reaffirming the state's continued recognition of the families' sacrifices. The murals of young men in uniform exemplify the dangerous binary of the state's specific form of commemorative propaganda: epic and authoritative in size and scope, but banal in their permanent position in the cityscape, scarcely noticed by local passersby. The prosaic nature of the monuments and their integration into the Iranian landscape signals the deep inscription of the Iran-Iraq War into the public realm, a visual arena where the billboards dotting the many urban highways alternate between images of shampoo bottles and television sets and sweeping panoramas of soldiers walking off into the sunset, bright, painterly colors used in a strange juxtaposition with the mournful imagery depicted. It is through such a positioning in the public spaces that the ubiquity and permanence of these images has rendered them no longer shocking, but banal, their potency and efficacy arising not from their ability to be noticed and effective but from their infiltration of the everyday: their "everydayness" rendering them a part of national consciousness.

Ultimately, by reinscribing the narrative of the "Holy Defense" into the still-unfolding narrative of postrevolutionary Iran—rendering visible the memories of the absent young men (they have not died, they have been turned into image, the body robbed of the opportunity to be corpse but only spirit, transformed into paint and color), names of otherwise innocuous streets and public squares are turned into signifiers of war, such that utterances of war-related phenomena infiltrate everyday conversation (Where is the drug store? Behind the Garden of the Martyrs)—the state may continue to operate under the logic of war or, more specifically, under the logic of threat. Indeed, by continually reinserting the visual and linguistic presence of the Iran-Iraq War into the present day, not only is the state formulating an origin story for the Islamic Republic, a nation forged in defiance of both the imperial powers and Saddam's Sunni-secular army, it also proposes the idea that the continued existence of the nation rests upon the ability to keep these forces at bay. To remain ever vigilant: such is both the promise and the command of the authority figures, and it is this reason that demands the nation operate through a logic of threat.[10]

To begin, a logic of threat implies a logic tied to a specific temporal matrix, for the notion of an imminent threat undeniably implies that the future is at risk, the possibility that the state of things may cease to exist in their current manifestation. Thus, a logic of threat implies both the promise of a possibility of a future as well as the possibility of its destruction, the present constructed in order to preserve its past. By operating under the assumption of an ever-present threat, then, these commemorative tactics of the state speak less to the present than to the future; in other words, these summonings—visual and rhetorical—of past trauma are engaged most directly not with the present, but with the future: the contemporary realm subsumed under the weight of both the past and the future, serving only as placeholder. On the one hand, the past is felt so acutely in the everyday that the present is only able to situate itself as a sort of remainder, that which exists as aftermath, as if perpetually caught within the immediate moment after the catastrophe. Furthermore, as result of this, the enemy and cause of injury that existed in the past remains ever near: hence the immanence and imminence of threat, until the primary goal of the vulnerable present is to position itself in such a way as to preserve the possibility of a future. Thus, remembrance within Iran emerges as a way to subsume the present under both the future and the past.

As has been extensively written about, there are many other forms of memorialization offering opportunities for the inscription of the past into the present within postrevolutionary Iran, most notably the commemoration of the Karbala narrative, a story of sacrifice and martyrdom that lays some of the conceptual and spiritual cornerstones of Shi'ism. I focus here, however briefly, on the commemoration of the Iran-Iraq War due to (1) its occurrence in the immediate past, such that individual memories persist in a substantial portion of the population, although there is a generational shift occurring;[11] and (2) its ability to operate on both the personal and national registers, an event that impacted the vast majority of those living within Iranian borders on an intimate level, providing a personal experience by which to judge/measure that the national narrative presented.

Considering the importance of commemoration within the construction and preservation of the national narrative of postrevolutionary Iran, it would appear that the Sufis' reaction to the destruction of the meeting place at Takhteh-Foulad would exist in direct opposition to such an emphasis on preservation and insertion of past traumatic events into the contemporary realm. Indeed, a cursory glance would seem to display a series of neat binaries: an active forgetting versus an active remembrance, a willful amnesia over willful remembrance, rejection over affirmation. Where the clerical establishment has chosen the path of memorialization, reconstructing visuals to render the absent present, the Sufis have embarked upon an arguably more challenging arc to render the present absent, most notably when the physical ruins remained around them. And while it is certainly undeniable that the choices and actions of these two groups contain deep intellectual differences, upon closer examination, it may be argued that the positions of both contain certain theological resonances. Contrary to the binaries presented, it may be argued that there exists a certain Shi'i mode of thinking, which I hope to address here.

Ja'fari versus Nimatullahi Understanding of Shi'i Remembrance

> *Zekr* is the heart of Shi'ism, and Sufism is the heart of Shi'ism.
>
> SEYED MUSTAFA AZMAYESH, *MORVARID-E SUFI-GARI* (2008)

There is remembrance, and there is *zekr*. And, as the above quotes articulate, the two are not the same.

Up until this point, I have been translating "*zekr*" as "remembrance" or "mindfulness"; here, however, it is clear that to consider *zekr* as a form of remembrance or memory proves a poor understanding: it is rather something only "akin to memory." If we understand memory as an act of preservation, a process by which to crystallize and store that which has come to pass, then *zekr* instead proves a phenomenon that not only maintains knowledge but "*renders it present*." *Zekr* appears as an intellectual exercise whereby a specific instance of stored knowledge is brought forward, a summoning to both reaffirm and reenter into the present that has been kept. Following this, as al-Isfahani explains, there exist two types of *zekr*, one that "follows forgetfulness" and another that does not involve forgetting at all, but instead "expresses a continuous remembering." Thus, to rearticulate, we see not only distinctions between *zekr* and memory, but within *zekr* itself, a distinction that may be all the more transparent when we consider the ways in which these two interpretations are adopted by the government of the Islamic Republic and the Sufis respectively. And while the importance of *zekr* within Sufi practice has been demonstrated thus far, before examining these divisions more closely it is worthwhile to understand the "rendering present" of *zekr* that is evident within more "orthodox" forms of Shi'i jurisprudence.

To begin more generally, within the Qur'an *zekr* is often translated as an "invocation,"[12] as seen in the following passages:

> And invoke the Name of thy Lord morning and evening. (76:25)
> And invoke the Name of thy Lord, devoting thyself to Him with utter devotion. (73:8)
> O ye who believe! Invoke God with much invocation. (33:41)
> Call upon thy Lord in humility and in secret. (7:55)
> And invoke thy Lord within thyself, in humility and awe, and beneath thy breath, in the morning and in the night. (7:205)

Zekr as invocation emerges hence as a method to achieve a ceaseless form of devotion, a practice to be done "morning and evening," in order to reaffirm the place of the divine throughout the day. The interior, possibly silent or inaudible, form of invocation is also emphasized, where the calling upon is conducted "in humility and in secret," and "beneath thy breath," an intimate form of summoning that possesses a physical as well as spiritual proximity to the faithful, sounds barely escaping beyond the mouth, the words as fragile as a memory. Perhaps all acts of remembrance contain an element of invocation, where that which was once known is again beckoned forward, but it might be argued that the intentionality behind this kind of willful calling forward would set it apart from other forms of remembrance, even if there are certain resonances within both.

Within the text of *Nahj Al Balaghe*,[13] the collection of letters, sermons, and sayings attributed to Imam Ali and the second holiest text within Ja'fari Shi'ism, the importance of a "continuous remembering" is also seen:

> And establish the prayers for the sake of My remembrance. (20:14)
> Remember God with much remembrance. (33:41)
> Prayer keepeth one from indecency and evil, while the remembrance of God is greater. (29:45).
> And remember the name of his Lord, so prayeth. (87:15)

Then He gave him heart with memory, tongue to talk and eye to see with, in order that he may take lesson (from whatever is around him) and understand it and follow the admonition and abstain from evil. (Sermon 82)

Although this is only a small selection of passages that refer to remembrance, Imam Ali frequently discusses the theme throughout the text, especially in relation to prayer, in several instances placing hierarchizing memory over prayer. In particular, "remember God with much remembrance" is similar to the translation of the *aya* in the Qur'an to "invoke God with much invocation," such that the verb and the noun are one and the same, suggesting that the act is a means unto itself. Perhaps most revealing of memory as rendering present is the idea of "heart with memory" in the passage from Sermon 82,[14] indicating that an act of recollection draws from an a priori source, that the heart, center of emotion, spirituality, and, often, instinct, would be able to bring forth the name and presence of the divine, rather than the mind.

With these too few examples of the role of remembrance within the spiritual texts of Ja'fari Shi'ism, what I have hoped to demonstrate here is that *zekr* indicates not only the act of remembrance but a remembrance intentionally summoned forward, a mindfulness as integrally tied to the creation of knowledge as it is to the preservation of knowledge. Furthermore, as previously discussed, it has been the objective of the Iranian government to continually reinsert the episodes of the past into the present, the images and memories reinserted into the consciousness of Iranians for as long as deemed productive. In both cases too, both forms of invocation are dependent upon a "*zekr* of the tongue," one that implies a memory reimagined in such a way that it is made and/or exists external to oneself, through either a whispered utterance, a spiritual belief/thought made tangible, or an elaborate visual depiction rendered large onto the side of a building, grabbing the attention of otherwise distracted passersby. Ultimately, it is clear to see the parallels between the political tactics of the current regime and the spiritual directives of the texts that guide them, such that Shi'i remembrance remains as involved with the present and future as with the past.

Returning to the al-Isfahani quote, let us now turn to the second form of *zekr* mentioned, the *zekr* of the heart, that which "follows forgetfulness." Notice too, that this form of *zekr* is still closely linked to remembrance, but is distinct from the "continuous remembering" of the previous form. Indeed, by following forgetfulness, it would appear that it would indicate some sort of break, a rupture in the mindfulness, only to be reaffirmed again. In other words: in order to reformulate and re-create that moment of recognition, it needs to vanish just so that it may reemerge again, its disappearance as crucial as its reappearance, the prescription of an epistemological void so that the individual may experience the reemergence of that mindfulness. Similarly, the Sufis have done something similar, perhaps a strange inverse: they remember to forget. Just as the Qur'an commands one to "invoke the name of God," the sheikhs advised the faithful to actively try and extinguish the memory of the *hosseiniyeh*, an invocation of forgetting. Ultimately, if it may be argued that the Sufis have implemented a form of active forgetting, or willful amnesia, as I have been calling it here, then, just as the *zekr* as mindfulness may involve disremembering, so too may a willful amnesia involve a sort of layer of remembrance as well.

Furthermore, it appears as if the two Shi'i groups in question have both turned to the concept and practice of *zekr* in order to fulfill their respective objectives: one to reinscribe the traumas of the past into the present, giving evidence for the need for a strong, central government to ensure that these traumas may not be experienced again; the other in order to declare their disinterest and disengagement with the sociopolitical as well as material realm. Rather than positioning the groups as wholly heterodox and orthodox, the clerical establishment in opposition to the mystical outliers, here we see both entities utilizing different interpretations of Shi'i epistemology, demonstrating slight shifts in their understanding of a deeply complex and nuanced idea. Thus, when attempting to understand the dynamic between this particular Sufi order and the governing authority, whether they be the central government or local municipality, through the prism of *zekr*, it is clear that such modes of oppositional thinking prove insufficient. We might consider in the place of this binary a particular discursive tradition, one where two groups, whose faiths both claim to be the "heart of Shi'ism," draw upon a long history of the importance of remembrance within Shi'i scholarship, culminating in differing interpretations of the same theme. One embracing the "remembrance to forget," the other a more direct, perhaps less circular form of recollection. The similarities in tactics then must also be noted as much as the divergences, as ultimately both Sufi and Ja'fari are adding to the multiplicity of interpretations of Shi'ism in Iran today.

An Impossible Apolitics

Abandon these tales of yesterday and tomorrow.
Now is the time to change yourself!

SHAH NIMATULLAH VALI, IN JAVAD NURBAKHSH,
MA'ARIF-I SUFIYA (1983)

Until the coronavirus pandemic swept through the world, individual Sufis still gathered outside the grave on Fridays for evening prayers. They gathered not as a group, but individually, going to a small alleyway behind the new wall, but primarily praying inside the cemetery. "We did not want to attract attention," I was told at the time, "but we don't think they will bother us if we don't go in a large group." When asked again about the destruction of the *tekiyeh* and what has happened since, the responses are still wildly mixed, largely depending on the individual's relationship to myself.

Let us reconsider Takhteh-Foulad and the events that transpired there. Most notably, up until this moment we have focused mainly on the Sufis' reaction to the razing of the site, and how we might understand their decision to disremember the building. In these concluding spaces, however, it is worth examining the incident more wholly from beginning to end, from the initial sign posted upon the door to their continued praying in the alleyway. In looking at the larger narrative there appears to be a turning point in the tactics and responses employed, before the destruction and after, a stark contrast in their actions and reactions. Initially, the Sufis employed a number of tactics in their attempts to prevent the demolition: appealing to the authorities, looking to family connections within the bureaucracy, various avenues of dialogue and negotiations that culminated with the confrontation on the night of the destruction. Such methods of direct engagement are typical techniques by which individuals and collectives may attempt to thwart the actions of the political bodies that govern them, and the order embraced these methods wholeheartedly. Why then, in the aftermath of the devastation at Takhteh-Foulad, after such resistance had been mounted—sleeping through cold nights, risking arrest or worse—did their oppositional consciousness seem to dissipate so quickly?

One might offer that it did not disappear, it merely changed forms.

Perhaps not even changed forms, but perhaps what occurred was a shift: a shift in the way that the order wished to view the incident. Initially, the matter was approached on what might be called a societal or bureaucratic level, where attempts were made to navigate the various institutes and to contact appropriate authorities, all means by which they might confront the municipality directly. Just as the municipality claimed the reason for the destruction was "beautification" of the neighborhood, meaning the building was destroyed for purely civil purposes, so too did the Sufis approach the instance as an entirely civil matter, ultimately resulting in an act not dissimilar to civil disobedience, action met with counteraction.

After the demolition, however, the mystics never contacted the authorities again, spoke only to a few media figures immediately after the event and then, at least in theory, spoke of the matter no further. This public silence, however, did not imply that the Sufis were no longer concerned with what transpired at Takhteh-Foulad, nor had they dismissed it completely. The incident was rather approached from an entirely different light, the terms of the debate reconfigured wholly: now the removal of the *hosseini-yeh* would be approached through a mystical lens. Rather than confrontation, there is evasion; rather than direct opposition, a strange sideways tactic has been espoused, the sociopolitical realm abandoned in favor of one with which it was largely unconcerned. It is in this way that the Sufi order has rendered the municipality's actions impotent: One can never lose if they have never played at all.

Is this resistance? There are shades of defiance here, undoubtedly, if we are to understand resistance as actions or thoughts explicitly reactionary to some oppositional force. More often, resistance is framed as a persecuted group taking some form of active measure in response to a governing body that has impinged upon their autonomy or self-preservation in some way or form; and one might argue that the mystics' response to the Isfahani municipal government, working in tandem with the national government, would prove just such an example. The Sufis' ultimate response, however, or nonresponse, their very deliberate actions to "ignore" the event in their own way, adds a layer of ambiguity that might problematize such a categorization. If resistance is deliberative action in response to antagonistic forces, how does deliberative forgetting register?

Beyond simply resistance, however, this might be understood as a tactic first and foremost. What is a tactic? Both method and maneuver, it is an act that is calculated, purposeful, and intentional. A tactic is something that is designed to respond to a certain dilemma or obstacle, and hence is molded by the contours of the problem it wishes to navigate, the formation of a conceptual counterpoint. Thus, when considering the mystics' actions, one might categorize them as a form of tactical endeavor, one that involves a certain mode of resistance but is not wholly defined by it. In other words, their decision to not directly engage with the municipal government and the larger systems of power was a form of resistance by the fact that they chose to prioritize their metaphysical needs first—the primacy of the remembrance of God—thereby demonstrating the impotency and irrelevance of the state in light of their own epistemological and spiritual framework. Just as they did with their civil tactics, they continued to approach the incident through careful deliberation after the destruction, merely shifting their response to consider what the building was addressing all along: the spiritual needs of the faithful. In this way, the entire incident has been reframed as a spiritual exercise, as devoid of politics as they might make it, an unknowing of memory, which, given the context, is a highly politicized act.

Unknowing of Memory

What does it mean to unknow a memory? The strangest of exercises, to question oneself at such profound registers, acting as both skeptic and believer, both pushing and pulling against a single idea, refuting information that exists on the most fundamental of levels. Ultimately, this form of refutation of knowledge implements an instance of self-doubt so severe that it undermines not only the ontological status of places and things, but one's own cognitive faculties and emotions, propelling one to question the very nature of their own reality. Indeed, such an upending of reality—outside of some form of psychotic break—is only possible when the parameters of what constitutes "reality" itself might be reconfigured. To demand such malleability from the Real undermines the understanding of reality as a totality, that which is unchanging and exists as a temporally and ontologically contained whole. In this instance, then, we must turn to Sufi understandings of what constitutes that which might be considered "real." Furthermore, we must also consider the epistemologies demanded by such systems of reality, and it is in this way that we turn to mystical logic; it is here that we might see how the dream logic is in play. Before that, however, let us revisit mystical notions of the real.

As previously discussed, within contemporary mysticism one of the primary debates revolves around the discernment of that which is real and that which is imagined, that which is veiled and that which is revealed. And perhaps the aspect that we must keep first and foremost in our minds is that the Sufis believe that such a thing that might be called reality *does exist,* but it is only the most enlightened beings who are able to experience it as such. Beyond this, just as there are stations on the path, there exists various stations of reality that become transparent as one advances further along the path, as if one's sight was slowly coming into focus. A more commonly used analogy, however, is the idea of wakefulness and dreaming, or that those who have reached *tawhid* are the only beings who are considered ever truly awake. As such, very few are ever said to have achieved full wakefulness, only saints and other holy figures, as even the *qotbs* and sheikhs are seen as only positioned higher on the path. It is safe to assume, then, that the Sufis practicing at Takhteh-Foulad would have considered themselves enshrouded from the real, residing instead in a state of dozing somnolence, and it is from this vantage point that we might consider the epistemological foundations guiding their actions.

The mystics have attempted to manipulate the real because the Ral is not available to them, merely a strange dreamworld that is itself an illusion. One of the key aspects of Sufism is the recognition of the inaccessibility of the Real. With Takhteh-Foulad, they affirm its illusory nature by exploiting the artifice and illusion that comprises this elusive in-between, partially revealed stage.[15] Furthermore, it is imperative to realize the power of subjectivity ensconced within this worldview: not only for manipulating the illusion, but for constructing it as well. And it is here, then, where the ontological and the existential are collapsed into one, that the dream logic takes hold: if all life is a dream, then it may be as you dream it. If reality is unavailable to us and we are thus only able to understand the external world as a dream, then only oneiric thinking might be used to both affirm and navigate such a realm.

Furthermore, not only is it the thinker/dreamer who constructs this strange space, as Bachelard has noted, but there is also no difference between them: "The dreamer is the double consciousness of his well-being and of the happy world. His cogito is not divided into the dialectic of subject and object."[16] In other words, the dreamer constructs both self and world. Certainly, the phenomenological implications of both the Sufis' thought and Bachelard are great: the difference is that the Sufis believe that there is in fact an a priori reality—it is merely out of reach—whereas Bachelard would disavow any forms of apriority altogether. The similarities lie instead in the fact that both "journeys" are driven entirely by the subject; time and time again it is the individual and the individual alone who is made responsible for his spiritual development. Bachelard distinguishes between the dream and reverie: the former overtakes us, unconscious thoughts dominating conscious thoughts, whereas reverie is more akin to a daydream, a mode of conscious thinking implemented by the individual, active dreaming versus passive dreaming: "In such encounters, a Poetics of Reverie becomes conscious of its tasks: causing consolidations of imagined worlds, developing the audacity of constructive reverie, affirming itself in a dreamer's clear consciousness, coordinating liberties, finding some true thing in all the indisciplines of language, opening all the prisons of the being so that the human possesses all becomings. Those are just so many often contradictory tasks lying between what concentrates the being and what exalts it."[17] Within an unknowing of memory, no less of a claim is made than the supremacy of the imaginary over the actual. The gentle daydream, in its implementation, rendered bold. In offering a group solution as to how to react to the destruction of their meeting place, the sheikhs have offered a united imaginary front, a "consolidation," as Bachelard notes, of a dream. If reverie is conscious dreaming, then a poetics of reverie is the careful assemblage and shepherding of these ephemeral thoughts, as a conductor moving notes through the air.

And so we have found ourselves in the "audacity of constructive reverie," by a small group of individuals who insisted on what might be called a dream, an idea "suggested" to them by their spiritual leaders, those they trust the most. And although there were those within the order who did not put into practice these ideas, none refuted or challenged them, none made the case for another tactic. Those who did not attempt to "actively forget" simply acknowledged that it was too difficult for them to do so. Otherwise, they joined the rest in forgoing the memory of their space, the memory of its destruction, so that they might more closely adhere to the *zekr* that had been proscribed to them. Such is the audacity of the politics of apolitics.

When even a memory may be unlearned, a greater risk has been revealed: when the knowledge of a memory may be overturned, then the actuality of all greater knowledge too remains malleable, open, and at risk. As is understood within Sufi thought, to possess knowledge of something does not represent possession of an absolute, but rather an open engagement with a thought. To return once more to a previously quoted passage by Majzub'alishah: "Literally, *erfan* [gnosis] is knowing. Yet knowing has different stages . . . gnosis is not an absolute matter. It is something that, as the philosophers say, is graduated (*tashkiki*) such as light and faith, which have degrees. . . . More than anything else . . . this process continues endlessly."[18] Again, we see here both knowledge and the project of mysticism as synonymous entities, so closely intertwined as to be inseparable, both dedicated to the implementation of the practice of the irresolution of thought.

Thus, by invoking their own mystical epistemologies, the Sufis at Takhteh-Foulad have contested not only the actions of the authorities, but the finality of the event itself. They have here applied the ideas within the *zekr* ritual—that forgetting may also be understood to be intimately tied to remembrance, such that one might actively forget just as one might actively remember—as well as those ideas pertaining to the unreality of the world to respond to the destruction of the *tekiyeh* on their own terms. There exist many stories of what transpired, or what did not transpire, at Takhteh-Foulad, and the Sufis' disavowal of the authorities' actions have in the end invoked a strange political turn. On the one hand, we witness the implementation of apolitics at its most extreme, the most blatant form of disengagement, one what might even venture to say denial, of a politically motivated series of actions that had a directly negative outcome on the group itself. And it might be safe to stop there, to simply categorize the actions of a spiritual group uninterested in the broader social realm as a part of a larger system of belief. On the other hand, we have a group who has essentially denied the authorities any agency and in a sense has stripped them of their power by refuting the very actions that allow them to reassert their dominance.

In the end, however, it might be argued that either assessment remains contingent upon the question of perspective: from the perspective of the authorities and the broader Iranian sociopolitical sphere, a group has deemed the actions of the state apparatus irrelevant—despite its directly negative outcome on its own affairs—and such a maneuver might be viewed as a distinctly political act, one that reaffirms the dialectics of power through its very denial. From the perspective of the Sufis, however, or perhaps more specifically the perspective put forward by the sheikhs, this has been viewed first and foremost as an exercise in mystical thought and practice, an occasion where the potential within their own epistemologies to help navigate a world at times hostile to such ideals has been carried out to the fullest extent.

5 Unknowing of Place

> And you have spread yourself upon everywhere,
> and where has lost its where-ness.
>
> MANSUR AL-HALLAJ, *ANA AL-HAQQ RECONSIDERED* (1972)

> In the auditory category, we have here an immense sound-
> miniature, the miniature of an entire cosmos that speaks
> softly. Faced with such a miniature of world sounds as this, a
> phenomenologist must systematically point out all that goes
> beyond perception, organically as well as objectively.
>
> GASTON BACHELARD, *THE POETICS OF SPACE* (1994)

A sound emerges. Faint at first, the type of noise that operates more as question than sensation, prompting one to seek confirmation: Do you hear that? It is late afternoon and, as in most Iranian urban residential areas, the neighborhood is largely quiet, the stillness punctuated only by the occasional car or passerby. Only distance is keeping us from hearing this sound then, and our movements forward allow its tones to come into sharper relief.

We have been listening for this sound, so its emergence does not come as a surprise. As we walk toward it we pass rows of middle-class apartment buildings, the most popular form of housing in Iran, one after the other, with cars lining the perimeter of the street. Sometimes the buildings are set back from the street, a garden protected by high walls in front of the building, others without a walled garden. While it's not typical to hear music being broadcast, it is not enough to cause alarm or a deep surprise, simply something to be observed and noted. We have been told to listen for this sound, to follow it to its source, and so that is what we are doing.

Its increase in volume allows the noises to come into focus and assume form: a quiet song of a *daf*, a large frame drum. It is played by tapping and rolling the fingers and knuckles in various formations against the skin of the drum, punctuated by short slaps and caresses by a flattened palm. The sound it produces is not unlike that of rain on a rooftop.

"Ah, this must be their alley [*kucheh*]," my companion, Nickoo, notes.

The two of us move more slowly, trying to identify which building the music—no longer just sounds now—emanates from, until finally we settle on a shorter building with speckled gray stone and a front garden. The *daf* drumming is clearly coming from this garden, penetrating the thick stone wall and spilling out into the street. We've found our destination.

"Oh good, we found it, that wasn't too bad."

On the pedestrian gate, the family names for the apartments inside are smudged and largely worn away, and we scan them fruitlessly. This is the building, but which apartment is not clear. And while the rollicking and rolling sound of the gentle *daf* has summoned us to this spot, outside a white wall and gray brick building, technology will guide us the rest of the way.

Nickoo takes out her cell phone. "Can you buzz us in?"

A harsh buzz sounds, a clanging lock releases, and the door snaps slightly open. We enter the doorway and make our way inside. As we walk through the courtyard, we pass a small personal stereo on top of a chair, playing music. It is positioned near the front of the courtyard, but not directly behind the wall, not close enough to block the sound that emanates from it. We make our way inside the building.

Inside the apartment, we are the last to arrive and are greeted with an almost festive atmosphere. About a dozen people are seated along the ground and on the sofa, talking and laughing among themselves, seated not in the formal guest room, with its sharp edges and reflective surfaces, but squeezed into the smaller and softer living room, where the body might relax along with the furniture. Although of the people who are there only some are family, there is no question this room is the appropriate choice. There are books scattered around too—some dog-eared, some new—as ubiquitous as the cups of tea and snacks filling the space.

"So you found us!"

"Of course! I received excellent directions!"

"It was loud enough, then? We didn't want to annoy the neighbors, but we wanted to make sure you heard it from the street. I actually went out into the street to check."

"No, you had it at just the right volume."

"So, it turned out well." And then, with a laugh: "You see what kinds of things we have to think of in Iran!?"

This small group of young people had been holding such creatively organized reading groups for a little less than three months, and then had stopped, citing the difficulty in coordinating everyone's schedules as the main reason for discontinuing the sessions.

The group was composed of approximately fifteen young people, both men and women, who ranged in age from nineteen to thirty-four. Of this core group, about ten had attended a "formal" Sufi gathering, meaning a gathering organized and led by a Sufi sheikh, at least once, and of that group half were either "officially" members of an order, or children of official members. During their meetings, they read aloud and discussed selections from the canon of medieval Persian poetry, sometimes choosing pieces beforehand, other times choosing at random. They concluded each session with what is called a *fal:* a sort of fortune-telling game, very common throughout the country and certainly not an activity exclusive to the Sufi community, involving a book of the poetry of Hafez that is passed around. After this discussion of everyone's fate, the session would come to a close or the already relaxed atmosphere would shift into a purely social gathering.

My focus here is less the content of such meetings, but more the curious way in which the sessions were organized and made known to their members. More specifically, what led to the decision to take such pains to broadcast their locations audibly rather than simply deciding upon a predetermined location? What does such a tactic reveal about their understanding of *ma'rifat,* and how might it give rise to an alternative "Sufi space"?

When I spoke to my interlocutors, I asked them why and how they decided upon their unique method of convening. In their responses to me, they told me about their desire to devise a "Sufi way of meeting." Afsaneh, a woman in her midtwenties who carried with her a well-worn family copy of a volume of Rumi's *Masnavi,* described it as follows: "We get together [*jam mishim*] and discuss themes of these mystical works [*matn-e erfani*], so shouldn't the way we come together be related to that?" Central to their discussions was the importance of wandering (*sargardan, suluk*)[1] and listening (*sama*), two concepts that have long held places of importance within mystical epistemologies.

And these young Sufis took a very particular hermeneutic stance toward the concept of wandering: they approach it in the literal sense, meaning wandering is understood to require actual physical movements of the body and dislocation of place. This is in contrast with other Sufi thinkers who approach wandering in a figurative or nonliteral sense, typically as a metaphor for one's personal journey to achieve union with God (*tawhid*). This embrace of a literal interpretation of wandering is also noteworthy, as itinerancy has long fallen out of favor with the overwhelming majority of Sufis in Iran over the last hundred years, with all—save for the odd *qalandar* (wandering ascetic) here and there—living sedentary lives. Instead, these young Sufis' interpretation of both wandering and *sama* is one that favors materialism and sensoriality over metaphor and indexicality.[2] As Bita, a middle-school teacher in her late twenties who taught English- and French-language classes on the side, told me: "It's the only time I walk slow." This observation of her slowness, which could only become apparent through a physical instantiation of wandering, was clearly significant enough to Bita that she remarked upon it and that it meant something to her. Literal interpretation is too often viewed as a result of a lack of imagination, a dour form of interpretation that leaves little room for real engagement, but here there was a lightness to our conversations, a sense of play and fun, which will be discussed in greater detail in a later section.

By examining the example of this small group and their creative application of theories of mystical ideas, we might better understand the ways that a Sufi community has reinterpreted the mystical ideals of old to create an alternative Islamic space in postrevolutionary Iran. What are the markers, both visible and invisible, that demarcate the boundaries of this transient Sufi space, a listened-for soundscape that appears and disappears at the will of its organizers? How can listening be used to generate a different form of collective space? In what way is movement involved in this enterprise? Are these imagined spaces and, if so, how does that fact relate to perception as related to the real? In analyzing these questions, we may be able to understand the aesthetics as an epistemic practice, one tied to the questioning of unknowing, as well as the advantages and disadvantages of operating within a space that remains never fully known, perhaps even to the Sufis themselves.

This chapter traces the construction of a listened-for soundscape, one whose building blocks are sound, movement, and the hermeneutic imagination. Here, mystical epistemologies have emerged as a form of urban inscription, one where ideas, originating in the textual and conceptual spheres, have been translated into spatial form to create a Sufi soundscape. An inscription and a carving, they have marked the streets, the vibrations of the sounds leaving an invisible residue on the homes and alleyways. And, just as we have seen before with texts, bodies, and memories, here too space and place become unbounded entities. There is an unknowing of place, one that acts again as the contestation of finitude, this time through the construction of a soundscape that is both a contained and uncontained entity, a reconfiguration of streets and alleyways into a shape-shifting and ever inchoate aural sphere.

To better understand this construction, I will first investigate the conditions and circumstances that inspired the participants to imagine and instantiate such an activity, whereupon the actions of the municipal government (*shahrdari*) initiated a reimagining of collective Sufi space. From there, I analyze how the group's hermeneutics are broadly informed by a particular critical lens toward their own tradition, one that, in a shift from that of their own order, favors the literal over the metaphorical. For the rest of the chapter, I focus on how two key concepts, intentional listening (*sama*) and wandering (*sargardan*), are specifically utilized in the construction of this collective space, providing both a philosophical and an aesthetic framework that together accentuate the tenuous and amorphous nature of the soundscape, shaped by the political stakes of meeting and the processes and ideals of spiritual transformations. I conclude by returning to the broader context by investigating what it means for such a space to exist within postrevolutionary Iran.

Before moving into deeper analytical waters, a note regarding the aforementioned concepts: mystical wandering, known as *suluk* or *sargardan*, and intentional listening, known as *sama*,[3] which we have seen briefly before. Here, *sama* refers more specifically to a form of audition that should be understood as (1) distinct from the more passive hearing, and (2) not only an engaged form of listening, but one that is accompanied by the highest intentionality and attention (*tavajo*) of the listener, an intention to achieve a sense of the ultimate union with God (*tawhid*).

Wandering, an extremely common metaphor within Sufi thought, signifies the means of traveling on the "Sufi path" of spiritual development. It is not a linear journey that one takes when pursuing such abstract goals, but one of a meandering and even directionless nature. At the same time, however, these wanderings are to be understood not as aimless, but purposeful.

In this way, they move toward a paradox: intentional wanderings. A space that remains never fully known to its own inhabitants, there are clear resonances here with forms of thinking and knowledge that reveal not answers but further questions, another seemingly paradoxical phenomenon of a knowledge that reveals not a finalized thought but an awareness that one knows nothing, as one does when considering the divine. Through creating these aesthetic and material experiences, bursting forth from the Sufi canon and subsequently shaped through their own hermeneutics, these young Sufis have created a space that remains ever inchoate and transient, one that is marked as much by its ability to appear as it is by its ability to disappear.

Whither Resistance? Catalysts and Cancellations

The original impetus to organize the meetings at all came in the wake of the cancellation of official Sufi gatherings at a sheikh's house in a residential neighborhood by the local authorities. During these weekly meetings, group prayers were said and either a sermon (*sokhanrani*) was delivered by an elder (*pir*) or a CD of a sermon by a spiritual leader (*qotb*) was played. Such gatherings had been going on for years, and the order had been convening in that particular location for close to a decade, when one day a person came from the local authorities and stated that the Sufis were no longer to hold their gatherings at this location. When asked why, the official reason given was that it was clear that a residential home was being used for commercial purposes, and so they must desist immediately.[4] The mystics attempted to assure the official that nothing was being sold on the premises, nor was anyone paying to attend—in other words, the home was not being used for "commercial" purposes as they understood it. The authority figure, however, remained unconvinced and repeated his order. Not wishing to pursue the matter further, the Sufis ended the meetings entirely.

After these official meetings were stopped, the order no longer met in any "official" capacity, and the sheikhs recommended traveling to Tehran to attend large gatherings instead. On holidays and other special occasions, however, people would still gather locally, usually in a gender-segregated capacity, and invite either a sheikh or a female elder to deliver a sermon or lead a poetry reading, prayer sessions, or mourning ritual. These gatherings, however, were infrequent. The collective described in this article, however, did continue to meet on a regular basis.

It is important to note that it is quite possible that these creatively organized gatherings probably would not have occurred had the original, larger meetings not been disbanded in the first place. Indeed, had the local authorities not responded in the way they did, had the legal standing in Iran been more clear, perhaps the young people would never have taken the initiative. Or perhaps they would have taken up this unique form of listening practice on their own. It is impossible to know.

As such, one could posit that this soundscape should be understood primarily in light of this cancellation, arguing that this interpretation and application of Sufi concept acts as a mystical response to local politics first and foremost, where mystical epistemologies provide the solution to what is essentially a problem between a local group and the authorities. I am uncomfortable to center my analysis around this narrative for two reasons.

First and foremost, the actions of the state (*dowlat*), or even how the municipal authorities (*shahrdari*) might pose a problem (*geer bedan*, in the colloquial), were almost entirely absent from my conversations with my interlocutors. When asked why and how they decided upon their unique method of assembling, their responses consisted of discussions around engaging with mystical ideals they encountered in texts and sermons; of envisioning a "Sufi way of meeting." The only ways the actions of the municipality came into the conversations was as a starting point: "After the meetings were cancelled." So while the dispersal of the original, larger meetings certainly acted as a catalyst, my conversations with my interlocutors reveal that "responding" to the cancellations was not really a priority for them.

Second, I fear that such a framing—understanding the soundscape primarily as a response to the municipality—runs into very tired tropes of "resistance." This not only belies the deeply complicated, fragmented, and disparate relationships between mystical groups, broadly writ, and the Iranian authorities in both their national and local instantiations, but also does injustice to the complexity of the epistemologies employed by the Sufis themselves. There are abstruse theological concepts at play here; to categorize such hermeneutic stances under the umbrella of "resistance" is to reduce the complexity of their thinking to a simple "us v. them" paradigm. Perhaps theological experimentation is not as interesting to some analysts as "state power," but it was clearly the former for the Sufi collective themselves. As such, I have centered my analysis around how the interpretation and application of mystical epistemologies gave rise to the construction of a transient Sufi soundscape.

Of Games and History, or Fun with Hermeneutics

I met with my interlocutors on a number of occasions, usually in a group setting, to discuss their decision-making process, to understand how such a unique method of convening came about. In their responses to me, they spoke of the importance of wandering, of listening with an open heart, and of their affections for the Sufis of old, how in centuries past certain mystics would travel from city to city for years at a time, sometimes searching for the perfect teacher with whom to study, sometimes adhering to itinerancy for their entire lives. "We all love the story of how [the mystical poets] Shams and Rumi met," Nazanin told me, describing the apocryphal first encounter between the wandering *darvish* Shams and the sedentary Rumi, where the former proceeds to upend the latter's previously respectable life. "If they hadn't met, if Shams hadn't gone to Konya [the city where Rumi lived], we wouldn't even know who Rumi is, he would just be some jurist. Travel (*safar*) and wandering are so important." Amir Hossein added playfully, "We pay our respects to the Sufi masters (*pir-ha*) of old! *And* we learn about wandering."

Through their utilization of the "classical" Sufi concepts of *sama* and *wandering* (*suluk, sargardan*), the youth here, like countless others before them, are participating in an engagement with and summoning forward of their own history. In drawing from their canon so unambiguously, they are demonstrating a clear desire to position themselves as operating within Sufi discourses. They are calling upon well-established conceptual matrices to operate as both guides and anchors, and thereby confirming their desire to cement and affirm their ties to the Sufi tradition. As has been done innumerable times for millennia prior, an established idea served as inspiration for further creation.

The literalness with which they approach the ideas, especially wandering, is particularly noteworthy. The idea of wandering is central to Nimatullahi Sufism but physical wandering within the orders has not been a primary concern for over a hundred years, if not longer. Indeed, we return again to that seminal 1939 text, *Pand-e Saleh* (Saleh's Advice), where idleness and begging,[5] the sometimes accompaniments to wandering, were discouraged. In the text, Shaykh Saleh Alishah describes the accusations leveled against them by Sufism's detractors: "They try to present dervishes to certain people as a form of idleness and shamelessness; as being a burden to society; as not being bound to the customs [adab] of religion and the laws; as not observing the manners of religiosity; and as opposing civilization. They do this so as to humiliate dervishes before all groups, so that some seekers [taleban] might consider their words true and believe in them and thus be led astray from the Truth."[6]

Although the practice had already been in decline for some time at the time of its publication in 1939, Saleh's Advice cements the transition of Nimatullahi Sufism from a close-knit circle of men devoting their entire lives to spiritual development (tawhid) to a form of religious practice compatible with the lives of "respectable" people. Thus, the era of the itinerant holy man was already coming to a close, leaving only the rare individual, deemed alternately eccentric or devout, to pursue the life of rootlessness. I should also note, however, that physical wandering was never explicitly banned or condemned in and of itself, and so to take it up is not necessarily a refutation of modern Sufi practice.

Given that these peripatetic practices have long fallen out of living memory, then, what drew these young mystics to carry out such meanderings? Was it some sort of revivalist impulse? A means of recreating an older, potentially more romantic form of Sufism, where being a darvish often structured one's entire life, rather than the Sufism of today where it is incorporated into a life that is otherwise completely unremarkable from most other Iranians'? Rather than paying homage to their illustrious ancestors or the Sufism of generations past, however, their immediate answer was perhaps a bit less lofty: they thought it would be fun, but also a means to connect to the project of Sufism as a whole. While the project was absolutely conceived with mystical ideals and practices in mind, and hence situates itself firmly within the discursive practices of the order, there was never once a mention of extending the activity beyond the group themselves—that is, bringing it to the larger Sufi community in their city or elsewhere. When conceiving of the wandering/listening project, the group wanted to do something fun or cool, bahal as they recounted to me, rather than envisioning some grand scheme for the future of Sufism in Iran.

"Do you think of it as a kind of game (bazi)?" I asked my interlocutors. "No, not from the outset, we weren't thinking of it like that, but I guess it's kind of a game or puzzle," Shervin replied.

Nazanin countered: "Well, no, I don't think so. Our wandering isn't really a *game* in the sense that's it just for fun, or has no real consequences. It's like a game in that there is something to solve or find, and it's interesting, but ideally it's like a type of practice."

"Is it really so serious as that?" Fatima queried.

"Why not?" replied Nazanin.

"Yeah, I don't think it's a game, we thought it was a Sufi way of meeting. It's not always the easiest way, but it's the most engaged, and allows you to connect to your surroundings," offered Babak.

"It's certainly the only time I wander or listen carefully during the day."

"Well, that's because you have a job, I wander around all the time! *Bikaram dige*, I don't have anything to do!"

"Is it the same type of wandering though as *our* wandering?"

"Well . . . well sometimes, sometimes yes, sometimes no. Depends on my day, my mood."

I interject here: "What do you mean by a different type of wandering?"

Fatima explained: "One type is just aimless [*bi-eradeh*] wandering, that's not the kind we're interested in, the other is searching for something but you don't know what that something is yet. That's our type of wandering."

"So for meetings it's not the ideal type of wandering, but it's still something more similar than to aimless wandering."

"See, it's not a type of game then, is it," said Nazanin.

"No, no, I guess it's not. All right, you were right!" Shervin conceded with laugh.

Game or not, there was a lightness to our conversations, a sense of play and fun. As they discussed my questions out loud together, there was a convivial air among the friends, and a youthful enthusiasm that marked our conversations about their unique hermeneutic stance. "Fun" and "Islamic hermeneutics" are not two terms that are often associated with each other, but the playful—yet still thoughtful, still informed—attitude of my interlocutors made "fun with hermeneutics" a very real thing. Nur Amali Ibrahim, in his study of Islamic Indonesian university groups, similarly found that student collectives provided "playful spaces that permit the emergence of unusual and nontraditional forms of piety."[7] It is worth noting that both with the case study presented here and with Ibrahim's interlocutors, there was no authority figure present, no teacher or guide, therein freeing the youths from the pressure to ascertain the "right" or "best" interpretation. Instead, they were free to debate and experiment as peers and equals. This is not to say that such creativity does not happen in more formal classroom settings, as Odabaei's and Tawasil's ethnographic work in Iranian seminaries has shown,[8] but simply that there is a particular dynamic that characterizes young people coming together discussing ideas without an authority figure present. It is in this way that the Sufi soundscape first came together vis-à-vis mystical epistemologies, with a sense of exploration and lightness, with one eye toward the gravitas of the past and another toward what was "cool" in the present.

The Literal as Experimental

As evidenced by my interlocutors' comments, there are many types of wandering: aimless, intentional, existential. One characteristic these iterations all share, however, is that they are composed of acts of physical movement. And while this may seem to be an obvious statement, it is significant within the world of Islamic mysticism. As mentioned earlier, wandering within Sufi thought—while a central question for many thinkers—often remains in the realm of metaphor or within that nebulous space between the literal and the metaphoric.[9] For this group of young Sufis, however, wandering is understood in the literal sense, operating as a decisive activity that must be actualized by the movement of one's body, offering a form of knowledge and experience that would not have been obtained otherwise.

I should clarify what I mean by "literal" interpretation, as literalism within Islam is a category that is often deeply misunderstood outside of theological circles. Typically, it is considered in terms of Islamic legal theory (*usul al-fiqh*), where the meaning of the text is said to be apparent or manifest (*zahir*) within the printed or recited words and the rules of grammar that apply to them. This form of exegetical practice is often contrasted with those schools of jurisprudence that emphasize rational argumentation (*aql*) or a concealed internal meaning (*batin*), seemingly positing literalism as the uncritical alternative to the deep thinkers of nonliteralist schools of thought. This understanding of external or literal meaning (*zahir*), however, is a misconstruction. To begin, it grossly simplifies the disparate and highly sophisticated hermeneutics of those who analyze the "exterior" meaning of the text. Following a literalist interpretation does not mean that one does not carry out any analysis of the text; rather that one's *form* of analysis is derived from a specific hermeneutics and epistemology, one that typically privileges language over context, linguistics over reference-based argumentation, *haqiqa* (literal trope) over *majaz* (figurative, nonliteral). As Mahmood notes, within so-called literalist Qur'anic hermeneutics, it is not that meanings are laid bare, but that a "certain form of literacy" is developed.[10]

In his excellent *Islam and Literalism*, Robert Gleave offers a slightly different take on the term. While he acknowledges that "literalist" is an imperfect analogue to interpretations that favor *zahir* (apparent, external) "meanings," he defends its use by noting that he uses it as an "analytical tool which . . . does capture one of the elements of the tradition nicely. . . . Since literal meaning . . . [is a] common phrase, used in everyday parlance as well as secondary literature, the idea of literality can act as a starting point through which a book in the English language can discuss a world expressed almost exclusively through the medium of technical Arabic,"[11] and I would agree with this assessment. Despite its potential limitations, the use of the designator "literalist," even as an imperfect approximate for *zahir* or *haqiqa*, allows us the opportunity to think more closely about what "apparent" definitions really mean, a moment to highlight the nuance and care that goes into such thoughtful interpretations, and how a literalist or apparent interpretation might differ from one that is centered around the idea of the metaphorical or "hidden."

When analyzing this case study, however, what I am referring to as their "literal interpretation" is distinct in that it is not related to exegesis or any form of textual analysis at all. Rather, it is their interpretation of a concept—in this case *sargardan* or *sama*—that favors materialism and sensoriality over metaphor and indexicality. These young people approach wandering (*sargardan*) at the level of allegory as well as a material practice that highlights the potential for transformation of the self through an engagement with the profane Real. Just as literal interpretations of the text offer an opportunity for further analysis, so too does literal interpretation of wandering offer an opportunity for the Sufi hermeneutic imagination to exert itself onto the streets of the city.

When they walk through the neighborhoods, straining to hear the sounds from the meeting place, the Sufis are engaging in a form of devotional activity, turning an idea that they had first encountered as metaphor into actuality. Through their wandering and listening, the streets are transfigured into a place with the potential for sacral interaction, if only for the Sufis themselves, if only momentarily. Moreover, in emphasizing the material over the abstract in their devotion—or, perhaps more accurately, the material *alongside* the abstract—it appears that they are privileging experiences of immanence. The material world here operates as a realm to search for, and hence interact with, the divine, therein bringing two disparate ontological planes in sight of one another. This is not a simple empiricism at play here, but when fused with their conceptual framework becomes the radical materialism of immanence. As Deleuze has written: "Empiricism is by no means a reaction against concepts. . . . On the contrary, it undertakes the most insane creation of concepts ever."[12] Just as many anthropologists have noted the transfigurative potential of engagements with matter and material,[13] so too can a literalist understanding of Islam possess a similar capacity for inventive play.

Literalism is too often seen as synonymous with the absence of critical thought, a black hole of interpretation where the word offers not inspiration but command, often of a proscriptive variety. Here we see a literal interpretation of a classic Sufi concept (favored over an allegorical one) brought forth as a creative and theologically sound solution to create a space of their own. Indeed, through these experimentations with the literal and fun with hermeneutics, these young people are challenging the idea of the boundedness of space, affirming the potential of materiality as a malleable entity, one which they can assemble and disassemble at will.

Intentional Wanderings

> I went to the master's street and said "Where is the master?"
> They said, "The master is a lover and is drunk and wandering
> from street to street. "
>
> RUMI, IN ARBERRY, *MYSTICAL POEMS OF RUMI* (2010)

> It is not one truth or another that lacks, or truth in general; nor is it doubt
> that leads us or despair that immobilizes us. The wanderer's country is not
> truth, but exile; he lives outside, on the other side which is by no means
> a beyond, rather the contrary. He remains separated, where the deep of
> dissimulation reigns, that elemental obscurity through which no way can
> be made and which because of that makes its awful way through him.
>
> MAURICE BLANCHOT, *THE WRITING OF THE DISASTER* (1982)

In the introduction of this book, I cited a quote from the Nimatullahi Soltanalishahi quob Nur'Ali Tabandeh: "gnosis (*erfan*) . . . is a process [that] continues endlessly."[14] It is an important reminder that within the project of Nimatullahi mysticism, the path and the object are the same; the journey and objective of Sufism are seen as intrinsically and inseparably linked together. Indeed, as Sufi knowledge is characterized by a lack of finality of thought, so too is the journey to achieve this thought never-ending, fully achieved only by saints. If Sufism is defined as the obtainment of mystical knowledge, and such knowledge is defined as ever expansive and definitively fully unobtainable except for saint figures, then Sufism itself is constituted as an endless process.

For this reason, the metaphors of journeying, pathways, and wandering are ubiquitous in Sufi philosophy, for the Nimatullahi but also more broadly. Perhaps the most obvious example of this is that the word for "order," as in "Sufi order," in Persian is *tariqa*, whose meaning is "path." The literal translation of what gets called a "Sufi order" is thus "Sufi path." That the name that they have given to their own organizational body is that of "path" is not insignificant. To join this assembly of people it is thus implied that one is not simply joining a designated group but is embarking upon a designated *route*, one which acts as, if not a destination, a means to some form of directionality. In this way, they are emphasizing motion over collectivities, an avenue over assembly.

Moreover, one of the many monikers the Sufis use to describe themselves is "wayfarers" or "wanderers of the path." Thus, not only is the name of the organizational body of the Sufis indicative of the importance of the concept of movement, but the people themselves are referred to as travelers and journeymen, those whose lives are structured around transience. When you become a Sufi you become a wanderer, and epistemological itinerancy becomes your life principle.

The word most commonly used for wandering is *sargardan*, which literally translates as "the turning of the head." In other words, wandering is "the turning of the head." To move in such a fashion indicates not merely a forward motion, but a disoriented one, potentially even provoking a circular or spiral motion. I think it is safe to assume too that the potential side effect of dizziness or light-headedness that such head-turning might produce is not entirely unintentional, as (the proper forms of) intoxication and even disorientation are valued experiences within Sufism (indicative as they are of the experience of states [*hal*] one achieves when concentrating on or upon contact with the mysteries of the divine). By invoking the word *sargardan* (rather than other names for wandering, i.e., *siyar*, etc.), the head—and, in turn, thought—is being involved in this process as well. Thus, it is significant to note too that these wanderings demand not only endless movement, an unthinking and infinite unfolding, but a more specific type of journey, one tied to the development and experience of a certain form of knowledge.

Unsurprisingly then, yet another moniker for Sufism per my interlocutors is "the path of substantial evolution." Not only is the path itself an endless "journey," but it involves the process of change of the individual upon the path. A substantial evolution of the self, a becoming through wandering. Subjectivity, just as the form of knowledge with which it engages, is also something that mutates, evolves, remains ever transient, in a state of constant emergence, or at least ideally so.

To return to the words of the Nimatullahi sheikh Seyed Mustafa Azmayesh, who has also written much about journeying and comments specifically on the self-contained nature of the mystical path: "The starting point and the goal, the subject and object are fixed. To put it in other words, I travel from me to Me, in me and by me. I am the point of departure; I am the goal, the journey and the traveler." In a separate piece, he also writes, "Sufism or mysticism in general is a form of travel: a travel from the alienated self to the alternate, real self."[15]

I would return here too to comments made by my interlocutors mentioned earlier in the article that also shed light on the epistemological intricacies of Sufi wandering. As Fatima stated, the Sufis are not interested in "just aimless [bi-eradeh] wandering, that's not the kind we're interested in, the other is searching for something but you don't know what that something is yet. That's our type of wandering."

A clear distinction is being made here. For Fatima, these movements are decidedly not aimless, as the concept of wandering might suggest, but intentional; they are intentional wanderings. Nazanin supports Fatima's assertion when she pushes back against Babak's claim that he wanders around all the time because he is unemployed; as Nazanin asks him: "Is it the same type of wandering though as *our* wandering?" Babak concurs that it is not.

Intentional wandering is a more focused, more directed form of searching, even as the paths to union with God (*tawhid*) remain endless. Azmayesh further affirms this point in his description of the path to reach mystical gnosis (*erfan*) as one which contains infinite possibility: "Sufism ... cannot be compared to a straight road leading from 'A' to 'B.' As described before, it is an individual path. Moreover, the sheikh will, instead of presenting him an answer or a solution, confront the student with the jungle of life and place him in the midst of a multitude of possibilities in order to find his own way."[16] Here, then, the sheikh does not give the disciple a linear trajectory, but offers instead a labyrinth of possibilities, providing more convolution rather than clarity, so that the individual must formulate his own course.

In embracing the seemingly paradoxical concept of intentional wan-derings, these young Sufis are adopting a hermeneutical stance that favors the labyrinthine over the straightforward. As a result, the space they have constructed similarly privileges diffusion over cohesion, movement rather than stasis, and is never fully known or predictable. In doing so, they have demonstrated their commitment to Sufi ideals over efficacy and familiarity.

Open Sounds: *Sama* and Transformation

Urban residential neighborhoods in Iran, with the notable exception of Tehran, are quiet. In a surprise to many unfamiliar with Iranian cities, even working-class neighborhoods in Iran have a relatively low noise level. In the poorer northern neighborhoods of Isfahan, like Zeinabieh for exam-ple, with their higher density of residents and small brick adobe houses of a few rooms, the majority of the streets and winding alleyways are not particularly noisy at all. This is due in large part to the fact that shops and other commercial activities are separated from residential areas, with the occasional small store embedded between houses and apartment build-ings. I would equate the sound level of residential neighborhoods in Ira-nian cities to that of American suburbs. Incidental noises—a car starting, passersby chatting, children playing in the alleyways (*kucheh-ha*)—can be heard, but generally things are quiet. The Sufis' listened-for soundscape is thus made possible by the relative auditory calm of their neighborhoods, as the middle-class enclaves described in this case study are indeed no ex-ception in terms of noise level.

The appropriate forms of housing were also necessary in order for the broadcasting of music to occur. Such an endeavor would not be possible if they lived on the outskirts of the city in the massive housing complexes where many educated and upwardly mobile young professionals live, where there are no real streets to wander as such, but simply very large apartment buildings rising up out of the ground, with very little develop-ment around them. Most of these new tower (*borj*) apartments do not have the traditional courtyard or enclosed front yard of many middle-class apartment buildings in Iranian cities, but have lobbies that lead out directly into the street. The majority of working-class homes also do not possess a front courtyard (although some share an inner courtyard with their next-door neighbors), and so while they would have an easier time broadcasting music than those in housing complexes, this Sufi soundscape may have taken a different shape if it took place in primarily working-class neighborhoods.

I highlight these conditions as we turn our attention now to listening and listening practices, so we might better understand the ways that the music was able to travel. This listened-for soundscape would only be possible under these appropriate auditory and spatial configurations that exist in the participants' residential areas.

Of course, this is not the only influencing factor. The Sufis' utilization of audition emerges from a long tradition of listening within Islamic practice more broadly, a topic that has drawn the attention of scholars for quite some time.[17] One need only look to the pedagogical techniques,[18] sermons and circulation, Qur'anic recitation practices, or even the original revelation and transmission of the Qur'an for a few examples of the centrality of audition throughout Islamic history and philosophy. Of course, in the Sufi tradition, this has often been discussed in the context of the *zekr* ceremony or other ceremonial contexts.[19] In this sense, the Iranian Sufis are again drawing from well-established customs developed before their time. For this analysis, however, I will be tracing the ways that mystical epistemologies are being utilized to form an alternative, if ever tenuous, Islamic space within Iran, with a particular focus on *sama*, intentional listening. How can listening be used as a catalyst for transformation? What are the physical attributes of sound that allow for the formulation of an ephemeral and inchoate space, one that allows for a space/place that can appear and disappear, creating a momentarily cohesive Sufi space but one that can also quickly disassemble? I investigate this material dimension not only to understand the ways in which the soundscape is shaped by the local environment, proscribed by the specific lines and shapes of the neighborhood, but to highlight the ways in which the auditory lends itself to particular forms of transience, making it difficult to fully map, trace, or know the space.

Before this, a note about the music that was utilized. To put it in plain terms, the Sufis were not particularly invested in the music or poetry recitation that was broadcast. As my interlocutors told me, "No, no one really discusses what to play beforehand; it's basically traditional [*sonati*] music or poetry."[20] Sara confirmed this idea: "Yeah, we don't pay much attention to what song or CD is being played specifically, we just listen for its sound and figure out where it's coming from." Bita continued, "I mean, we're not going to play some pop music, just something appropriate [*monaseb*]." "What counts as appropriate?" I pressed. "Something that sets the mood for reading the *Masnavi* [Rumi], just something traditional or *erfani*.[21] It would be pretty ridiculous if we were playing [dance pop star] Arash and then we wanted to read poetry." The seductive beats of the international dance scene excluded, the stylistic indices of the music, then, are not of major concern here. By referring to that which is *monaseb*, or appropriate for the occasion, as any form of "traditional" music, this includes a huge range of possibilities. Beyond the casual approach to music or poetry selection too, the devices utilized—primarily boom boxes or iPod speakers—are not particularly difficult to come by. The sound is transformed from a typical audio CD of music or poetry recitation into a marker of a soundscape through the audition of the Sufis themselves. Although it is certainly through the help of media technologies that this particular group is able to organize themselves, to focus on such in this particular instance would be to disregard the major concerns of the project as a whole.

Space, Audition, Islam

There have been numerous works that explore sound and hearing within Islamic communities, spaces, and places, and this project shares resonances with many of them, particularly those works that analyze instances where the listener is transformed by sound, and the sound is transformed by the listener. In this way, this project is in line with Charles Hirschkind's masterful exploration of the mediation and impact of cassette sermons in Cairo.[22] Not only is their potential for development of the self through the act of audition but, just as the Sufis followed listened-for sounds, so too are these sermons indeed highly sought after by those who listened to and for them.

The differences arise in that the soundscape of the Sufis is not an example of a Hirschkindian counterpublic. As he describes it, a counterpublic is a "discursive arena" that is both embedded within and also a result of the larger material, religious, and political landscapes of contemporary Egypt. These are not self-organized endeavors, but phenomena that emerge and disappear out of the noises of the everyday, only coming into being when "the disciplining power of ethical speech" of the cassette sermon encounters an ethical listener.

Conversely, the Sufis are broadcasting the sounds themselves for their own listening/recognition. This is sound as willed occurrence, self-generated and unrecognizable to all but the select few who seek it out. Indeed, one of the key distinctive features of this Sufi space is its position as a *listened-for* soundscape, one that is formulated through a sort of aural search party by its inhabitants. These are desired sounds that are sought out by their listeners. This type of soundscape is decidedly distinct from those constituted by ambient street noise, a background hum that is felt through the more passive hearing, where one can both tune in and tune out or, in the case of denizens of extremely loud, Muslim-majority metropolises, a deafening cacophony that one learns how to audibly manage, or be overwhelmed by it in the process. Indeed, these sorts of ambient soundscapes tend to produce various forms of audition, as Brian Larkin has astutely pointed out in his discussion of the development of "inattention" in Nigeria,[23] where people move in and out of listening/hearing mode as they traverse the city streets, and it is in such cases that the use of media technology allows for such a soundscape to exist at all. Moreover, it is important to remember that the auditory spaces invoked within this Sufi community here differ from most standard definitions of "an acoustic environment,"[24] due to the fact that the musical sounds conjured in the homes are decidedly intentional as opposed to incidental.

What of the *azan*, the Islamic call to prayer? Could these sounds be seen as a formulation of a kind of *azan* soundscape? The voice of the *mu'azzen*, he who recites the call to prayer, also provides a summoning and signaling to a site, and in this way the *azan* is certainly a listened-for sound. But the *azan* is as predictable and expected as the day is long, it is something that not only marks the moment for prayer but the very passing of the day itself. A sound remarkable for its inevitability, one listens for the *azan* as one waits for the end of the workday.[25] The rhythms of the broadcast of *azan* are thus structured very differently than those of the Sufi-sounds, deeply interwoven into that of the quotidian experience. And it is a noise whose signification is recognizable by all, even by strangers in the city. When it is not there, it is a sign of serious disruption. When the Sufi sounds are not there, only a select few will notice.

Expansive Potential of the Sound-Space

"When you are focusing on trying to find the meeting place, you know the source of the music, you experience the neighborhood in a different way," said Bita. I asked my interlocutors to describe the experience of wandering around, listening for the sounds and trying to locate the source. Some, like Bita, noticed that they viewed the alleyways and streets in a different light. I am also reminded of Babak's earlier statement: "It's not always the easiest way, but it's the most engaged, and allows you to connect to your surroundings."

Others, like Nickoo, said they remained hyperaware of the sound, and tended to ignore the surroundings. "I'm concentrating so much on the sound, it's kind of like the neighborhood is irrelevant." Fatima chimed in, "Yes, it's like I'm not even seeing it [the place]. It's like when listening becomes the primary sense, it doesn't even matter what you see." Clearly, here it is the ear that leads, and the eye follows. In both sets of experiences—becoming hyperaware of their surroundings or becoming irrelevant of their surroundings—it is clear that a transformation of the experience of the space occurs. When you experience a place primarily through listening, there are certain challenges and opportunities that present themselves. Gone are the fixed boundaries of the visual landscapes, replaced with a mutable and, in this case, temporary entity.

Theories of auditory space abound, both inside and outside the Islamic tradition. In 1973, Marshall McLuhan, who, along with Edward Carpenter, was one of the first to write about acoustic space, observed that "auditory space has no point of favored focus. It's a sphere without fixed boundaries, space made by the thing itself, not space containing the thing."[26] To begin to understand the experience of an auditory space, one must also consider the material nature of sound itself, or sound as a tangible, corporeal phenomenon, one that is substantial enough and significant enough to encompass and relegate an entire spatial horizon. Sound remains in flux and in motion, an invisible entity composed of a series of vibrations that remain uncontained and unlocatable but still perceptible.

Indeed, the tenuous nature of sound is reaffirmed by its tendency to remain in flux—and thereby constantly in progress and ultimately undefined—at all times. In considering this curious aspect of sound, then, the question might be posed as to how this might affect the *perception* of sound. David Toop proposes the following, framing his argument here in terms of perception, rather than sound itself: "For one thing, each kind of perception bears a fundamentally different relationship to motion and stasis, since sound, contrary to sight, presupposes movement from the outset . . . sound by its very nature necessarily implies a displacement or agitation, however minimal."[27] In other words, because sound as a phenomenon exists in such an ephemeral, transitional state, it may be argued that its existence relies more on perception than a static object that may be viewed visually.[28] Thus, emerging from the mutable constitution of sound is the particular importance of perception *within the establishment of the soundscape.*

In considering the idea of the hearing act as a mode of inquisition into the realm of the vanishing, how might this then apply to this Sufi community of Isfahan? At the most fundamental level, it is important to remember that the vast majority of the musical performances occur in the evening. In this sense, the auditory declarations of the audible landscape of Isfahan might only be heard during the evening hours, such that were one to listen for them during the day they would be greeted only with the everyday sounds of the residential neighborhoods. Thus to hear this soundscape is to capture a temporary entity, one made available only for approximately thirty minutes, leaving the listener doubting whether they might have heard anything at all. It becomes an unknown space even for those who have created it.

Consequently, it may be said that, although through its very activation the sonic is able to overtake or arguably even create its own space, these auditory vibrations are similarly shaped and affected by the physical boundaries that they confront. The volume, too, is of tantamount importance: loud enough to be heard by passersby, but not loud enough to draw unwanted attention, set at just that level to be audible for those who might be listening for it.

And so sound emerges here as the shape-shifter, forever altering its form, oftentimes mimicking the spaces around it, those spaces of containment, but ultimately remaining formless. It would appear, then, that perhaps auditory space is not necessarily invisible, yet rather inherently unrecognizable. A camouflaged architectonics, at once enigmatic and encoded, it strays beyond the totality of comprehension, drawn instead toward the peripheries of the unnamable. In other words, the soundscape is always in disguise. It is in this way too that the paradox of concealment and revealing of the Sufis' strategy occurs: they are hiding in plain sight.

They broadcast their presence in the most literal of terms, announcing their presence to and drawing the attention of anyone who might be in the neighborhood. And yet the sounds are only decipherable to those who understand their significance, remaining hidden in their innocuous form of an audio recording. If it were live music, however, surely, they would draw more attention.

But what might it be like to inhabit such a space? One that seems difficult to recognize, and yet so easily apprehended? Counterintuitively, I would argue that to come upon such an encounter would ultimately result in a feeling of maximal proximity; for when something is placed into question, no choice remains but that of engagement, thereby cementing a fierce reciprocity with the sensorial object, an acute nearness that collapses the inner and the outer, as Julian Henriques articulates: "Acoustic space . . . is a kind of space you are inside as well as outside and it is inside of you as well as you being inside it. In fact with sound it simply does not make sense to think of having an inside and an outside in the way that the visual sensory modality, with its preoccupations with surfaces, restricts us."[29] And so, auditory space continues the phenomenological tendencies of the sensorial event and the listening act that ultimately gives rise to it.

Finally, one last outcome of the auditory space as a desired space is the privatization and personalization of an instance, the broadcasting of music into a neighborhood street, of what is otherwise the public realm. Indeed, upon experiencing the music at hand, a sense of intimacy is created between the recording and the listener, between the individual listener and herself, in this last instance as a result of the introspection/cognition involved in the listening act. In addition, remembering the small size of the group—oftentimes amounting to fewer than a dozen individuals—this was already rendered an unintentionally private space at the outset. Thus, it is this small gathering that is able to transform an already confidential space into one of heightened immediacy. In a way, one is reminded of a quote by Kafka, wherein he writes: "Like a game of tag where the only 'home' is a tree on the far side of the ocean. But why did they set forth from that place?—It is on the coast that the billows crash most fiercely. So narrow a room do they have there, and so unconquerable."[30] In these contested sites, the soundscape gives rise to a space of the utmost vitalism, caught between an exchange of subject and object, remaining impenetrable and unknowing to all but those inhabit it.

Ultimately, the proposition of a silent/secret yet audible landscape begs a paradox: that, in the final scope, this underground aspect of the Sufi community enhances spatial experience rather than reduces it. Inasmuch as it circumscribes a masked arena, it also produces itself as an expanse, one that remains seamless and volatile, indefinite and unbound. Such is the potential contained with an unknowing of place.

In the Islamic Republic of Iran, Islam is being constantly debated, configured, and altered in a seemingly endless number of ways. Although the state maintains clear control of the organization and the image of their own particular narrative, to say that alternative Islamic discourses do not exist is a gross generalization as demonstrated by the young people discussed in this chapter. Moreover, it is to religious ideals and philosophies

FIGURE 5.1 Underground shrine, unnamed for anonymity.

that these Sufis have turned to navigate a moment of interference, inserting seemingly socially irrelevant mystical practices and ideas into the sociopolitical arena.

It is in this way that Sufi space has come into being when mystical ideas met local politics. In some sense, it resembles the formation of a shadow. Just as a shadow is formed when light touches a material object, a reflection and outcome of the relationship and positionality between two distinct phenomena, so too does this particular Sufi space come into being when the mystical imagination confronts the sociopolitical arena of an Iranian city. As shadow (space), it thus contains the possibility to disappear and reappear at the pleasure of the points of interaction, shifting shape and direction in accordance with the angle and potency of the light.

In doing so, this creative navigation of local politics has escaped the binaries of both resistance-acquiescence as well as the transcendent-material. Regarding the former, to say this is a form of resistance would be a misreading of the Sufis' intentions when establishing their unique method of convening; namely, to do something that is fun or cool (*bahal*) and something in the path of Sufism or Sufis (*darvishi, dar tariqa faqiha*). While it is certainly a *response* to an outside authority, and hence entangled in the dynamics of local politics, the nature of their reply is perhaps better categorized as a mode of navigation than the direct and targeted intentions that a resistance might imply. Acquiescence does not fit either, as such a stance would require a cessation of the meetings entirely.

And then there is lightness, and then there is play. In a highly creative endeavor, the Sufis have constructed a space that, if one were to plot it, would consist of a map of different spots throughout the city, each spot being marked by a series of meandering lines, coming together to resemble something close to a blur. Another analysis could have taken this entire endeavor to be a sort of art piece or performance, one played out on the streets of Isfahan. Which begs a question: What does this map of blurry spots mean for the larger socioreligious sphere within Iran? For those outside the confines of this small group, does the group's inventiveness possess any consequence or impact? On a practical level, I think it is safe to say probably very little, as people go about their daily lives, unaware of these goings-on. And yet still . . . the sound is there, asserting itself onto the streets—unassuming as it is, its true purpose masked to all save those searching for it—demonstrating the potential for a transformed city soundscape, even if all that is heard is a modest echo. As Rumi writes: "We all were parts of Adam at one time/In paradise we all have heard these songs/Though clay and water fill us up with doubts/We still remember something of those songs."[31]

Postscript (*Reng*)

Improvisation and Unknowing

> Improvisation: a necessary experimentation with context . . .
> an awareness of playing the potential and possibility of any
> moment with the tools at hand.
>
> DANIEL FISCHLIN AND ERIC PORTER, "IMPROVISATION AND
> GLOBAL SITES OF DIFFERENCE" (2016)

> . . . We have found the traceless and thrown away all traces . . .
>
> RUMI

As mentioned earlier, the music that this small group of Sufis broadcast was by and large "traditional" (*sonati*) or "classical" (*assil*) Iranian music, music that often falls under the category of improvised music. The performances could be rollicking and fast-paced, all percussive frame drums and frenzied stringed santours, or as delicate and gentle-natured as a beguiling flute (*ney*) solo, but all contained at least some element of performance that was not largely predetermined beforehand.

What is improvised music? Often contrasted with composition, improvised music is notoriously difficult to define.[1] While often synonymous with spontaneity or extemporaneity, in the Iranian context at least it would be inaccurate to understand improvisation as a form of performance where the notes and rhythms, melodies and harmonies, are created completely ex nihilo. Musicologist Laudan Nooshin has explored this point more thoroughly and masterfully than anyone, noting how the term "improvised" (*bedaheh navazi*) often fails to capture not only the years and years of training that musicians undergo before becoming proficient and skilled enough to improvise but also the complex musical schematics involved.[2] With this system in mind, we may better understand how even music that is not reliant upon a predetermined score still has an origin point, as Nooshin explains:

> This essentialization of improvisation—treating it as one particular kind of music which is somehow distinct from composition—is problematic for a number of reasons. For one thing, many of its defining elements are not absolute, but relative. For example, much debate has surrounded one of the central defining concepts of improvisation—spontaneity—and in particular the exact meaning of the term, the extent to which particular performances are truly spontaneous, whether spontaneity can be judged from the sound alone, and so on. . . . *Moreover, any "spontaneity" is clearly mediated and shaped through musical and cultural norms, as well as through musicians idiosyncrasies, the physical limitations and possibilities of instruments or voice, interaction with other musicians and the audience, and so forth* (emphasis mine).[3]

In other words, even that which must be created seemingly out of the ether, immediately and in coordination with other musicians (who also do not have a score in front of them), comes into existence formulated by sets of ideas and formulae. This is not to undercut the creativity of the musicians, far from it: I can think of no more difficult task than to create an artwork in real-time, to continually produce and progress onward in the way you deem the most vital without knowing what the very near future holds, to know when to provoke your fellow musicians and when to follow and respond, all in the presence of an audience following your every move.

And so, when considering improvisation, I would offer that we approach it as operating within these multiple registers, arising out of *something* but never wholly predetermined, or if we might turn to Laudan Nooshin once more, "the idea of improvisation as something grounded—as freedom underpinned by knowledge of [the musical system] *radif*."[4] When creating in real time, you move in directions that have not been previously decided upon, paths that have never been trod before (and may never be again), reacting to external forces and cues based on the training you have received and nothing more.

And as we contemplate this improvised music, I would offer the idea of considering improvisation outside of a musical context, to consider what is involved when one must act immediately, to react to one's surroundings without a full understanding of what might result and how things might go. Improvisation is based on a mastery of technique and an immense amount of training and the ability to trust your own instincts, moving forward in real time without having the luxury of thinking things over.

These Sufis of Iran navigate the broader world, these external forces and cues that they encounter, in a similar fashion. They pull not from musical *radifs* but from mystical epistemologies, these systems of thought that are debated, reflected upon, and contemplated so fully so that, one day, they can progress to other modes of thinking, an instinctual, immediate thinking, like the performers of improvised music who can produce art in a way that is distinct from other forms. These are mystics who embrace a form of *ma'rifat* that emphasizes the unknown and inchoate, that knowledge that foregrounds the incomprehensibility of the divine and the limit of human thought. As the improvisers create/perform differently than those operating from a score, so too do these Sufis utilize a distinct form of knowledge that, through its need to question, conceives of thought as a question without answer that moves ever forward, a formless, generative endeavor, moving forward as the improvisers do. As Rumi has said: "Form comes out from Formlessness: Then it returns, for unto Him we are returning."[5] As unknowing dissembles that with which it comes into contact (to unknow something is exactly that, to put the object of one's analysis to question), it lays out no clear path, leaving you no choice but to improvise.

And what of the external factors and elements to which one must respond? Improvisation requires not only a form of moving forward without any clear path in front of you, but also the ability to respond to external stimuli and obstacles in ways they find most vital. For these Sufis, these forces include the shapes of alleyways, the municipal government, discourses of identity politics, ideas of textual authority, an understanding of one's own body, and more: these are just some of the external cues that shape the Sufis' utilization of their epistemologies. The ways they navigate life in contemporary Iran are thus shaped by their epistemologies of disassemblages as well as these forces they encounter.

And so there is movement forward. Through busy thoroughfares and quiet residential streets, via rapid metros and the viselike grip of standstill traffic, during hectic mornings and the slow torpor of the postsiesta afternoon, there is movement. For when all human thought is put to question in an affirmation of the supremacy of God, when all knowledge must be contested, and yet what results is not paralysis but activation . . . there is movement. As one works one's way through the world, improvising and armed with unknowing, a long and sightless walk awaits, pathways formed and unformed, heard and unheard, seen and unseen. . . .

NOTES

Introduction

1. Azmayesh, *Morvarid-e Sufi-gari*, 71.

2. Majzub'alishah, "Sufigari, Shi'igari, Erfan," 15.

3. This translation, with a few modifications of mine, is based on that of Nasrollah Pourjavady. Ghazzali, *Sawanih*, 26–27.

4. A further note on translation: I have translated *ma'rifat* as "non-knowledge" and "unknowing" rather than "gnosis" for a few reasons. First, gnosis itself is an extremely vague term, and one that often requires unpacking. More importantly, the word "gnosis" is derived from "Gnosticism," a collection of beliefs within Hellenistic strains of early Judeo-Christian thought (Aldo, "Free Will According to the Gnostics," 174–95; Thomassen, *The Coherence of "Gnosticism"*; Merkur, *Gnosis*). While there are of course intriguing parallels between Christian and Islamic esotericism, translating *ma'rifat* as "gnosis" risks erasing the specificity of its development within the Islamic tradition. My second reason is that there are thousands of interpretations of what *ma'rifat* entails, some of which may run counter to the ideas espoused in this book, and so I translate *ma'rifat* as unknowing to reaffirm that it is this particular interpretation of *ma'rifat* that is being explored herein. In other words, when I refer to either *ma'rifat* or unknowing in this text, I am referring to that interpretation utilized by my interlocutors unless specified otherwise. Lastly, my choice of "unknowing" is inspired by Georges Bataille's idea of "nonknowledge," which he defines as "the undefinable, what thought cannot conceive . . . everything that is contrary to knowledge," or in other words, that which we do not know, which remains unknown to us. See Bataille, *The Unfinished System of Nonknowledge*, 131. The experience of this "undefined knowledge," however, is distinctly different from the experience of ignorance, as Bataille elaborates further: "When I speak of nonknowledge now, I mean essentially that I know nothing, and if that I am still talking, it is essentially insofar as I have a knowledge that brings me to nothing" (Bataille, *The Unfinished System of Nonknowledge*, 140). I have also utilized the gerund form to highlight the experiential nature of Sufi knowledge, reaffirming the way it operates as an active and participatory mode of thinking.

5. I avoid the term "Iranian Sufism" because this would imply a holistic study into Sufism in *all* its current manifestations, including groups like the Kurdish Sunni Orders, and I want to be clear that my manuscript does not claim to represent all mystical collectives and/or strains of thoughts that exist within Iran today.

6. Mittermaier, *Dreams that Matter*; Taneja, *Jinnealogy*; Doostdar, *The Iranian Metaphysicals*; Pandolfo, *Knot of the Soul*, 191.

7. Pandolfo, *Knot of the Soul*, 240.

8. I follow Devin Deweese's definition of a Sufi order as a group of initiated members who follow a single religious authority, and who can trace their organization back through a chain of authority figures to an original founding member (Deweese, "'Dis-ordering' Sufism in Early Modern Central Asia" and "Organizational Patterns and Developments within Sufi Communities"). Orders have often been closed to the public and/or nonmembers, but that tended not to be my experience in Iran.

9. According to the 2008 Library of Congress Country Profile, Iran's demographic was 65 percent Persian, 16 percent Azeri Turk, 7 percent Kurd, 6 percent Lur, 2 percent Arab, 2 percent Baluchi, 1 percent Turkmen, 1 percent Qashai, and less than 1 percent Armenian, Assyrian, and Georgian.

10. This includes an acceptance and reverence for the twelve Imams of Twelver (Ithna-ashari) Shi'ism, belief in ideas such as divine justice (*adalat*), *velayat* (authority), *ijtihad* (legal reasoning) adherence to all Shi'i holidays, veneration of saints, prayer formations, and more. For works that provide an overview of Twelver as well as Zaydi and Ismaili Shi'ism in English, see the works of Najam Haidar, *The Origins of the Shi'a* and *Shi'i Islam*, and Amir-Moezzi, *The Spirituality of Shi'i Islam*.

11. For more discussions of how to define an order, see Deweese, "'Dis-ordering' Sufism," and "Organizational Patterns and Developments"; Ernst and Lawrence, *Sufi Martyrs of Love*; Green, "Emerging Approaches to the Sufi Traditions of South Asia," 123–48; Green, *Sufism*.

12. Kiani, *Tarikhe Khanegha Dar Iran*; Abisaab, *Converting Persia*; Connell, *The Nimatullahi Sayyids of Taft*; Lewisohn, "An Introduction to the History of Modern Persian Sufism, Part I," 437–64; Zarrinkub, *Jostojou dar tassavof-e Iran*; Nurbakhsh, *Masters of the Path*.

13. Doostdar, *The Iranian Metaphysicals*.

14. Haeri, *Say What Your Longing Heart Desires*, 144–45.

15. These included:*Sufism: Meaning, Knowledge, Unity; Ma'arifa Sufiya; Sufi Symbolism*, Vol. 8, *Insations, Revelations, Lights*.

16. Haeri, *Say What Your Longing Heart Desires*; Shams, *A Revolution in Rhyme*; Manoukian, *City of Knowledge in Twentieth Century Iran*; Olszewska, *The Pearl of Dari*; Fischer, *Mute Dreams, Blind Owls, and Dispersed Knowledges*; Fischer and Abedi, *Debating Muslims*.

17. Prior to 1979 the seminaries were famously not state run (although it might be argued they had a certain copacetic relationship with the Shah), and one was able to study

mysticism with a teacher, sometimes in a formal classroom setting, sometimes in private lessons. See Fischer, *Iran*, for more on the history of the Qom seminary in twentieth-century Iran. Today there are both state-run and independent seminaries, with *tasavvuf* debated and discussed in both.

18. Walbridge, *The Most Learned of the Shia*; Fischer, *Iran*; Asghari, "Islamic Philosophy and Sufism in the Contemporary Shia Seminary and Their Opponents (1850–present)."

19. Majzub'alishah, "Sufigari, Shi'igari, Erfan," 18.

20. Mittermaier, "Dreams from Elsewhere," 249.

21. Pandolfo, *Knot of the Soul*.

22. Manoukian, "Thinking with the Impersonal," 212.

23. *Hu* refers to an invocation of the name of God, a shortened version of Allah-Hu, and is often used as a declarative during moments of emotional intensity.

24. The idea that existence is marked by an interplay between the Real and the Unreal is not exclusive to Nimatullahi Sufism but is a widely discussed conceptual matrix analyzed by such luminaries of mystical thought as al-Ghazzali, Ibn Arabi, Rumi, and many others.

25. Lévi-Strauss, *Tristes Tropiques*.

26. Boyarin, *The Ethnography of Reading*, 6. An early proponent of situating the project of ethnography at the nexus between anthropology, literary studies, and critical theory, in his work Boyarin has tackled how thought processes and thinking through reading might be understood as a form of human "practice."

27. Fischer and Abedi, *Debating Muslims*; Messick, *The Calligraphic State* and *Shari'a Scripts*.

28. See Fabian, *Out of Our Minds*; Mittermaier, "The Book of Visions," 229–47.

29. See Hull, *Government of Paper*; Das and Poole, "Anthropology in the Margins of the State," 140–44; Gupta, *Red Tape*.

30. See Rosen, "Ethnographies of Reading," 1059–83.

31. Manoukian, *City of Knowledge*, 205.

32. Absent from this discussion is the obfuscation of meaning within Persian poetry for reasons *outside* the Sufi tradition. The employment of rhetorical devices like metaphor (*est'areh*), simile (*tashbih*), figurative speech (*majaz*), and analogy (*tamthil*)—all tropes that may be said to "hide" meaning—is an essential skill of any sophisticated writer. Indeed, the field of classical Persian literary theory is a rich and well-developed discipline, and for some literary theorists such as Jurjani (d. 1078) and Mohammad al-Raduyani (d. 1100), the more complicated and obtuse the wordplay, the better. As Seyed-Gohrab has written, however, the employment of these tropes were valued not only for their originality and sophistication, but because they provided "puzzles" for their audiences to unravel, a chance for the erudite reader to demonstrate their analytical skills and engage with the poem on a deeper level as they would solve the riddle behind the words

(Seyed-Gohrab, ed., *Metaphor and Imagery in Persian Poetry*). I would argue that there is a stark difference between such valorization of metaphor/obscured meaning as a puzzle to be resolved and what the Sufis would believe: namely, that obscured meanings are there not to be solved but to allow for further—nay, endless—opportunities for engagement.

33. Haeri, *Say What Your Longing Heart Desires*; Fischer, *Mute Dreams, Blind Owls*.

34. The distinction between a Sufi philosopher and a Sufi poet is not necessarily an easy one to make. Here, I base the distinction on the different written forms employed by the two groups as the key determining factor.

35. Junayd Baghdadi and Ahmad Ghazzali are considered sheikhs of the order and, given their prolific output, are hence a natural reference for the sheikhs. Ibn Arabi, a self-identified Sunni from Al-Andalus and perhaps one of the most influential and widely read Sufis of all time, is more curious. His popularity is due not only to the widespread analysis of his writings in Iran at the time, particularly for the jurists of the School of Isfahan, but also that Shah Nimatullah Vali, the namesake of the order, in fact translated Ibn Arabi's masterwork, *Bezels of Wisdom* (*Fusus al-Hikam*), into Persian and commented upon it (see Nasr, *Sufi Essays*).

36. Tamimi Arab, "A Minaret of Light," 136–63. Lee, "Technology and the Production of Islamic Space," 86–100.

37. Hirschkind, *The Ethical Soundscape*.

38. Hirschkind, "Hearing Modernity"; Larkin, "Techniques of Inattention," 989–1015; Khan, "The Acoustics of Muslim Striving," 571–94; Spadola, *The Calls of Islam*.

39. Erlmann, "But What of the Ethnographic Ear?," 1–20; Bull and Back, eds., *The Auditory Culture Reader*.

40. Clifford, "Introduction: Partial Truths," 12.

41. Attali, *Noise*.

42. Taussig, *Mimesis and Alterity*.

43. Deleuze, *Difference and Repetition*, xix.

Chapter One. Sufism in Iran, Iran in Sufism

1. Doostdar, *Iranian Metaphysicals*.

2. Safi, *The Politics of Knowledge in Premodern Islam*.

3. Babayan, *Mystics, Monarchs, and Messiahs*.

4. Megan Specia, "Who Are Sufi Muslims and Why Do Some Extremists Hate Them?" *New York Times*, Nov. 17, 2017.

5. The Safavids date back to Safi-ad-din Ardaabil (d. 1334), who transformed the Zahediya Sufi Order to bear his name. It was only when Shakyh Junayd assumed leadership in 1447

that they turned to vying for political power at all, until the Safavid Shah Ismaili took power, beating out several rival groups in the wake of the collapse of Timur. Melville, *Safavid Persia*.

6. Bayat, *Mysticism and Dissent*; De Jong and Radtke, *Islamic Mysticism Contested*.

7. Arjomand, *The Shadow of God and the Hidden Imam*; Bayat, *Mysticism and Dissent*.

8. Chahardahi, *Selsel-ehha-yi Ṣufiyah-e Iran*.

9. Anzali, "*Mysticism*" in Iran.

10. I should note that Anzali's theory is in contrast to that of Zarrinkub, one of the preeminent historians of Sufism in Iran. In his classic 1972 work, *Iranian Sufism in Historical Perspective*, Zarrinkub argues that the disdain for the category of *sufigari* arises because of Iranians' inherent dislike for organized Sufism, therein eschewing *sufigari* for the more dispersed phenomenon of *erfan*. Zarrinkub, alongside other figures like literary historian Shafi'i Kadkani, also use *erfan* and *tasavvuf* interchangeably, failing to note a serious difference between the terms. See Zarrinkub, *Tassavof-i irani dar manzare tarkhie-an*; Shafi'i Kadkani, *Advar-e shehr-e farsi*.

11. Corbin, *En Islam Iranian*, vol. 1, *Le Shî'isme duodécimain*; Corbin, *The Voyage and the Messenger*; Nasr, "Philosophy in Islam," 57–80.

12. Corbin, "Confessions extatiques de Mir Damad," 331–78, and "La place de Molla Sadra Shiraza dans la philosophie iranienne," 81–113; Nasr, "The School of Iṣpahān," 904–32; Anari, *Maktab-e Eṣfahan dar šahr-sāzi*. See also Khatami, *From a Sadraean Point of View*.

13. As Knysh points out, Ibn Arabi never used "*wahdat al-wujud*" himself but is largely credited with the phrase. Knysh, "'Irfan' Revisited," 631–53.

14. Indeed, there were some groups that were vying for political power. Remember that the Safavid themselves arose out of a Sufi order that then turned its attention to the political realm. See Abisaab, *Converting Persia*.

15. Van Den Bos, *Mystic Regimes*.

16. Yazdi, "Irfan va Hikmat."

17. Sabzavari, *Shahr-I Mazuma*.

18. Algar, "The Fusion of the Gnostic and Politics in the Life of Imam Khomeini."

19. Knysh, "'Irfan' Revisited," 631–53.

20. Knysh, "'Irfan' Revisited," 634.

21. Ruhollah Khomeini, *Misbaḥ al-hidaya ila al-khilafa wa al-wilaya*.

22. Fischer, *Iran*, 242.

23. Knysh, "'Irfan' Revisited," 651.

24. A series of five televised lectures broadcast from December 1979 to January 1980; see Khomeini, *Islam and Revolution*.

25. Khomeini, *Islam and Revolution*, 365.

26. Khomeini, *Islam and Revolution*, 366.

27. Najafian, "Poetic Nation."

28. According to Najafian, what is available from Khomeini's poetry is from two eras: the love poems (*ghazals*) he wrote as a young man, and the poetry he composed in the late 1980s during the final period of his life. The fifty-five years' worth of poetry he composed in between, however, remains lost, or at least unpublished.

29. The translations are credited to Dr. Ghulam Reza Avani.

30. Tihrani, *Shining Sun*.

31. Ehteshami and Rizvi, "Beyond the Letter," 443–60.

32. Tihrani, *Shining Sun*, 70.

33. Asghari, "Islamic Philosophy and Sufism in the Contemporary Shia Seminary and their Opponents (1850–present)."

34. Tihrani, *Ruh-e Mujarrad*.

35. Vakili goes into detail about this on his personal website: https://mhva.ir/about/. The site is titled "Shaykh Mohammad Hassan Vakil: The Source for Information on the Hojjat-al Islam al-Muslameen (Shaykh Mohammad Hassan Vakil: Paygha Etelaat Resani Hojjatalislam al-Muslameen)." It houses a number of Ostad Hojjat al-eslam Vakili's publications, links to purchase his books, audio, and visual recordings of his various sermons and lectures, his biography, and links to his social media accounts.

36. Vakili, *Mohayaldin; Shi'i Khales*. See also Vakili, *Maktab-I Tafkiki: Tarikh va Naqd*.

37. See Ashtiyani, "Naqd-i Tahafut-i Ghazzāli." For an introduction to his work, see Ashtiyani, *Erfan*. For more on the anti-Sufi Tafkiki school, see Rizvi, "'Only the Imam Knows Best,'" 487–503.

38. For more on Amoli's views on everything from jurisprudence to the role of Mahdism in the contemporary, see the website of his foundation, the Esra International Foundation of Revelatory Sciences, http://javadi.esra.ir/home.

39. "Vijegi-haye Erfani-e Imam Khomeini Az Manzar-e Ayatollah Javadi Amoli," http://javadi.esra.ir/-/ های-عرفان-امام-خمینی-قدس-سره-از-منظر-ایت-الله-جوادی-آملی. The official website of Ayatollah Javadi Amoli features recordings of his sermons, his latest statements, ways to contact his office, and of course his writings.

40. http://javadi.esra.ir/-/ معرفت-عرفان-شناسی،-حقیقی-شهود-ذات-است-بین-خدا-و-خلق-هیچ-حجابی خلق-خود-مگر-نیست.

41. For more, see the work of Odabaei, "The Outside (Kharij) of Tradition in the Aftermath of the Revolution," 296–311, and "Giving Words."

42. Haeri, *Say What Your Longing Heart Desires*.

43. Doostdar, *Iranian Metaphysicals*, 3.

44. Doostdar, *Iranian Metaphysicals*, 149–51.

45. Doostdar, *Iranian Metaphysicals*, 153.

46. Shams, *A Revolution in Rhyme*, 189.

47. Shams, *A Revolution in Rhyme*, 202.

48. Shams, *A Revolution in Rhyme*, 194.

49. Shams, *A Revolution in Rhyme*, 194.

50. Hazrat Nur'Ali often added a caveat to labeling Shah Nimatullah Vali as the "founder" of the order for, despite it bearing his name, Nur'Ali claimed that the real founder was in fact Imam Ali, the son-in-law of the prophet Muhammad.

51. Anonymous, *Zendigename Shah Nimatullahi Vali*.

52. Another theory holds that the Nimatullahi Sufis of Iran felt disconnected from their spiritual leader in the Deccan, prompting them to request a representative be sent from India. See Pourjavady and Wilson, "Isma'ilis and Ni'matullahis," 113–35, for more on this period.

53. Indeed, Shah Nimatullah and his successors were Sunni. In subsequent years, the Nimatullahi would explain this small fact away by noting that (1) Shah Nimatullah recognized Imam Ali as the beginning of the chain of succession (*silsileh*), thereby providing enough evidence for Shi'i qualifications according to later *qotbs*; and (2) Shah Nimatullahi also traced his own lineage back to Imam Musa Kazem, the seventh Shi'i Imam, giving him the status of *seyed* (or descendent of the prophet), to further pad his Shi'i bona fides.

54. Tabandeh, "The Rise of Nimatullahi Shi'ite Sufism," 126–43.

55. Mottahadeh, *The Mantle of the Prophet*; Momen, *An Introduction to Shi'i Islam*; Cole, *Sacred Space and Holy War*.

56. Tabandeh, "The Rise of Nimatullahi Shi'ite Sufism," 165. See also Tabandeh, *The Rise of the Ni'matullāhī Order*.

57. Rizvi, "Before the Safavid-Ottoman Conflict," 113–26.

58. Anonymous, *Zendigename Shah Nimatullahi Vali*.

59. Shirwani, *Kashf al-Ma'arif*.

60. Tabandeh, "The Rise of Nimatullahi Shi'ite Sufism," 240.

61. Chahardahi, *Selsel-ehha-yi Sufiyah-e Iran*; Van Den Bos, *Mystic Regimes*, 77.

62. Cancian, "'I'm Only a Village Farmer and a Dervish,'" 136–38.

63. Van Den Bos, *Mystic Regimes*, 88.

64. Van Den Bos, *Mystic Regimes*, 87; Saleh Ali Shah, *Pand-e Saleh*, 7.

65. Van Den Bos, *Mystic Regimes*, 89.

66. Kasravi, *Sufigari*.

67. Van Den Bos, *Mystic Regimes*, 122.

68. Eilers, "Educational and Cultural Development in Iran During the Pahlavi Era," 310–31.

69. Eilers, "Educational and Cultural Development in Iran During the Pahlavi Era," 303–31; Lewisohn, "An Introduction to the History of Modern Persian Sufism, Part II," 36–59.

70. Reza-Ali Shah, *Nazar-e mazhabi be e'lamiye-ye huquq-e bashar*, 48.

71. The term was coined by Ahmad Fardid and made popular through the highly influential 1962 essay of the same name by Jalal Al-e Ahmad.

72. The story is also recounted in a 1994 sermon of Mahbub Ali Shah. See also Van Den Bos, *Mystic Regimes*, 141.

73. Mahbub Ali Shah, *Khorshid-e Tabande*, 81.

74. Van Den Bos, *Mystic Regimes*, 156.

75. Given the number of assassinations that occurred in the years following the revolution, there were unfortunately plenty of opportunities for such activities; see Dabashi, *Theology of Discontent*; Keddie, *Modern Iran*.

76. Constitution of the Islamic Republic of Iran, Article 13, Section 1, "General Principles."

77. Despite this legal recognition, these groups have at times faced difficulties, especially in regard to inheritance laws and public ceremonies. For more see Sanasarian, *Religious Minorities in Iran*, vol. 13.

78. The Twelver Ja'fari school, the official religion of Iran, is a form of Shi'i Islam. It is so named because of its recognition of the twelve Imams who claim lineage to Imam Ali, the son-in-law of the Prophet Muhammad, and refers to the influential sixth Imam, Jafar al-Sadeq.

79. Constitution of the Islamic Republic of Iran, Article 12, Section 1, "General Principles."

80. Momen and Smith, "The Baha'i Faith 1957–1988," 63–91.

81. Tavakoli-Targhi, "Refashioning Iran," 77–101; Keddie, *Modern Iran*. Others have refuted these claims: Momen, *An Introduction to Shi'i Islam*, 2004.

82. Van Den Bos, *Mystic Regimes*.

83. For more, see Hermann and Rezai, "Constitution en vaqf d'une 'mosquée sanctuaire' ne'matollāhī à Téhéran à l'époque pahlavī," 293–306.

84. The practice of using residential spaces for religious ceremonies organized by lay people, without the help of any official channels or clergymen, is extremely common among Iranians and is certainly not exclusive to Sufis. It is more often used for *azadari* (mourning or lamentation) or *roozekhaneh* (literally house of prayer). Typically, it is owned by a person of some wealth, one who is able to afford an extra house or apartment, and then is used by a wide network of family and friends. In certain instances, the house that children may inherit from parents may be used for *mahdaviye*. More often than not, however, these ceremonies are simply held in people's own homes, the complaints of

neighbors notwithstanding. The name *mahdaviye* is derived from the name of the twelfth and final Imam, Imam Mehdi, so that it means literally "place of Mehdi."

85. The word *fozul* translates as both adjective and noun, "nosy" and "busybody," usually indicating a harmless, if irritating, person. Sometimes, however, as in the usage here, it is meant to suggest something a bit more sinister, an individual who may report any sort of activity they may deem suspicious to a wide array of authorities, most likely the Ershad or Komiteh, both official policing bodies that monitor "un-Islamic activities."

86. I was asked not to reveal this line. In decades past, the particular quatrain changed from week to week, but the practice eventually became too complicated.

87. This is the honorific most commonly used to address the spiritual leader. The word *hazrat*, Arabic for "presence," is used often in reference to the twelve Imams and other holy figures, i.e., Hazrat Zahra. When used here, it can be translated as roughly "His Presence," the word "agha" meaning "sir" or "mister."

88. This is significant as it marks a distinction from the dress of the clerical establishment, who wear both the brown robe and the turban to mark their clerical status. Tellingly, the Sufi sheikhs and *pir*s have voluntarily stopped wearing the *ammameh* during the past twenty years in order to demonstrate their distinction from the clerics.

Chapter Two. Unknowing of Text, Unknowing of Authority

1. For more on modern *doreh* circles, see Haeri, *Say What Your Longing Heart Desires*; Tawasil, "The Howzevi (Seminarian) Women in Iran"; Osanloo, *The Politics of Women's Rights in Iran*.

2. Imam Jafar al-Sadeq is a key historical figure in many Sufi and Shi'i discourses, and, among other things, is known for emphasizing the idea of political quietism and esotericism within Shi'ism. For more see Amir-Moezzi, *The Divine Guide in Early Shi'ism*.

3. For more, see Lewisohn, *The Heritage of Sufism*.

4. Kiani, *Tarikhe Khanegha Dar Iran*.

5. Van Den Bos, *Mystic Regimes*; Anzali, *"Mysticism" in Iran*.

6. Green, *Sufism*; Ridgeon, *Morals and Mysticism in Persian Sufism*; Karamustafa, *Sufism*.

7. Odabaei, "Giving Words."

8. As previously mentioned, Sheikh Noroozi is part of a very extensive tradition of Sufis who advocate for thinking beyond the intellect and there are strains of more esoterically inclined Shi'i *tafsir* where one can find similar sentiments. For example, the idea of learning through *kashf*, which is typically translated as unveiling but can also operate as a form of epistemology. And Sayyed Haydar Amoli argues for a spiritual unveiling (*kashf ma 'navi*) as a means to bypass the limitations of the intellect and reality, and it is only through this bypassing that one is able to comprehend the divine (Amoli, *Jami' al-asrar wa-manba' al-anwar lil-ma'arif al-muta'llih al-wali*). Allameh Tabatabai has also

written on the concept of *kashf*, and Sajjad Rizvi has intriguingly translated Tabatabai's understanding of *kashf* as "inner revelation," suggesting a type of awareness that comes (as in a revelation) to oneself in such a way that it was not consciously summoned. (Rizvi, "Striving Beyond the Balance [*al-Mizan*]," 65). More specifically, Rizvi describes how, in Tabatabai's *Risalat al-Walayat*, "The epistemological hierarchy is clear, and follows in ascending order: the senses, the intellect, inner revelation (*kashf*) and vision (*shuhud*). Tabatabai then cites numerous Qur'anic verses and hadiths that support his contention" ("Striving Beyond the Balance [*al-Mizan*]," 65). I highlight both these examples to note that the idea of thinking beyond the intellect does not operate only within Sufi circles. The resonances between *kashf* and the inner heart, as well as other concepts like intuition à la al-Ghazali, surely require further attention.

9. Golestaneh, "'Text and Contest'," 197–224.

10. The wandering mystic Shams encountered Rumi in Konya in AD 1244. According to a number of Sufi traditions, after they spent a number of years together, Shams departed Konya suddenly under mysterious conditions. Rumi was anguished at the loss of Shams from his life, and continued to attribute much of his poetry to Shams, even many years after his muse and mentor's departure. See Lewis, *Rumi—Past and Present, East and West*; Chittick, *The Sufi Doctrine of Rumi*.

11. This is a reference to a verse from the eleventh-century poet Baba Taher.

12. To provide just one example, in her discussion of Sufi exegesis as a form of mirroring, where the content of the Qur'an may only be revealed/unveiled when the reader is pure of heart, Annabel Keeler has described how it is the force of the ideas that command and shape the readings. Keeler, "Sufi Tafsir as a Mirror," 1–21. See also Knysh, "Sufism and the Quran," 137–59; Godlas, "Sufism," 418–29; and Böwering, *The Mystical Vision of Existence in Classical Islam*.

13. Many have claimed that theses *ayas* were included to distinguish the Qur'an from pre-Islamic forms of Arabic poetry, especially the odes. Bateson, *Structural Continuity in Poetry*.

14. Analyzing Qur'anic references within Islamic poetry is a task without end, so much so that the best approach would be to look to the studies of individual poets to better understand. I would particularly recommend looking to non-English sources in this instance, with the works of Allameh Tabatabai on Hafez being a particularly rich source.

15. Perhaps the most prolific cataloger of Sufi Qur'anic hermeneutics is Gerard Böwering, who categorizes the development of this genre into five separate periods: (1) the era of the "precursors," individuals like Imam Jafar al-Sadeq, (2) the era of al-Sulami, (3) the era of institutionalized Sufism, (4) Persianate and non-Arab Sufism, and (5) the era of Sufism in "decline." I must admit I find this categorization problematic for a number of reasons, not only because it supports the "rise and fall" motive of "Islamic civilization," but because of the Arabic-centric nature of its positioning. For other works on Sufi Qur'anic Hermeneutics, see Keeler et al., *The Spirit and the Letter*; Cancian, *Approaches to the Qur'an in Contemporary Iran*, which contains excellent contemporary Sufi Qur'anic tafsir as well; and Cancian, "Translation, Authority and Exegesis in Modern Iranian Sufism."

16. Jamal Elias has thoughtfully countered this idea of Sufi *tafsir* as a genre unto itself, arguing that such an idea does not critically investigate what is meant both by the term "Sufi" and the term "genre." Instead, he advocates for these esoterically inclined commentaries to be considered in light of their contemporaries, especially given the fact that many of these Sufis cited many non-Sufis' works in their writings, rather than being forced into a potentially more ahistorical and overdetermined Sufi genre. Elias, "Sufi Tafsir Reconsidered."

17. It is also sometimes translated as "inner meaning of the esoteric meaning" (Steigerwald, "Twelver Shiʿi Taʾwil," 449); or "esoteric of the esoteric" (Andani, "A Survey of Ismaili Studies, Part 1," 191–206).

18. Elias, "Sufi Tafsir Reconsidered."

19. Elias, "Sufi Tafsir Reconsidered," 48.

20. Both have written extensively on Hallaj.

21. Mittermaier, *Dreams That Matter.*

22. Bachelard, *Poetics of Space,* 15.

23. Haleem, *The Qurʾan,* 34.

24. Golestaneh, "Text and Contest."

25. Ricoeur, "The Model of the Text," 108.

26. Kant, *Critique of Judgement.*

27. Ahmed, *What Is Islam?,* 283.

28. Ahmed, *What Is Islam?,* 284.

Chapter Three. Unknowing of Self, Unknowing of Body

1. Böwering disputes this. Bistami's writings are quite limited, but his influence is outsized, and he is cited by many prolific writers such as Attar, Sarraj, and others.

2. Losensky translation in Sells, *Early Islamic Mysticism,* 234.

3. Torab, "Piety as Gendered Agency," 235–52; Haeri, "The Private Performance of 'Salat' Prayers," 5–34.

4. The beggar's bowl, or *kashkul,* was carried by wandering mystics in Iran. *Kashkuls* are legible to both Sufis and non-Sufis as being emblematic of mysticism, and are used to connote devotion to a life of spiritual and material poverty.

5. Sells, *Early Islamic Mysticism,* 240.

6. Keeler, *Sufi Hermeneutics.*

7. Nurbakhsh, "Sufism and Psychoanalysis," 211–12.

8. Azmayesh, *Morvarid-e Sufi-gari,* 24.

9. Ernst, *Words of Ecstasy in Sufism*; Ernst, *Hallaj*.

10. Abdel-Kader, *The Life, Personality and Writings of Al-Junayd*, 84; emphasis added.

11. See Maybudi, Sarraj, among others.

12. Sells, *Early Islamic Mysticism*, 240.

13. Tabatabai, Allameh, *Risalat-e Wilayat*.

14. Slightly complicating matters is the fact that many Iranians, Sufi and non-Sufi, will actually visit graves of saints in order to ask for their children to receive good grades, even if for Setare and Sara such a request would fall into the "insignificant" category.

15. I should also note that, to my knowledge, the phrase "the heart of God" (*del-e khoda*) is not a common one with Sufi thought, Persian poetry, or really any mystical literature at all. Although I may be mistaken, there is a chance it is a phrase of Minoo's own devising or a slight malapropism.

16. Although radio became available to private homes in the 1940s, many households, if not the majority, still did not have one. See Mokhtari-Isfahani, *Sargozasht-e Radio Dar Iran beh Revayat-e Esnaad* .

17. Al-e Ahmad, *Gharb-zadagi*. For more on Al-e Ahmad's influence see Boroujerdi, "Gharbzadegi"; Dabashi, *Theology of Discontent*; Gheissari, *Iranian Intellectuals in the Twentieth Century*. Though popularized by Al-e Ahmad, the term was coined by Ahmad Fardid.

18. Vahdat, "Return to Which Self?," 55–71.

19. A lecture entitled "Bazgasht bi Khishtan" ("Return to Self"), two articles in the newspaper *Kayan*, "Bazgasht bi Khish" ("Return to Self"), and an article entitled "Bazghasht bi Kodoom Khish" ("Return to Which Self"), all available in Shariati, *Nivishtah'i Ali Shariati*, 4.

20. Rahnema, *An Islamic Utopian*; Ghamari-Tabrizi, "Contentious Public Religion," 504–23.

21. Shariati, *Nivishtah'i Ali Shariati*, 4.

22. Shariati, *Vares-I Adam*, 215.

23. Davari, "A Return to Which Self?," 103.

24. Davari "A Return to Which Self?," 89.

25. Khanlarzadeh, "Theology of Revolution," 504.

26. Khanlarzadeh, "Theology of Revolution," 505.

27. Ghamari-Tabrizi, *Foucault in Iran*, 91. For more on Shariati and mysticism see also Ghamari-Tabrizi, "Moderneti Erfaani" and Rahnema, *An Islamic Utopian*.

28. Golestaneh, "'To Be Transformed into Thought Itself.'"

29. Golestaneh, "'To Be Transformed into Thought Itself.'"

30. Odabaei, "The Outside (Kharij) of Tradition"; Bajoghli, *Iran Reframed*. Of course, there are many individuals within Iran, inside and outside the political establishment,

who would shake their heads at the "shallowness" of the young population, decrying them as social media addicts and the like, and there have been several cases tying this to Western influence, but as a whole it is very different.

31. Numerologically, 121 "translates" into "Help me [Imam] Ali."

32. al-Ghazzali, "On Listening to Music," 17.

33. al-Ghazzali, "On Listening to Music."

34. At this juncture, one might suggest a separate study of the various forms of listening within Islamic practice in light of this unique instance of Sufi audition within the *zekr* ritual. In particular, the role of audition within the pedagogical tradition (see Messick, *The Calligraphic State*); the sermon tradition (see Hirschkind, *The Ethical Soundscape*); or even the original revelation of the Qu'ran might prove compelling points of comparison. In addition, I would like to reassert that al-Ghazzali is not offering a definitive type of listening with this quote—indeed, he goes to great lengths to delineate several forms of "unlawful listening" within "On Listening to Music"—but is in fact positing that, in certain contexts, audition contains this imaginative potential.

35. al-Ghazzali, "On Listening to Music," 26.

36. al-Ghazzali, "On Listening to Music," 29.

37. al-Ghazzali, "On Listening to Music," 12.

38. al-Ghazzali, "On Listening to Music," 22.

39. Nurbakhsh, *Sufi Symbolism*, 3:189.

40. al-Ghazzali, "On Listening to Music," 20.

41. al-Ghazzali, "On Listening to Music," 11.

42. al-Ghazzali, "On Listening to Music," 22.

43. Netton, *Sufi Ritual*, 35.

44. Schimmel, *Mystical Dimensions of Islam*, 172.

45. Shannon, *Among the Jasmine Trees*, 122.

46. Derrida, *Positions*; Dabashi, *Truth and Narrative*.

47. Deleuze, *Pure Immanence*; Deleuze and Guatarri, *A Thousand Plateaus*.

48. Shannon, *Among the Jasmine Trees*, 118.

49. Schimmel, *Mystical Dimensions of Islam*, 168.

50. Asad, *Genealogies of Religion*; Hirschkind, *The Ethical Soundscape*; Mahmood, "Rehearsed Spontaneity and the Conventionality of Ritual," 827–53.

51. Bell, *Ritual*.

52. Asad, "Interview with Saba Mahmood."

53. While Asad might take issue with positing Sufism as a distinct epistemological mode of thought, having criticized the way in which Sufi and Salafi modes of thought are often

put in opposition to one another (see Mahmood, "Interview with Talal Asad"), he himself does offer the following distinction: "I think that most Salafi reformers would be critical of Sufism when it transgressed one of the basic doctrines of Islam: the separation between God and human beings. I've heard criticism of Sufi practices that seemed to imply the possibility of complete union with God as opposed to the possibility of complete openness to God. I think that that is the crucial point for many people who are critical of Sufism." (Mahmood, "Interview with Talal Asad.")

54. al-Rumi in Trimingham, *The Sufi Orders of Islam*, 80.

55. My use of the term "mimesis" is based upon the definition set forth by Michael Taussig in *Mimesis and Alterity*, where he describes it as "the faculty to copy, imitate, make models, explore difference, yield into and become Other. The wonder of mimesis lies in the copy drawing on the character and power of the original, to the point whereby the representation may even assume that character and that power" (xiii). And while Taussig discusses the mimetic faculty as occurring between disparate cultures in a postcolonial context, I would offer here that the "Other" in question might be understood to be God or, more specifically, the experience of God.

56. Azmayesh, *Morvarid-e Sufi-gari*, 34.

57. Azmayesh, *Morvarid-e Sufi-gari*, 29.

58. Azmayesh, *Morvarid-e Sufi-gari*, 38.

59. Taussig, *What Color is the Sacred?*, 14.

60. Azmayesh, *Morvarid-e Sufi-gari*, 89–90.

61. Taussig, *Mimesis and Alterity*, 53.

62. Azmayesh, *Morvarid-e Sufi-gari*, 39.

63. Cage, *Silence*, 38.

64. Azmayesh, *Morvarid-e Sufi-gari*, 36.

Chapter Four. Unknowing of Memory

1. The term *hosseiniyeh* translates into "place of Hossein," referencing the third Imam Hossein and one of Shi'i Islam's holiest figures. The building was referred to interchangeably as a *hosseiniyeh* (temple), tomb (*tekiyeh*), and shrine, but was generally used as a multipurpose meeting place for the order.

2. The English-language press materials of the Takhteh-Foulad Cultural Organization as well as the Takhteh-Foulad Encyclopedia Office give the site the official title of "Takhteh-Foulad Historical, Cultural, and Religious Complex" and alternately describe it as a necropolis and cemetery. I employ both terms to describe it here.

3. Prior to the twentieth century, Sufi meeting places and temples were founded almost exclusively with funding from the *vaghf*, a religious endowment or charitable trust

nominally under the control of the clergy and based in *sharia* law. During the Safavid era when Takhteh-Foulad was built, however, the *sadr*, or religious authority, was appointed by the Shah (Ebrahimnejad, *Medicine, Public Health, and the Qājār State*; Floor, "The 'ṣadr' or head of the Safavid religious administration, judiciary and endowments and other members of the religious institution"), and it was ultimately the nobility who maintained control over such endeavors. A similar allocation of powers remained in existence until the Islamic Revolution, when the clergy, often working through the municipal government, assumed control. While the decision to fund such projects remains in the hands of the state, the organizations that they housed would often remain autonomous or semiautonomous, perhaps the most famous example being the Nimatullahi Sufi *hosseiniyeh* in the center of Tehran in Park-e Shahr, founded during the Pahlavi era in the twentieth century, which remains at least nominally "autonomous" today. The meeting place (*hosseiniyeh*) at Takhteh-Foulad maintains a unique status among other shrines and temples constructed before 1979 in that, while the cemetery complex of Takhteh-Foulad has a *vaghf-nameh* (founding document), the Sufi *hosseiniyeh* housed within it itself possesses no such documentation. As a result, it is categorized as a part of the Takhteh-Foulad complex as a property of the municipal government (*shahrdari* records), rather than as a private or semiprivate entity.

4. See, for example, Benjamin, *The Arcades Project*, and Nietzsche, *Thus Spoke Zarathustra*, 103–439.

5. Dabaghi, *Takht-e Foulad*, ix.

6. Ghaem, *Isfahan, Iran*.

7. There are many other shrines that people visit, asking for happy marriages for their themselves and their children, good heath, and comfortable homes, among other things.

8. Doostdar, *The Iranian Metaphysicals*.

9. Karimi, "Imagining Warfare, Imaging Welfare," 47–63; Khosronejad, *Unburied Memories*; Moosavi, "How to Write Death," 9–31; Partovi, "Martyrdom and the 'Good Life'" in the Iranian Cinema of Sacred Defense," 513–32; Varzi, *Warring Souls*. See also Aghaie, *The Martyrs of Karbala*.

10. For more on this, see Massumi, "The Political Ontology of Threat," 52–70.

11. According to *The World Factbook*, 37 percent of the population is under twenty-four years of age (2020 estimate). CIA, "Field Listing—Age Structure," *The World Factbook*, https://www.cia.gov/the-world-factbook/field/age-structure/.

12. Haleem, *The Qur'an*.

13. Taghi-Jaafari, *Tarjome va Tafsir-e Nahj Al Balaghe*.

14. Taghi-Jaafari, *Tarjome va Tafsir-e Nahj Al Balaghe*.

15. I would distinguish this stage, despite its in-between status, from that which is called a liminal space. If we understand liminality as a form of rupture from reality, then the Sufis'

experience of the Unreal would be distinctly different. They operate not within a break from reality but one that is wholly separate from it, the "Unreal" at all times.

16. Bachelard, *The Poetics of Reverie*, 158.

17. Bachelard, *The Poetics of Reverie*.

18. Majzub'alishah, "Sufigari, Shi'igari, Erfan," 15.

Chapter Five. Unknowing of Place

1. Wandering, in both the metaphorical and literal senses, has been associated with Islamic mysticism since its earliest days. So central was the idea of wandering in early medieval Sufism that the famed Persian theologian al-Hujwiri (d. 1077) divides Sufis into two categories: settled (*muqimon*) and wanderers, or travelers (*musafarin*). For certain orders, such as the Qalandariyya, it is their key characteristic, as its followers adhered to a life of itinerancy (see Dahlén, "The Holy Fool in Medieval Islam," 63–81). Even for those more sedentary mystics, such as Jalal al-din Rumi or Hafez, the idea of wandering (*sargardan, suluk*) is a central concern in their writing, often acting as a metaphor for the project of mysticism as a whole, characterized as it often is as an endeavor of journeying and restlessness, full of longing.

2. This is not to suggest that that which gets called a metaphor within mystical literature does not come with its own highly complex set of issues. For the purposes of this book, however, I am limiting the discussion to that of the literal. For more on the question of metaphor within Sufism, see Sells, "Ibn'Arabi's Polished Mirror"; Kugle, *Sufis and Saints' Bodies*; Seyed-Gohrab, *Metaphor and Imagery in Persian Poetry*.

3. *Sama* is sometimes associated with a remembrance (*zekr*) ritual or listening to music specifically (see Avery, *A Psychology of Early Sufi Sama*; Werbner, "Stamping the Earth with the Name of Allah"), and has often generated much controversy over the centuries, having been commented on by the likes of influential mystics such as al-Hujwiri, al-Ghazzali, and Rumi (see Suvorova, *Muslim Saints of South Asia*; Keshavarz, *Reading Mystical Lyric*).

4. Interview by author, December 2009. I have not been able to locate any written record of this decree. Although revealed to me by my interlocutors, no written record exists, or at least none that I was able to locate or access. I can confirm that they had been meeting at the sheikh's house prior to the forced cancellations of the meetings. I am not including dates in order to further obscure the identities of my interlocutors.

5. The practice of begging by "holy men" was not frowned upon in many circles until the late nineteenth century. For more see Tabandeh, "The Rise of Nimatullahi Shi'ite Sufism in Early Nineteenth-Century Qajar Persia."

6. Saleh Ali Shah, *Pand-e Saleh*, xi.

7. Ibrahim, *Improvisational Islam*, 22.

8. Odabaei, "The Outside (Kharij) of Tradition"; Tawasil, "The Howzevi (Seminarian) Women in Iran."

9. One of the foremost debates within Sufi scholarship is the question of literalism versus the metaphoric. For example, a common trope is to describe states of ecstasy or intoxication as integral to the mystical experiences, with invocations of wine-bearers (*saqi*) and wine-houses (*sharabkhaneh*). Scholars have debated for centuries as to whether we understand these lines of prose to be extolling *actual* intoxication, where wine is utilized as a catalyst to come closer to the divine, or simply as a metaphor used to evoke mystical experience. See Saeidi and Unwin, "Persian Wine Tradition and Symbolism," 97–114; Seyed-Gohrab, *Metaphor and Imagery in Persian Poetry*.

10. Mahmood, "Secularism, Hermeneutics, and Empire," 340.

11. Gleave, *Islam and Literalism*, viii.

12. Deleuze, *Difference and Repetition*, 204.

13. Taussig, *What Color Is the Sacred?*; McLean, "Black Goo," 589–619; Stewart, *Ordinary Affects*.

14. Majzub'alishah, "Sufigari, Shi'igari, Erfan," 15.

15. Azmayesh, *The Teachings of a Sufi Master*, 12.

16. Azmayesh, *Morvarid-e Sufi-gari*, 17.

17. Al-Faruqi, "Music, Musicians and Muslim Law," 3–36; Nelson, "Reciter and Listener," 41–47.

18. For pedagogical techniques, see Messick, *The Calligraphic State*; for sermons and circulation, see Hirschkind, "Hearing Modernity," 131, and Hirschkind, *The Ethical Soundscape*; for Qur'anic recitation practices, see Graham and Kermani, "Part One: Recitation of the Quran."

19. See Kapchan, *Traveling Spirit Masters* and "The Promise of Sonic Translation," 467–83; Frischkopf, "Tarab ('Enchantment') in the Mystic Sufi Chant of Egypt," 233–69; Qureshi, *Sufi Music of India and Pakistan*, vol. 1.

20. "Traditional" (*sonati*) Iranian music typically refers to music that utilizes Persian instruments, is based upon the classical harmonic minor form, and has the *radif* rhythm structure. See Azadehfar, *Rhythmic Structure in Iranian Music*.

21. *Irfan*, derived from the Arabic *ma'rifat*, literally means knowledge or gnosis, but in the colloquial sense often refers to the mystical tradition in the Persian humanities, i.e., medieval Persian poetry. For more on the distinction between the interconnected categories of *irfan*, *tasavvuf*, and Sufism, see Anzali, *"Mysticism" in Iran*.

22. Hirschkind, *The Ethical Soundscape*.

23. Larkin, "Techniques of Inattention."

24. Schafer, *The Tuning of the World*, 13.

25. And yet, as Naveeda Khan has pointed out, the *azan* can also provoke reactions of indifference or outright hostility ("The Acoustics of Muslim Striving," 587). See also Spadola, *The Calls of Islam*; Lee, "Technology and the Production of Islamic Space," 86–100; Eisenberg, "Islam, Sound and Space," 186–202

26. McLuhan, *Media Research*, 41.

27. Toop, *Haunted Weather*, 58.

28. Connor, "Edison's Teeth."

29. Henriques, "Sonic Dominance and the Reggae Sound System Session," 459.

30. Kafka, *Blue Octavo Notebooks*, 46.

31. Rumi, *Masnavi*, 736–37.

Postscript (*Reng*). Improvisation and Unknowing

1. In the *Oxford Handbook of Critical Improvisation Studies*, editors George Lewis and Benjamin Piekut very clearly state that they offer no working definition: "This *Handbook* makes no explicit attempt to negotiate a single overarching definition of improvisation. Rather, as we see it, the critical study of improvisation seeks to examine improvisation's effects, interrogate its discourses, interpret narratives and histories related to it, discover implications of those narratives and histories, and uncover its ideologies." Lewis and Piekut, *Oxford Handbook of Critical Improvisation Studies*, Introduction.

2. Iranian classical music is based on the *dastgah* system, which is a musical modal system organized around the rearranging of several hundred melodic motifs (*gusheh*). Different *dastgahs* may then come together to form a collection known as a *radif*. Jean During describes the *dastgah* as "a collection of discrete and heterogeneous elements organized into a hierarchy that is entirely coherent though nevertheless flexible." Jean During, "Dastgah," *Encyclopedia Iranica*, https://iranicaonline.org/articles/dastgah. For more on this see Farhat, *The Dastgah Concept in Persian Music*.

3. Nooshin, "Improvisation as 'Other,'" 253; emphasis added.

4. Nooshin, "Improvisation as 'Other,'" 263.

5. Rumi, *Masnavi*, 2:156.

Abdel-Kader, Ali Hassan, ed. *The Life, Personality and Writings of Al-Junayd*. Cambridge, UK: Gibb Memorial Trust, 2014.

Abisaab, Rula Jurdi. *Converting Persia: Religion and Power in the Safavid Empire*. London: I. B. Tauris, 2004.

Aghaie, Kamran Scot. *The Martyrs of Karbala: Shi'i Symbols and Rituals in Modern Iran*. Seattle: University of Washington Press, 2004.

Ahmed, Shahab. *What Is Islam? The Importance of Being Islamic*. Princeton, NJ: Princeton University Press, 2015.

Al-e Ahmad, Jalal. *Gharb-zadagi: maqalah*. Tehran: Azad, 1341/1962.

Algar, Hamid. "The Fusion of the Gnostic and Politics in the Life of Imam Khomeini." *Al-Tawhid*, 1988.

Amir-Moezzi, Mohammad Ali. *The Divine Guide in Early Shi'ism: The Sources of Esotericism in Islam*. Albany: State University of New York Press, 1994.

Amir-Moezzi, Mohammad Ali. *The Spirituality of Shi'i Islam: Beliefs and Practices*. London: I. B. Tauris, 2011.

Amoli, Seyyed Haydar. Jami' al-asrar wa-manba' al-anwar lil-ma'arif al-muta'llih al-wali. Tehran: Qadir, 1377/1998.

Anari, Zahra. *Maktab-e Esfahan dar šahr-sāzi*. Tehran: Entesharat, 2001.

Andani, Khalil. "A Survey of Ismaili Studies, Part 1: Early Ismailism and Fatimid Ismailism." *Religion Compass* 10, no. 8 (2016): 191–206.

Anonymous. *Zendigename Shah Nimatullahi Vali*. Tehran: Entesharat-e Haqiqat, 2007.

Anzali, Ata. *"Mysticism" in Iran: The Safavid Roots of a Modern Concept*. Columbia: University of South Carolina Press, 2017.

Arjomand, Said Amir. *The Shadow of God and the Hidden Imam: Religion, Political Order, and Societal Change in Shi'ite Iran from the Beginning to 1890*. Chicago: University of Chicago Press, 1984.

Asad, Talal. *Genealogies of Religion: Discipline and Reasons of Power in Christianity and Islam*. Baltimore: Johns Hopkins University Press, 1993.

Asad, Talal. "Modern Power and the Reconfigurations of Religious Traditions: An Interview with Saba Mahmood." *Stanford Electronic Humanities Review* 5, no. 1 (1996). http://web.stanford.edu/group/SHR/5-1/text/asad.html.

Asghari, Seyed Amir. "Islamic Philosophy and Sufism in the Contemporary Shia Seminary and Their Opponents (1850–present)." PhD diss., Indiana University, Bloomington, 2022.

Ashtiyani, Jalal al-Din. *Erfan: Gnosticism, Mysticism.* Tehran: Shirkat-Sihami-Intishar, 1386/2007.

Ashtiani, Jalal al-Din. "Naqd-i Tahafut-i Ghazzālī." *Kayhan Andishe,* no. 14 (1366/1987).

Attali, Jacques. *Noise: The Political Economy of Music.* Manchester, UK: Manchester University Press, 1985.

Avery, Kenneth S. *A Psychology of Early Sufi Sama: Listening and Altered States.* London: Routledge, 2004.

Azadehfar, Mohammad Reza. *Rhythmic Structure in Iranian Music.* Tehran: University of Tehran Press, 2011.

Azmayesh, Seyed Mustafa. *History of Evolution in the Nematolahi Organization.* Netherlands: Ketab-khaneh Tasavuf Press, 2002.

Azmayesh, Seyed Mustafa. *Morvarid-e Sufi-gari.* London: Mehraby, 2008.

Azmayesh, Seyed Mustafa. *The Teachings of a Sufi Master.* London: Mehraby, 2005.

Babayan, Kathryn. *Mystics, Monarchs, and Messiahs: Cultural Landscapes of Early Modern Iran.* Cambridge, MA: Harvard University Press, 2002.

Bachelard, Gaston. *The Poetics of Reverie.* Boston: Beacon Press, 1971.

Bachelard, Gaston. *The Poetics of Space.* Boston: Beacon Press, 1994.

Bajoghli, Narges. *Iran Reframed: Anxieties of Power in the Islamic Republic.* Stanford, CA: Stanford University Press, 2019.

Bataille, Georges. "The Torment." In *Inner Experience,* translated by Stuart Kendall, 31–62. New York: State University of New York Press, 1998.

Bataille, Georges. *The Unfinished System of Nonknowledge.* Minneapolis: University of Minnesota Press, 2001.

Bateson, Mary Catherine. *Structural Continuity in Poetry: A Linguistic Study of Five Pre-Islamic Arabic Odes.* Berlin: De Gruyter Mouton, 2019.

Bayat, Mangol. *Mysticism and Dissent: Socioreligious Thought in Qajar Iran.* Syracuse, NY: Syracuse University Press, 1982.

Bell, Catherine M. *Ritual: Perspectives and Dimensions.* New York: Oxford University Press, 1997.

Benjamin, Walter. *The Arcades Project.* Cambridge, MA: Belknap Press, 2002.

Blanchot, Maurice. *The Writing of the Disaster.* Paris: Gallimard, 1982.

Boroujerdi, Mehrzad. "Gharbzadegi: The Dominant Intellectual Discourse of Pre- and Post-Revolutionary Iran." In *Iran: Political Culture in the Islamic Republic,* edited by Samih K. Farsoun and Mehrdad Mashayekhi. New York: Routledge, 1992.

Böwering, G. *The Mystical Vision of Existence in Classical Islam: The Qurʾānic Hermeneutics of the Ṣūfī Sahl At-Tustarī (d. 283/896).* Berlin: De Gruyter, 1980.

Boyarin, Jonathan, ed. *The Ethnography of Reading.* Oakland, CA: University of California Press, 1993.

Bull, Michael. *Sounding Out the City: Personal Stereos and the Management of Everyday Life (Materializing Culture).* New York: Berg, 2004.

Bull, Michael, and Les Back. "Introduction: Into Sound." In *The Auditory Culture Reader,* 1–20. New York: Berg, 2004.

Cage, John. *Silence.* Middletown, CT: Wesleyan University Press, 1961.

Cancian, Alessandro, ed. *Approaches to the Our'an in Contemporary Iran*. New York: Oxford Univesity Press, in association with the Institute of Ismaili Studies, 2019.

Cancian, Alessandro. "'I'm Only a Village Farmer and a Dervish': Between Political Quietism and Spiritual Leadership: Early Modern Shī'ī Sufism and the Challenge of Modernity." In *Political Quietism in Islam: Sunni and Shi'i Practice and Thought*, edited by Saud Al-Sarhan, 131–44. New York: I. B. Tauris, 2019.

Cancian, Alessandro. "Translation, Authority and Exegesis in Modern Iranian Sufism: Two Iranian Sufi Masters in Dialogue." *Journal of Persianate Studies* 7, no. 1 (2014): 88–106.

Carter, Paul. "Ambiguous Traces, Mishearing, and Auditory Space." In *Hearing Cultures: Essays on Sound, Listening, and Modernity*, edited by Veit Erlmann, 43–63. Oxford: Berg, 2004.

Chahardahi, Mudarrisi Mortaza. *Selsel-ehha-yi Ṣufiyah-e Iran*. Tehran: Entesharat-e Batunak, 1981.

Chahardahi, Mudarrisi Mortaza. "Selsel-e tasavvuf-e Iran." *Vahid* 11, no. 3: 253–59.

Chahardahi, Mudarrisi Mortaza. "Selsel-eye Nematollahi Munes'alishahi." *Vahid* 11, no. 5: 526–31.

Chittick, William C. *The Sufi Doctrine of Rumi*. Bloomington, IN: World Wisdom, 2005.

Clifford, James. "Introduction: Partial Truths." In *Writing Culture: The Poetics and Politics of Ethnography*, edited by James Clifford and George E. Marcus, 12. Berkeley: University of California Press, 1986.

Cole, Juan. *Sacred Space and Holy War*. New York: I. B. Tauris, 2007.

Connell, Michael Paul. *The Nimatullahi Sayyids of Taft: A Study of the Evolution of a Late Medieval Iranian Sufi Tariqah*. PhD diss., Harvard University, 2004.

Connor, Steven. "Edison's Teeth: Touching Hearing." In *Hearing Cultures: Essays on Sound, Listening, and Modernity*, ed, by Veit Erlmann, 153–72. Oxford: Berg, 2004.

Corbin, Henry. "Confessions extatiques de Mir Damad, maître de théologie à Ispahan." *Melanges Louis Massignon*, ob. 1041/1631–1632, Institut Français de Damas, 1956.

Corbin, Henry. *En Islam Iranien. Aspects situels et philosophiques*. Vol. 1: *Le Shī'isme duodécimain*. Paris: Editions Gallimard, 1991.

Corbin, Henry. "La place de Molla Sadra Shiraza dans la philosophie iranienne." *Studia Islamica* 18 (1962): 81–113.

Corbin, Henry. *The Voyage and the Messenger: Iran and Philosophy*. Berkeley, CA: North Atlantic Books, 1998.

Crapanzano, Vincent. *Imaginative Horizons: An Essay in Literary-Philosophical Anthropology*. Chicago: University of Chicago Press, 2004.

Dabaghi, Azizollah. *Takht-e Foulad: The Treasury of Culture*. Pamphlet. Isfahan: Municipal Government of Isfahan Publication, 2009.

Dabashi, Hamid. *Theology of Discontent: The Ideological Foundations of the Islamic Revolution in Iran*. New York: New York University Press, 1993.

Dabashi, Hamid. *Truth and Narrative: The Untimely Thoughts of Ayn al-Qudat al-Hamadhani*. London: Curzon Press, 1999.

Daher, Rami. *Tourism in the Middle East*. Bristol: Channel View, 2007.

Dahlén, Ask. "The Holy Fool in Medieval Islam: The Qalandarīyāt of Fakhr al-dīn'Arāqī." *Orientalia Suecana* 53 (2004): 63–81.

Das, Veena, and Deborah Poole. "Anthropology in the Margins of the State." *PoLAR: Political and Legal Anthropology Review* 30, no. 1 (2004): 140–44.

Davari, Arash. "A Return to Which Self? 'Ali Shari'ati and Frantz Fanon on the Political Ethics of Insurrectionary Violence." *Comparative Studies of South Asia, Africa and the Middle East* 34, no. 1 (2014): 86–105.

De Bruijn, J. T. P. "The Qalandariyyat in Persian Mystical Poetry, from Sana Onwards." In *The Legacy of Mediaeval Persian Sufism*, edited by Leonard Lewinson, 75–86. London: Khaniqahi-Nimatullahi Publications, 1992.

De Jong, Frederick, and Bernd Radtke. *Islamic Mysticism Contested: Thirteen Centuries of Controversies and Polemics*. Boston: Brill, 1999.

Deleuze, Gilles. *Difference and Repetition*. Translated by Paul Patton. New York: Columbia University Press, 1994.

Deleuze, Gilles. *Pure Immanence: Essays on a Life*. Translated by Anne Boyman. New York: Zone Books, 2001.

Deleuze, Gilles, and Felix Guattari. *A Thousand Plateaus: Capitalism and Schizophrenia*. Translated by Brian Massumi. Minneapolis: University of Minnesota Press, 1987.

Derrida, Jacques. *Positions*. Translated by Alan Bass. Chicago: University of Chicago Press, 1981.

Deweese, Devin. "'Dis-ordering' Sufism in Early Modern Central Asia: Suggestions for Rethinking the Sources and Social Structures of Sufi History in the 18th and 19th Centuries." *History and Culture of Central Asia* (2012): 259–79.

Deweese, Devin. "Organizational Patterns and Developments within Sufi Communities." In *The Wiley Blackwell History of Islam*, edited by Armando Salvatore, 329–50. Hoboken, NJ: Wiley, 2018.

Doostdar, Alireza. *The Iranian Metaphysicals: Explorations in Science, Islam, and the Uncanny*. Princeton, NJ: Princeton University Press, 2018.

During, Jean. "La musique iranienne: Tradition et évolution." *Editions Recherche sur les Civilisations: Mémoires Paris* 38 (1984).

During, Jean. "Dastgah." Encyclopedia Iranica, https://iranicaonline.org/articles/dastgah.

Ebrahimnejad, Hormoz. *Medicine, Public Health, and the Qājār State: Patterns of Medical Modernization in Nineteenth-Century Iran*. Vol. 4. New York: Brill, 2004.

Eilers, Wilhelm. "Educational and Cultural Development in Iran during the Pahlavi Era." In *Iran under the Pahlavis*, edited by G. Lenczowski, 303–31. Stanford, CA: Hoover Institution Press, 1977.

Eisenberg, Andrew. "Islam, Sound and Space." *Music, Sound and Space* (2013): 186–202.

Elias, Jamal J. "Sufi Tafsir Reconsidered: Exploring the Development of a Genre." *Journal of Qur'anic Studies* 12 (2010): 41–55.

Enteshami, Amin, and Sajjad Rizvi. "Beyond the Letter: Explanation (tafsīr) versus Adaptation (taṭbīq) in Ṭabāṭabā'ī's al-Mīzān." In *The Spirit and the Letter: Approaches to the Esoteric Interpretation of the Qur'an*, edited by Annabel Keeler, Sajjad H. Rizvi, and Martin Nguyen. Oxford: Oxford University Press, 2016.

Erlmann, Veit. "But What of the Ethnographic Ear? Anthropology, Sound and the Senses." In *Hearing Cultures: Essays on Sound, Listening, and Modernity*, edited by Veit Erlmann, 1–20. Oxford: Berg, 2004.

Erlmann, Veit, ed. *Hearing Cultures: Essays on Sound, Listening, and Modernity*. Oxford: Berg, 2004.

Ernst, Carl. *Hallaj: Poems of a Sufi Martyr*. Evanston, IL: Northwestern University Press, 2018.

Ernst, Carl. *The Shambhala Guide to Sufism*. Boston: Shambhala, 1997.

Ernst, Carl. *Words of Ecstasy in Sufism*. Albany: SUNY Press, 1985.

Ernst, Carl, and Bruce Lawrence. *Sufi Martyrs of Love: The Chishti Order in South Asia and Beyond*. New York: Springer, 2016.

Fabian, Johannes. *Out of Our Minds: Reason and Madness in the Exploration of Central Africa*. Oakland: University of California Press, 2000.

Farhat, Hormoz. *The Dastgah Concept in Persian Music*. Cambridge: Cambridge University Press, 1990.

Al-Faruqi, Lois Ibsen. "Music, Musicians and Muslim Law." *Asian Music* 17, no. 1 (1985): 3–36.

Fischer, Michael M. J. *Iran: From Religious Dispute to Revolution*. Cambridge, MA: Harvard University Press, 1980.

Fischer, Michael M. J. *Mute Dreams, Blind Owls, and Dispersed Knowledges: Persian Poesis in the Transnational Circuitry*. Durham, NC: Duke University Press, 2004.

Fischer, Michael M. J., and Mehdi Abdei. *Debating Muslims: Cultural Dialogues in Postmodernity and Tradition*. Madison: University of Wisconsin Press, 1990.

Fischlin, Daniel, and Eric Porter. "Improvisation and Global Sites of Difference: Ten Parables Verging on a Theory." *Critical Studies in Improvisation/Études critiques en improvisation* 11, nos. 1–2 (2016).

Floor, Willem. "The 'Sadr' or Head of the Safavid Religious Administration, Judiciary and Endowments and other Members of the Religious Institution." *Zeitschrift der Deutschen Morgenländischen Gesellschaft* 150, no. 2 (2000): 461–500.

Frischkopf, Michael. "Tarab ('Enchantment') in the Mystic Sufi Chant of Egypt." In *Colors of Enchantment: Theater, Dance, Music, and the Visual Arts of the Middle East*, edited by Sherifa Zuhur, 233–69. Cairo: American University in Cairo Press, 2011.

Ghaem, Asghar Montazerol. *Isfahan, Iran*. Brochure. Encyclopedia Office of Takht-eh Foulad Cultural, Historical, and Religious Organization, 2009.

Ghamari-Tabrizi, Behrooz. "Contentious Public Religion: Two Conceptions of Islam in Revolutionary Iran: Ali Shariati and Abdolkarim Soroush." *International Sociology* 19, no. 4 (2004): 504–23.

Ghamari-Tabrizi, Behrooz. *Foucault in Iran: Islamic Revolution after the Enlightenment* Minneapolis: University of Minnesota Press, 2016.

Ghamari-Tabrizi, Behrooz. "Moderneti Erfaani: Shariati Dar Jahan-e Valter Benjamin." *Etemad*, June 17, 2021.

al-Ghazzali, Abu Hamid Muhammad. "On Listening to Music." In *Alchemy of Happiness* (*Kimiya al-saadat*), translated by Muhammad Nur Abdus Salam. Chicago: Great Books of the Islamic World, 2002.

Ghazzali, Ahmad. *Sawanih: Inspirations from the World of Pure Spirits*, translated by Nasrollah Pourjavady. New York: Routledge, 2013.

Gheissari, Ali. *Iranian Intellectuals in the Twentieth Century*. Austin: University of Texas Press, 1998.

Gleave, Robert. *Islam and Literalism: Literal Meaning and Interpretation in Islamic Legal Theory*. Edinburgh: Edinburgh University Press, 2012.

Gleave, Robert. *Religion and Society in Qajar Iran*. New York: Routledge, 2004.

Godlas, Alan. "Ṣūfism." In *The Wiley Blackwell Companion to the Qur'ān*, edited by Andrew Rippin and Jawid Mojaddedi, 418–29. Hoboken, NJ: Wiley, 2017.

Golestaneh, Seema. "'Text and Contest': Theories of Secrecy and Dissimulation in the Archives of Sufi Iran." In *Shi'i Islam and Sufism: Classical Views and Modern Perspectives*, edited by Dennis Hermann and Mathieu Terrier, 197–223. London: I. B. Tauris, 2019.

Golestaneh, Seema. "'To Be Transformed into Thought Itself': Mystical and Political Becomings within Ali Shariati." *Philosophy and Global Affairs* (September 2022).

Graham, William, and Navid Kermani. "Part One: Recitation of the Quran." In *The Cambridge Companion to the Qur'ān*, edited by Jane Dammen, 115–42. Cambridge: Cambridge University Press, 2006.

Green, Nile. "Emerging Approaches to the Sufi Traditions of South Asia: Between Texts, Territories and the Transcendent." *South Asia Research* 24, no. 2 (2004): 123–48.

Green, Nile. *Sufism: A Global History*. Vol. 34. New York: Wiley, 2012.

Gupta, Akhil. *Red Tape: Bureaucracy, Structural Violence, and Poverty in India*. Durham, NC: Duke University Press, 2012.

Haeri, Niloofar. "The Private Performance of 'Salat' Prayers: Repetition, Time, and Meaning." *Anthropological Quarterly* (2013): 5–34.

Haeri, Niloofar. *Say What Your Longing Heart Desires: Women, Poetry, and Prayer in Iran*. Stanford, CA: Stanford University Press, 2020.

Haider, Najam Iftikar. *The Origins of the Shi'a: Identity, Ritual, and Sacred Space in Eighth-Century Kūfa*. New York: Cambridge University Press, 2011.

Haider, Najam. *Shi'i Islam: An Introduction*. Cambridge: Cambridge University Press, 2014.

Haleem, Muhammad A. S. Abdel, trans. *The Qur'an: English Translation and Parallel Arabic Text*. New York: Oxford University Press, 2010.

al-Hallaj, Husayn ibn Mansur. "Kitab Al-Tawasin." In *Ana al-Haqq Reconsidered*, edited by Gilani Kamran. Lahore, Pakistan: Naqsh-E-Awwal Kitab Ghar, 1972.

Henriques, Julian. "Sonic Dominance and the Reggae Sound System Session." In *The Auditory Culture Reader*, edited by Michael Bull and Les Back, 349–56. New York: Berg, 2004.

Hermann, Denis, and Omid Rezai. "Constitution en vaqf d'une 'mosquée sanctuaire' ne'matollāhī à Téhéran à l'époque pahlavī." *Iran* 46 (2008): 293–306.

Hirschkind, Charles. *The Ethical Soundscape: Cassette Sermons and Islamic Counterpublics*. New York: Columbia University Press, 2006.

Hirschkind, Charles. "Hearing Modernity: Egypt, Islam, and the Pious Ear." In *Hearing Cultures: Essays on Sound, Listening, and Modernity*, edited by Veit Erlmann, 131–52. New York: Berg, 2004.

Hull, Matthew S. *Government of Paper: The Materiality of Bureaucracy in Urban Pakistan*. Oakland: University of California Press, 2012.

al-Hujwiri, Ali B. Uthman. *Kashf al-Mahjub (The Revelation of the Veiled): An Early Persian Treatise on Sufism*. Translated by Reynold Nicholson. Cambridge, UK: Gibb Memorial Trust, 1999.

Husayni Tihrani, Sayyid Muhammad Husayn. *Shining Sun: In Memory of 'Allamah Tabataba'i*. Translated by Tawus Raja. London: ICAS Press, 2011.

Husayni Tihrani, Sayyid Muhammad Husayn. *Ruh-I Mujarrad: yadnameh-i muvahhid-i azim va arif-i Kabir, Hajj Sayyid Hashem Musavi Hadad*. Jalalabad, Afghanistan: Hikmat, 1414/1993.

Ibrahim, Nur Amali. *Improvisational Islam: Indonesian Youth in a Time of Possibility*. Ithaca, NY: Cornell University Press, 2018.

Jouili, Jeannette S., and Annelies Moors. "Introduction: Islamic Sounds and the Politics of Listening." *Anthropological Quarterly* 87, no. 4 (2014): 977–88.

Kafka, Franz. *Blue Octavo Notebooks*. New York: Exact Change, 2004.

Kant, Immanuel. *Critique of Judgement*. 1790. Translated by James Creed Meredith. Oxford: Oxford University Press, 2007.

Kapchan, Deborah. *Traveling Spirit Masters: Moroccan Gnawa Trance and Music in the Global Marketplace*. Middletown, CT: Wesleyan University Press, 2007.

Kapchan, Deborah. "The Promise of Sonic Translation: Performing the Festive Sacred in Morocco." *American Anthropologist* 110, no. 4 (2008): 467–83.

Karamustafa, Ahmet T. *Sufism*. Edinburgh: Edinburgh University Press, 2007.

Karimi, Pamela. "Imagining Warfare, Imaging Welfare: Tehran's Post–Iran-Iraq War Murals and Their Legacy." *Persica* 22 (2008): 47–63.

Kasravi, Ahmad. *Sufigari*. Tehran: Mebu-ati-uye Forroghi, 1963.

Keddie, Nikki. *Modern Iran: Roots and Results of Revolution*. New Haven, CT: Yale University Press, 2006.

Keeler, Annabel, Sajjad H. Rizvi, and Martin Nguyen. *The Spirit and the Letter: Approaches to the Esoteric Interpretation of the Qur'an*. Oxford: Oxford University Press, 2016.

Keeler, Annabel. *Sufi Hermeneutics: The Qur'an Commentary of Rashid al-Din Maybudï*. Oxford: Oxford University Press, 2006.

Keeler, Annabel. "Sūfī tafsīr as a Mirror: al-Qushayrī the Murshid in his Latācif al-ishārāt." *Journal of Qur'anic Studies* 8.1 (2006): 1–21.

Keshavarz, Fatemeh. *Reading Mystical Lyric: The Case of Jalal al-Din Rumi*. Columbia: University of South Carolina Press, 1998.

Khan, Naveeda. "The Acoustics of Muslim Striving: Loudspeaker Use in Ritual Practice in Pakistan." *Comparative Studies in Society and History* 53, no. 3 (2011): 571–94.

Khanlarzadeh, Mina. "Theology of Revolution: In Ali Shari'ati and Walter Benjamin's Political Thought." *Religions* 11.10 (2020): 504.

Khatami, Mahmoud. *From a Sadraean Point of View: Toward an Ontetic Elimination of the Subjectivistic Self*. London: London Academy of Iranian Studies, 2004.

Khomeini, Ruhollah. *Islam and Revolution: Writings and Declarations of Imam Khomeini*. Translated by Hamid Algar. Berkeley, CA: Mizan Press, 1981.

Khomeini, Ruhollah. *Islamic Government*. Translated by Hamid Algar. Tehran: The Institute for Compilation and Publication of Imam Khomeini's Works (International Affairs Division), 2002.

Khomeini, Ruhollah. *Misbah al-hidaya ila al-khilafa wa al-wilaya*. Tehran: Bonyad-e Imam Khomeini, 1993.

Khosronejad, Pedram. *Unburied Memories: The Politics of Bodies of Sacred Defense Martyrs in Iran*. New York: Routledge, 2013.

Kiani, Mohsen. *Tarikhe Khanegha Dar Iran*. Tehran: Tahoori, 2010.

Kirshenblatt-Gimblett, B. *Destination Culture: Tourism, Museums, and Heritage*. Berkeley: University of California Press, 1998.

Knysh, Alexander. "'Irfan' Revisited: Khomeini and the Legacy of Islamic Mystical Philosophy." *Middle East Journal* 46, no. 4 (1992): 631–53.

Knysh, Alexander D. "Sufism and the Quran." In *Encyclopedia of the Qur'an*, edited by Jane Dammen McAuliffe, 5:137–59. Boston: Brill, 2005.

Kugle, Scott A. *Sufis and Saints' Bodies: Mysticism, Corporeality, and Sacred Power in Islam*. Chapel Hill: University of North Carolina Press, 2011.

Larkin, Brian. "Techniques of Inattention: The Mediality of Loudspeakers in Nigeria." *Anthropological Quarterly* 87, no. 4 (2014): 989–1015.

Lee, Tong Soon. "Technology and the Production of Islamic Space: The Call to Prayer in Singapore." *Ethnomusicology* 43, no. 1 (1999): 86–100.

Lévi-Strauss, Claude. *Tristes Tropiques*. Paris: Librairie Plon, 1955; rev. ed., London: Penguin UK, 2011.

Lewis, Franklin D. *Rumi—Past and Present, East and West: The Life, Teachings, and Poetry of Jalâl al-Din Rumi*. New York: Simon and Schuster, 2007.

Lewis, George, and Benjamin Piekut. *The Oxford Handbook of Critical Improvisation Studies*. New York: Oxford University Press, 2016.

Lewisohn, Leonard. "An Introduction to the History of Modern Persian Sufism, Part I: The Nimatullahi Order: Persecution, Revival, and Schism." *Bulletin of the School for Oriental and African Studies* 61, no. 3 (1998): 437–64.

Lewisohn, Leonard. "An Introduction to the History of Modern Persian Sufism, Part II: A Sociocultural Profile of Sufism, from the Dhahabi Revival to the Present Day." *Bulletin of the School for Oriental and African Studies* 62, no. 1 (1999): 36–59.

Lewisohn, Leonard, ed. *The Heritage of Sufism*. Vol. 3, *Late Classical Persianate Sufism (1501–1750)*. New York: Simon and Schuster, 2018.

Lewisohn, Leonard. *Classical Persian Sufism from Its Origins to Rumi (700–1300) v. 1*. New York: Simon and Schuster, 2018.

Library of Congress Country Profile. "Iran, May 2008." https://www.loc.gov/resource/g7620.ct003101/

Magris, Aldo. "Free Will According to the Gnostics." In *Fate, Providence and Free Will: Philosophy and Religion in Dialogue in the Early Imperial Age*, edited by René Brouwer and Emmanuele Vimercati, 174–95. New York: Brill, 2020.

Magris, Aldo. "Gnosticism: Gnosticism from its Origins to the Middle Ages [Further Considerations]." In *Encyclopedia of Religion*, edited by Lindsay Jones, 3515–22. Detroit: Macmillan Reference USA, 2005.

Mahbub Ali Shah, Hajj Ali Tabandeh. *Ahd-e elahi*. Tehran: Entesharat-e Haqiqat, 1997.

Mahbub Ali Shah, Hajj Ali Tabandeh. *Ashura-Day Sermon*, Tehran: Entesharat-e Haqiqat, June 9, 1995.

Mahbub Ali Shah, Hajj Ali Tabandeh. *Declaration*. Tehran: Entesharat-e Haqiqat, October 18, 1992.

Mahbub Ali Shah, Hajj Ali Tabandeh. *Khorshid-e Tabande*. Tehran: Entesharat-e Haqiqat, 1994.

Mahbub Ali Shah, Hajj Ali Tabandeh. *Tariqat-e Sufiyan*. Tehran: Entesharat-e Haqiqat, 2002.

Mahmood, Saba. *Politics of Piety*. Princeton, NJ: Princeton University Press, 2004.

Mahmood, Saba. "Rehearsed Spontaneity and the Conventionality of Ritual: Disciplines of Salat." *American Ethnologist* 28, no. 4 (2001): 827–53.

Mahmood, Saba. "Secularism, Hermeneutics, and Empire: The Politics of Islamic Reformation." *Public Culture* 18, no. 2 (2006): 323–47.

Majzub'alishah, Hajj Nur'Ali Tabandeh. "Sufigari, Shi'igari, Erfan." *Erfàn-e Iran* 2, no. 7 (2000): 11–23.

Majzub'alishah, Hajj Nur'Ali Tabandeh. *Tariqat-e Roshan*. Tehran: Khaneye Nimatullahi, 2009.

Majzub'alishah, Hajj Nur'Ali Tabandeh. Sermon, Amir Suleimaniye Husseiniyeh, January 17, 1997a.

Majzub'alishah, Hajj Nur'Ali Tabandeh. Sermon, Entesharat-e Haqiqat, February 2002.

Majzub'alishah, Hajj Nur'Ali Tabandeh. Sermon, Entesharat-e Haqiqat January 31, 2006.

Majzub'alishah, Hajj Nur'Ali Tabandeh. Sermon, Entesharat-e Haqiqat, March 1, 1997b.

Majzub'alishah, Hajj Nur'Ali Tabandeh. Sermon, Entesharat-e Haqiqat, March 21, 2013.

Majzub'alishah, Hajj Nur'Ali Tabandeh. "Tasavuf va Fiqh." Entesharat-e Haqiqat, Tehran, 2010.

Manoukian, Setrag. *City of Knowledge in Twentieth Century Iran: Shiraz, History and Poetry*. New York: Routledge, 2012.

Manoukian, Setrag. "Thinking with the Impersonal: An Ethnographic View from Iran." *Antropologia* 6, no. 1 n.s. (2019): 199–215.

Massumi, Brian. "The Political Ontology of Threat." In *The Affect Theory Reader*, edited by Melissa Gregg and Gregory J. Seigworth, 52–70. Durham, NC: Duke University Press, 2010.

McLean, Stuart. "Black Goo: Forceful Encounters with Matter in Europe's Muddy Margins." *Cultural Anthropology* 26, no. 4 (2011): 589–619.

McLuhan, Marshall. *Media Research: Technology, Art and Communication*. London: Routledge, 2014.

Melville, Charles, ed. *Safavid Persia: The History and Politics of an Islamic Society*. London: I. B. Tauris, 1996.

Merkur, Dan. *Gnosis: An Esoteric Tradition of Mystical Visions and Unions.* Albany: SUNY Press, 1993.

Messick, Brinkley. *The Calligraphic State: Textual Domination and History in a Muslim Society.* Los Angeles: University of California Press, 1996.

Messick, Brinkley. *Shari'a Scripts: A Historical Anthropology.* New York: Columbia University Press, 2018.

Milani, Milad. *Sufi Political Thought.* London: Routledge, 2017.

Mittermaier, Amira. "The Book of Visions: Dreams, Poetry, and Prophecy in Contemporary Egypt." *International Journal of Middle East Studies* 39, no. 2 (2007): 229–47.

Mittermaier, Amira. "Dreams from Elsewhere: Muslim Subjectivities beyond the Trope of Self-Cultivation." *Journal of the Royal Anthropological Institute* 18, no. 2 (2012): 247–65.

Mittermaier, Amira. *Dreams That Matter: An Anthropology of the Imagination in Contemporary Egypt.* Berkeley: University of California Press, 2010.

Mokhtari-Isfahani, Reza. *Sargozasht-e Radio Dar Iran beh Revayat-e Esnaad.* Tehran: Daftar-e Pajoohesh-haye Radio. 1389.

Momen, Moojan. *An Introduction to Shi'i Islam.* New Haven, CT: Yale University Press, 2004.

Momen, Moojan, and Peter Smith. "The Baha'i Faith 1957–1988: A Survey of Contemporary Developments." *Religion* 19, no. 1 (January 1989): 63–91.

Mottahedeh, Roy. *The Mantle of the Prophet: Religion and Politics in Iran.* Boston: Oneworld Publications, 1985.

Moosavi, Amir. "How to Write Death: Resignifying Martyrdom in Two Novels of the Iran-Iraq War." *Alif: Journal of Comparative Poetics* 35, no. 9 (2015): 9–31.

Najafian, Ahoo. "Poetic Nation: Iranian Soul and Historical Continuity." PhD diss., Stanford University, 2018.

Nasr, Seyyed Hossein. "The Meaning and Role of 'Philosophy' in Islam." *Studia Islamica* 37 (1973): 57–80.

Nasr, Seyyed Hossein. "The School of Iṣpahān." In *A History of Muslim Philosophy,* edited by Mian Mohammad Sharif, 904–32. Wiesbaden, Germany: Harrassowitz, 1966.

Nasr, Seyyed Hossein. *Sufi Essays.* Chicago: Kazi Publications, 1973.

Nelson, Kristina. "Reciter and Listener: Some Factors Shaping the Mujawwad Style of Qur'anic Recitation." *Ethnomusicology* 26, no. 1 (1982): 41–47.

Netton, Ian Richard. *Sufi Ritual: The Parallel Universe.* Richmond, UK: Curzon Press, 2000.

Nietzsche, Friedrich. *Thus Spoke Zarathustra.* In *The Portable Nietzsche,* translated by Walter Kaufmann, 103–439. New York: Penguin, 1982.

Nooshin, Laudin. "Improvisation as 'Other': Creativity, Knowledge and Power: The Case of Iranian Classical Music." *Journal of the Royal Musical Association* 128, no. 2 (2003): 242–96.

Nurbakhsh, Javad. *Ma'arif-i Sufiya.* London: Khaniqahi-Nimatullahi Publications, 1983.

Nurbakhsh, Javad. *Masters of the Path: A History of the Masters of the Nimatullahi Sufi Order.* New York: Khaniqahi-Nimatullahi Publications (KNP), 1980.

Nurbakhsh, Javad. *Sufism: Meaning, Knowledge, Unity.* New York: Khaniqahi-Nimatullahi Publications (KNP), 1981.

Nurbakhsh, Javad. "Sufism and Psychoanalysis. Part One: What Is Sufism?" *International Journal of Social Psychiatry* 24, no. 3 (1978): 204–12.

Nurbakhsh, Javad. *Sufi Symbolism: The Nurbakhsh Encyclopedia of Sufi Terminology*. Vol. 3, *Religions Terminology*. Lancaster, UK: Khaniqahi-Nimatullahi Publications, 1988.

Nurbakhsh, Javad. *Sufi Symbolism: The Nurbakhsh Encyclopedia of Sufi Terminology*. Vol. 8, *Insations, Revelations, Lights*. Lancaster, UK: KNP Press, 1995.

Odabaei, Milad. "Giving Words: Translation and History in Modern Iran." PhD diss. abstract, University of California, Berkeley, 2018.

Odabaei, Milad. "The Outside (Kharij) of Tradition in the Aftermath of the Revolution: Carl Schmitt and Islamic Knowledge in Postrevolutionary Iran." *Comparative Studies of South Asia, Africa and the Middle East* 39, no. 2 (2019): 296–311.

Olszewska, Zuzanna. *The Pearl of Dari: Poetry and Personhood among Young Afghans in Iran*. Bloomington: Indiana University Press, 2015.

Osanloo, Arzoo. *The Politics of Women's Rights in Iran*. Princeton, NJ: Princeton University Press, 2009.

Pandolfo, Stefania. *Impasse of the Angels: Scenes from a Moroccan Space of Memory*. Chicago: University of Chicago Press, 1997.

Pandolfo, Stefania. *Knot of the Soul: Madness, Psychoanalysis, Islam*. Chicago: University of Chicago Press, 2018.

Partovi, Pedram. "Martyrdom and the 'Good Life' in the Iranian Cinema of Sacred Defense." *Comparative Studies of South Asia, Africa and the Middle East* 28, no. 3 (2008): 513–32.

Pourjavady, Nasrollah, and Peter Lamborn Wilson. "Isma'ilis and Ni'matullahiis." *Studia Islamica* (1975): 113–35.

Pourjavady, Nasrollah, and Peter Lamborn Wilson. *Kings of Love: The History and Poetry of the Ni'matullāhī Sufi Order of Iran*. Tehran: Imperial Iranian Academy of Philosophy, 1978.

Qureshi, Regula Burckhardt. *Sufi Music of India and Pakistan: Sound, Context and Meaning in Qawwali*. Cambridge: Cambridge University Press, 1986.

Rahnema, Ali. *An Islamic Utopian: A Political Biography of Ali Shariati*. London: I. B. Tauris, 2000.

Reza-Ali Shah. *Gardesh-e Afghanistan va Pakistan*. Tehran: Chapkhaneye Heydari, 1975.

Reza-Ali Shah. *Nazar-e mazhabi be e'lamiye-ye huquq-e bashar (Negaresh-e Soltanhoseyn Tabandeh Gonabadi)*. Tehran: Chapkhaneye Peyruz, 1970.

Ricoeur, Paul. "The Model of the Text: Meaningful Action Considered as a Text." *Social Research*, 1971, 529–62.

Ridgeon, Lloyd. *Morals and Mysticism in Persian Sufism: A History of Sufi-futuwwat in Iran*. New York: Routledge, 2010.

Rizvi, Sajjad. "Being (*wujud*) and Sanctity (*wilaya*): Two Poles of Mystical Enquiry in Qajar Iran." In *Religion and Society in Qajar Iran*, edited by Robert Gleave. New York: Routledge, 2005.

Rizvi, Sajjad. "Before the Safavid-Ottoman Conflict: Jāmī and Sectarianism in Timurid Iran and Iraq." In *Jāmī in Regional Contexts: The Reception of 'Abd al-Raḥmān Jāmī's*

Works in the Islamicate World, ca. 9th/15th-14th/20th Century, edited by Thibaut d'Hubert and Alexandre Papas, 227–55. Boston: Brill, 2018.

Rizvi, Sajjad H. "'Only the Imam Knows Best': The Maktab-e Tajkīk's Attack on the Legitimacy of Philosophy in Iran." *Journal of the Royal Asiatic Society* (2012): 487–503.

Rizvi, Sajjad. "Striving Beyond the Balance (*al-Mizan*): Spiritual Practice in the Quran in Tabatab'i *Tariqa*." In *Approaches to the Our'an in Contemporary Iran*, edited by Alessandro Cancian, 41–76. New York: Oxford University Press, in association with the Institute of Ismaili Studies, 2019.

Rosen, Matthew. "Ethnographies of Reading: Beyond Literacy and Books." *Anthropological Quarterly* (2015): 1059–83.

Rumi, Jalal al-Din. *Mystical Poems of Rumi*. Translated by A. J. Arberry. Chicago: University of Chicago Press, 2010.

Saeidi, Ali, and Tim Unwin. "Persian Wine Tradition and Symbolism: Evidence from the Medieval Poetry of Hafiz." *Journal of Wine Research* 15, no. 2 (2004): 97–114.

Safi, Omid. *The Politics of Knowledge in Premodern Islam: Negotiating Identity and Religious Inquiry*. Chapel Hill: University of North Carolina, Press, 2006.

Saleh Ali Shah, Hajj Sheikh Mohammad Hassan. *Pand-e Saleh*. Tehran: Entesharat-e Haqiqat, 1372/1993.

Sanasarian, Eliz. *Religious Minorities in Iran*. Cambridge: Cambridge University Press, 2000.

Sands, Kristin Zahra. *Sufi Commentaries on the Qur'an in Classical Islam*. New York: Routledge, 2006.

Schafer, R. Murray. *The Tuning of the World*. New York: Random House, 1977.

Schimmel, Annemarie. *Mystical Dimensions of Islam*. Chapel Hill: University of North Carolina Press, 1975.

Sells, Michael. *Early Islamic Mysticism: Sufi, Qur'an, Mi'raj, Poetic and Theological Writings*. Mahwah, NJ: Paulist Press, 1996.

Sells, Michael. "Ibn'Arabi's Polished Mirror: Perspective Shift and Meaning Event." *Studia Islamica* 67, no. 121 (1988): 121–49.

Seyed-Gohrab, Ali Asghar, ed. *Metaphor and Imagery in Persian Poetry*. Vol. 6. Boston: Brill, 2011.

Shafi'i Kadkani, Mohammad Reza. *Advar-e shehr-e farsi*. Tehran: Tus, 1981.

Shah-Kazemi, Reza. *Justice and Remembrance: Introducing the Spirituality of Imam Ali*. London: Institute of Ismaili Studies, 2006.

Shams, Fatemeh. *A Revolution in Rhyme: Poetic Co-option under the Islamic Republic*. Oxford: Oxford University Press, 2021.

Shannon, Jonathan Holt. *Among the Jasmine Trees: Music and Modernity in Contemporary Syria*. Middletown, CT: Wesleyan University Press, 2006.

Shariati, Ali. *Nivishtah'i Ali Shariati, Majmu'ah-I asar*. Tehran: Ilham: Bunyad-e Farhangi-e Duktur Ali Shariat, 2010.

Shirazi, Muhammad Masum. *Tara'iq Al-Haqa'iq*. Tehran: Sana'i, 1966.

Shirwani, Zayn al-Abidin. *Kashf al-Ma'arif*. Tehran: Chapkhaneh Ferdowsi, 1971.

Sobhani, Ayatollah Jafar. *Doctrines of Shi'i Islam: A Compendium of Imami Beliefs and Practices*, translated and edited by Reza Shah-Kazemi. New York: I. B. Tauris: 2001.

Spadola, Emilio. *The Calls of Islam: Sufis, Islamists, and Mass Mediation in Urban Morocco.* Bloomington: Indiana University Press, 2013.

Steigerwald, Diana. "Twelver Shiʻ ı Taʻwıl." *The Wiley Blackwell Companion to the Qurʾān,* edited by Andrew Rippin and Jawid Mojaddedi, 449. Hoboken, NJ: Wiley, 2017.

Stewart, Kathleen. *Ordinary Affects.* Durham, NC: Duke University Press, 2007.

Sultanhoseyn, Hajj Tabandeh Gonabadi. *Tarikh va joghrafi-ye Gonabadi.* Tehran: Sazemen-e Chap-e Daneshah, 1969.

Suvorova, Anna. *Muslim Saints of South Asia: The Eleventh to Fifteenth Centuries.* London: Routledge, 2000.

Tabatabai, Allameh. *Tariq-e Erfan (Tarjome, Shehr, va Matn-e Resale- al-Wilayat Allameh Tabatabie).* Translated by Sadeq Hassanzadeh. Qom: Ayate-eshra, 1396.

Tabandeh, Reza. "The Rise of Nimatullahi Shiʻite Sufism in Early Nineteenth-Century Qajar Persia: Husayn Ali Shah, Majdhub Ali Shah, Mast Ali Shah and their Battle with Islamic Fundamentalism." PhD diss., University of Exeter, 2013.

Tabandeh, Reza. *The Rise of the Niʻmatullāhī Order: Shiʻite Sufi Masters against Islamic Fundamentalism in 19th-Century Persia.* Leiden: Leiden University Press, 2021.

Taghi-Jaafari, Mohammad. *Tarjome va Tafsir-e Nahj Al Balaghe.* Tehran: Feternesh Farhang va Islami, 1359/1980.

Taneja, Anand Vivek. *Jinnealogy: Time, Islam, and Ecological Thought in the Medieval Ruins of Delhi.* Stanford, CA: Stanford University Press, 2017.

Taussig, Michael. *Mimesis and Alterity: A Particular History of the Senses.* New York: Routledge, 1992.

Taussig, Michael. *What Color Is the Sacred?* Chicago: University of Chicago Press, 2009.

Tavakoli-Targhi, Mohamad. "Refashioning Iran: Language and Culture during the Constitutional Revolution." *Iranian Studies* 23, nos. 1–4 (1990): 77–101.

Tawasil, Amina. "The Howzevi (Seminarian) Women in Iran: Constituting and Reconstituting Paths." PhD diss., Columbia University, 2013.

Thomassen, Einar. *The Coherence of "Gnosticism."* Berlin: De Gruyter, 2020.

Toop, David. *Haunted Weather: Music, Silence, and Memory.* London: Serpent's Tail, 2004.

Torab, Azam. "Piety as Gendered Agency: A Study of Jalaseh Ritual Discourse in an Urban Neighbourhood in Iran." *Journal of the Royal Anthropological Institute,* 1996, 235–52.

Trimingham, J. Spencer. *The Sufi Orders of Islam.* Oxford: Oxford University Press, 1998.

Vahdat, Farzin. "Return to Which Self? Jalal Al-e Ahmad and the Discourse of Modernity." *Journal of Iranian Research and Analysis* 16, no. 2 (2000): 55–71.

Vakili, Hojjat al-Islam Mohammad Hasan. *Mohayaldin; Shiʻi Khales.* Mashhad: Institute for the Scientific Study of Islam, 2018.

Vakili, Hojjat al-Islam Mohammad Hasan. *Maktab-I Tafkiki: Tarikh va Naqd.* Tehran: Kanoon-e Andisheh Javan vabasteh be Moasse Kanoon Andisheh Javan Tehran, 1393/2014.

Van Den Bos, Matthijs. *Mystic Regimes: Sufism and the State in Iran, from the Late Qajar Era to the Islamic Republic.* London: Brill, 2002.

Varzi, Roxanne. *Warring Souls: Youth, Media, and Martyrdom in Post-Revolution Iran.* Durham, NC: Duke University Press, 2006.

Walbridge, Linda S., ed. *The Most Learned of the Shia: The Institution of the Marja' Taqlid.* Oxford: Oxford University Press, 2001.

Werbner, Pnina. "Stamping the Earth with the Name of Allah: Dhikr and the Sacralizing of Space among British Muslims." In *Making Muslim Space in North America and Europe*, edited by Barbara Daly Metcalf, 167–85. Los Angeles: University of California Press, 1996.

Yazdi, Ayatullah Muhammad Taqi Misbah. "Irfan va Hikmat." *Al-Tawhid* 14, no. 3 (1992).

Zarrinkub, Abdul Husayn. *Tassavof-i irani dar manzare tarkhie-an.* Tehran: Amir Kabir, 1972.

Zarrinkub, Abdul Husayn. *Jostojou dar tassavof-e Iran.* Tehran: Amir Kabir, 1984.

INDEX

Page numbers in italics refer to figures.

interpretation, 10, 11, 174; of dreams, 82, 83–86; ethnography and, 6; of *fana*, 114; layers of meaning and, 94; literal, 168, 175–77; of poetry, 21, 40, 71, 83, 84; of the Qur'an, 37, 75, 77–79, 89, 91, 125; reading as, 77–78. See also *tafsir*

intoxication, 68, 209n9

Iran, Islamic Republic of, 6, 28, 31, 156; construction of public memory in, 144; ethnic groups of, 9, 194n9; government effort to sanitize Shi'i practice, 145–46; housing in, 165; intellectual trends in, 117; Islam debated in, 186; nuclear program, 42; poetry as source of national pride, 92; status of religious minorities in, 53; Sufism in, 52; veterans and patriots of, 45

Iranian Revolution, 40, 118

Iranian Sufism in Historical Perspective (Zarrinkub, 1972), 197n10

Iran-Iraq War, 9, 45, 60, 144; Museum of Stone and, 141; Shi'i strategies of remembrance of, 152–55; as war of "the Holy Defense," 152

"'Irfan' Revisited: Khomeini and the Legacy of Islamic Mystical Philosophy" (Knysh), 36

Isfahan, xv, 8, 176, 188; cemeteries of, 141; as cultural capital of Islamic world, 144; municipal government (*shahrdari*), 137, 144, 160; seminaries of, 47. See also Takhteh-Foulad [Steel Throne] Cemetery

al-Isfahani, 155, 157, 158

Isfahani, Mirza Mahdi, 42

Islam, 70, 186, 206n53; anthropologies of, 7; embodied practice in, 130; Islamic philosophy (*hekmat*), 36; literalism in, 175; political Islam, 36, 38. See also Shi'ism; Sufism

Islam and Literature (Gleave), 176

Islam and Revolution (Khomeini, 1981), 29

Islamic Heritage Sites, 27

"Islamic Philosophy and Sufism in the Contemporary Shia Seminary and their Opponents (1850–present)" (Asghari), 41

Islamic Revolution, 45, 52, 54, 141

Ismaili, Shah, 197n5

Jafar al-Sadeq, Imam (sixth Shi'i imam), 12, 62, 65, 94, 200n78; esoteric orientation of, 63, 201n2; Qur'anic exegesis and, 76, 202n15

Ja'fari school of Shi'ism, 26, 28, 53, 144, 200n78; "continuous remembering" and, 155, 156, 157; *zekr* and, 156–58

Jews, 53

jinns (spirits), 7, 8, 16

Junayd, 103, 196n5

Junayd Baghdadi, 23, 105, 196n35

Jurjani, 195n32

Justice and Remembrance (Sarraj, 2006), 135

Kadkani, Shaf'i, 197n10

Kafka, Franz, 186

Kallilulah, Shah, 46–47

Kant, Immanuel, 92

Karbala, battle of, 141, 154

Karimi, Pamela, 152

kashf (spiritual unveiling), 201n8

Kashf al-Asrar (Maybudi), 104

Kasravi, Ahmad, 50

Kazem, Imam Musa (seventh Shi'i imam), 199n53

Keeler, Annabel, 202n12

Kerman, city of, 46

Kernel of the Kernel, The (Tabatabai), 78

Ketab al-Fana (Junayd), 105

Ketabkhane-ye Soltani library, 49

Khameini, Ayatollah, 146

Khan, Naveeda, 23, 210n25

khaneqah (Sufi meeting place), 50–51, 52, 54, 112, 135; cancellation by local authorities, 170–72; mystics living together in lodges, 63; report of session within, 55–58, 57; as Sufi places of worship, 101

Khanlarzadeh, Mina, 119

Khayyam, Omar, 74

Khomeini, Ayatollah Ruhollah, 12, 25, 33, 43, 51; as adherent of mysticism, 36; as gnostic Supreme Leader (*rahbar*), 36–39; *Islam and Revolution* (1981), 29; *Lamp Showing the Right Way* (1930), 37; poetry of, 37–38, 76, 198n28; on validity of mysticism, 29

Khosronejad, Pedram, 152

Kitab al-Asfar [*Book of Journeys*] (Sadra), 36–37

Knot of the Soul (Pandolfo), 7

knowledge, 8, 64, 65, 101, 178; amnesia and, 151; auditory body and, 132; circular exchange of, 91; contained in the heart, 83; creation and preservation of, 157; derived from poetry, 12; experiential, 133; forms of self and, 15; hierarchy of, 78; improvisation and, 191–92; interplay of knowing and not-knowing, 126, 127; interpretation of poetry and, 81; limit of, 5; mysticism as synonym for, 163–64; "secret of divine knowledge" (*sir-e ma'rifat*), 60; state of ecstasy in music and, 126; without teachers, 61; *zekr* and, 155

Nayrizi, Qutb al-Din, 41
Nazim al-Haqqani, Sheikh, 78
neo-Sufism, 44
Netton, Richard, 129
New Age, 11, 30, 44, 45
Nietzsche, Friedrich, 83, 143
Nigeria, 183
Nimatullahi Soltanalishahi Order, 4, 15, 122, 177; on inward and outward dimensions of religion, 15; *Saleh's Advice* as a foundational text of, 50
Nimatullahi Sufi Order, 10, 25, 32, 37, 52, 129; contrast with Ja'fari school on Shi'i remembrance, 155–58; departure from Iran, 34; history of, 46–47; India and, 199n52; Pahlavi regime and, 49–52; in Qajar era, 47–49; rituals and routine practices of, 55; *tawhid* (union with God) and, 103, 173; theories of remembrance, 144
Nimatullah Vali, Shah, 9, 10, 46, 47, 73, 102; lineage of, 199n53; poetry of, 12; shrine of, 46, 47; as translator and commentator, 196n35
noise, 18, 19, 56, 165–66, 182; ambient street noise, 183; in urban residential neighborhoods, 180. *See also* soundscapes
nonexistence (*naboodi*), 15, 111, 116, 117, 128; *fana* as, 113, 116; Tabatabai on merits of, 105; "tavern of ruin" and, 114; turn to, 27, 100
"nonknowledge," 60, 77, 127, 193n4
Nooshin, Laudan, 189–90
"Noroozi, Sheikh," 17, 18, 19, 59–61, 91, 201n8; on "inner heart" as best teacher, 93; students of, 70–74, 93; text without end and, 61–71
Nurbakhsh, Javad, 12, 104, 126
Nuri, Mulla Ali, 41
Nur Street collective, 101–3, 107, 111, 115, 120, 121

Odabaei, Milad, 175
Olszewska, Zuzanna, 12
ostad (master, professor), 30, 97–98; diminishing role of, 70; of poetry recitations, 79. See also *pir-murid* (teacher-student) relationship

Pahlavi, Mohammad Reza, 53
Pahlavi, Reza Shah, 49, 50
Pakistan, 51, 80–81
Pandolfo, Stefania, 7, 16
Partovi, Pedram, 152
path-of-love (*rah-e eshq*), 45
pedagogy, 26, 71, 87, 89, 92; history of *erfan* and, 73; limits of, 93

Persian language, 3, 11, 102, 112; calligraphy, 139; literature, 26. *See also* poetry, Persian
Piekut, Benjamin, 210n1
pir (Sufi masters), 56, 57, 58, 111, 170, 201n88
pir-murid (teacher-student) relationship, 49, 63, 64; enlightenment without a teacher, 72–73; Shams and Rumi, 73; varied nature of, 73
"Poetic Nation: Iranian Soul and Historical Continuity" (Najafian), 37
Poetics of Space, The (Bachelard, 1994), 165
poetry, Persian, 1, 19, 20, 43, 44, 136; as arena of Sufi infiltration, 44; *bayt* (lines), 62, 74, 91, 97; "bodily unconscious" and, 132; concealed wisdom in, 88; dream interpretation and, 83–86; esoteric meanings in, 21, 195n32; as form of literary exegesis, 76, 77, 202n13; *ghazals* (love poems), 91, 96; internal meaning (*batin*) in, 77, 78, 79; of Khomeini, 37–38, 76, 198n28; medieval canon, 23, 167; multiple meanings/interpretations of, 86–89; music and, 181, 182; poesis or poetics, 12; quoted in casual conversation, 74; recitation of, 79; of saints, 67; in sermons, 56; as source of national pride in Iran, 92; "tavern of ruin" as common phrase in, 113, 114; *tawhid* (union with God) and, 75; war poetry, 45; women's interpretations of Islam and, 43
politics, xi, 33, 42, 51, 52, 171; apolitics, 159, 163, 164; of dread, 138; electoral, 8; geopolitics, 109, 111; local, 171, 187
Porter, Eric, 189
postmodern literary theory, 26
Pourjavady, Nasrollah, 122
prayer beads (*tasbih*), 66, 97
prayer books (*ketab-e dua*), 43
"prison of the nafs" (*zendan-e nafs*), 115, 116
propaganda, 153

Qaderis (Sunni Kurdish Sufis), 9
Qajar dynasty, 47–49
qalandar (wandering ascetic), 31, 168
Qawwalis, 81
Qom, city/province of, xv, 13, 32; ayatollahs of, 76; seminary at, 37, 39, 42
qotbs (spiritual authority figures), 4, 15, 22, 55; burial places of, 136; formal portraits of, 97, 101, 102; in Nimatullahi Order, 31, 49; sermons of, 170; wakefulness and, 162. *See also* authority, spiritual

wakefulness and, 162; wandering and, 168; zekr ritual and, 115

Tehran, city of, 9, 55, 170; Ali Suleiymani Mosque, 52; noise in residential neighborhoods, 180; war museums and statues in, 153

tekiyeh [tomb] (Sufi meeting place), 135, 150, 151, 206n1; destruction of Takteh-Foulad tekiyeh, 146, 159; Seyed al-Araghaen tekiyeh, 140, 141

text, endlessness of, 67, 68

"third eye," 64

Tihrani, Seyed Mohammad Husayn Husayni, 12, 41

time, perception of, 127

Toop, David, 184

Torab, Azam, 101

"Torment, The" (Bataille, 1998), 121

transformation. See self, transformation of

Turkey, 48

al-Tustari, 76

Twelver Shi'ism, 9, 12, 13, 194n10; hazrat ("presence" of twelve imams), 56, 201n87; Iranian mystical thought divergent from, 25; jurisprudence of, 34; mysticism in relation to, 38–39. See also Ja'fari school of Shi'ism

ulama (clergy), 25, 29, 47–48

unconscious, the, 8

Universal Declaration of Human Rights, 51

unknowing (ma'rifat), 17, 67, 167, 193n4; affective and sensory dimensions of, 5; of the body, 121–23, 133; definitions of, 4–5, 6; as endless process, 5, 92; epistemologies of, 21; improvisation and, 189–92; interpretations of, 3–4, 10; known through experience, 64; of memory, 161–64; of self, 100, 104, 116; subjectivity and, 15; of text, 92. See also gnosis (erfan)

Unreal, the (khiyali, vehmi), 18–19, 21, 44, 105, 143, 195n24; fana and disappearance of, 106–11; as inauthenticity, 117; liminality and, 208n15; memory and, 144; travel to the Real from, 103

vaghf-nameh (founding document of endowment), 54, 207n3

Vakili, Mohammad Hasan, 41

Van den Bos, Matthijs, 52

Varzi, Roxanne, 152

wahdat al-wujud (unity of existence), 34

wajd (unveiling), 126, 127, 129

wanderers/wayfarers (salik/salik-ha), 13, 28, 31

wandering (sargardan, suluk), 6, 36–37, 41, 167, 208n1; of ascetics searching for perfect teacher, 172; begging and, 172–73, 208n5; as "classical" Sufi concept, 172; as game (bazi), 173–74; intentional, 170, 177–80; "literal" interpretation and, 176; monikers of Sufi self-description, 178–79; as vanishing practice, 173

Westernization, opposition to, 51

"Westoxification" [Gharbzadegi] (Al-e Ahmad), 117

Wittgenstein, Ludwig, 67

women, 43, 45, 58, 108

Writing of the Disaster, The (Blanchot, 1982), 135, 177

Yafe'i, Sheikh Abdollah, 46

Yazdi, Ayatollah Mohammad Taghi Mesbah, 36

Yazdi, Mirza Ali, 36

Zahabiyya Sufi Order, 41

Zahediya Sufi Order, 196n5

zaher (external meaning), 67, 76, 77, 79, 175, 176

Zahir od-Dowle Order, 51

zanjeer-zani (self-flagellating mourning practice), 146

Zarrinkub, Abdul Husayn, 197n10

Zayandeh river, xv–xvi

Zaydi school, 53

zekr (remembrance) ritual, 6, 26, 96–99, 103, 106, 143; dissolution of the self and, 100; forgetting and, 27–28, 128–30, 135, 164; as heart of Shi'ism, 155; incomprehensibility of the divine and, 124–25, 126; Ja'fari versus Nimatullahi understanding of, 155–58; at juncture of material and immaterial, 123; mimesis and, 131; as musical ritual, 5, 98; as negation of the Unreal, 109, 110; Nur Street collective and, 101, 102, 111; poetry and, 80; as quotidian practice, 112–13; reading and, 62; as release from everyday troubles, 107, 108, 109; remembrance of God (zekr-e khoda), 112, 115; sama (intentional listening) and, 128, 181; silent, 147; society and, 120; vocalization in, 123–26, 127; void and, 151. See also forgetting; memory

Zoroastrians, 53